LITTLE
CROW

Little Crow in 1851 by Frank Blackwell Mayer (1895)

LITTLE CROW

SPOKESMAN FOR THE SIOUX

GARY CLAYTON ANDERSON

MINNESOTA HISTORICAL SOCIETY PRESS
ST. PAUL · 1986

The paper used in this publication
meets the minimum requirements
of the American National Standard
for Information Sciences — Permanence
for Printed Library Materials,
ANSI Z39.48-1984.

MINNESOTA HISTORICAL SOCIETY PRESS
St. Paul 55101
© 1986 by Minnesota Historical Society
All rights reserved

Manufactured in the United States of America
10 9 8 7 6 5

International Standard Book Number:
0-87351-191-3 Cloth
0-87351-196-4 Paper

Library of Congress
Cataloging-in-Publication Data

Anderson, Gary Clayton, 1948–
    Little Crow, spokesman for the Sioux.
    Bibliography: p.
    Includes index.
    1. Little Crow, d. 1863. 2. Dakota Indians —
Biography. 3. Indians of North America — Minnesota —
Biography. I. Title.
E99.D1L732 1986   977.6'00497 [B]   86-795

To Laura

Contents

Illustrations

Maps

Acknowledgments

THE MINNESOTA HISTORICAL SOCIETY, through its editors and research fellows, played a major role in the conception and development of this book. I must give special thanks to Alan R. Woolworth, for many years a research fellow at the society. Alan provided intellectual as well as research aid, sending me photocopies of obscure material that in many cases helped bring Little Crow to life. Editor Sally Rubinstein worked tirelessly, checking sources and polishing my "prose." John McGuigan, the managing editor at MHS Press, kept me on schedule and, as unusual as it may seem, became a good friend during the process. At a critical point, the College of Liberal Arts of Texas A & M University awarded me a writing grant. Finally, colleagues Robert Calvert and Dale Knobel read various portions of the manuscript and offered well-defined criticism. Few writers have been blessed with more efficient and helpful editors and critics.

Introduction

ONE of the most difficult challenges facing historians today is to write the history of the dispossessed. Such people leave few records and are frequently viewed by the dominant culture as being worthy of nothing more than a footnote in the ever-moving vision of a nation's past. Traditional approaches to solving this problem have focused on writing about nameless "masses," be they slaves in the Old South or, in the case of the Indian, tribal groups. Obviously, the nature of government records and manuscript collections has mitigated against attempts at writing an individual's biography, traditionally an important historical genre. When biographies have been written, they often have been apologetic; because of the dearth of source material, minority leaders are usually portrayed as heroic "actors" in the larger context of a struggle against majority groups rather than as men or women with feelings and faults, who acted upon the dominant culture and tried to reshape it.

In the case of the American Indian, with few exceptions biographies have been written of men who became famous because they reacted to white aggression by leading resistance movements and capturing the imagination of the American public. The likes of Sitting Bull, Pontiac, Joseph, Black Hawk, and King Philip, just to name a few, provide the best examples. Alvin M. Josephy, Jr., immortalized leaders of this genre in his classic book, *The Patriot Chiefs*, a chronicle of the "great leaders" of the American Indian. While Josephy attempted to explain in his introduction that other leaders, mainly those who worked with Euro-Americans, also might be considered as having made important contributions, he concluded that so-called "good Indians" would never be the "great heroes" of the American Indian.[1] Only a selected few merited such status, and those generally had demonstrated prominence or success in war.

Certainly such apologetic biography has a place in scholarship. Josephy's book and others of its kind provide an important "ethnocentric" viewpoint. Yet the majority of Indian leaders never experienced the euphoria of a Sitting Bull or a Pontiac or even the limited success of a King Philip or

1

a Joseph. Biographies of supposedly less successful Indian leaders can be just as important, especially if they advance our understanding of the way in which leaders tried to shape interethnic relations, rather than simply react to them. The biography of Little Crow that follows, then, is not the story of a "patriot chief." Instead, it is about an important, intelligent, and tragic figure in history whose political career (1846–63) vividly illustrates the compromises, dilemmas, and often impossible situations that evolved in dealing with whites in the nineteenth century.

In addition, Little Crow is significant because of the dichotomy that he represents in history and the myths surrounding that dichotomy. He has become a symbol of Indian resistance and the failure of a government policy designed to assimilate the western Indians peacefully. The Dakota War of 1862, one of the bloodiest Indian wars in history, was in many ways the opening shot of a series of struggles on the northern Great Plains that culminated in the tragic affair known as Wounded Knee. Yet the war in Minnesota manifested such brutality that it is impossible for anyone who studies it to be unquestioningly supportive of the Indians, despite the unfulfilled promises of the government and the hardship that such breaches of faith created for the eastern Sioux people. Indeed, Little Crow's role in this cruel war has made an objective assessment of his life almost impossible. His end, as a trophy exhibited by the state, seemed at the time a more than fitting tribute to the triumph of "civilization" over "savagery."

Writers have had difficulty in dealing historically with this dual image. To some, Little Crow became a tragic but guilty figure who sanctioned brutality and justly deserved his ignominious fate.[2] To others, the killing of four hundred civilians, many of whom were women and children, was given less attention or even ignored, and emphasis was placed upon the mistreatment of the Dakota people and Little Crow as leader in a just cause.[3] When William Watts Folwell was researching his four-volume history of Minnesota in 1916, he recognized the difficulty of dealing with Little Crow. He wrote in a private letter, "Deceived by white men, discredited by his own people, he has been given an unjust character in history which should be corrected. . . . When the bitterness of the survivors of the days of 1862 shall have died out, this will probably be done." But when it came to assessing Little Crow in his exhaustive study of the war, Folwell concluded: "His ignoble end was not unfit."[4]

Still, in an age when not only the survivors of the war but many of their children have passed on, writing an objective biography of Little Crow remains a challenge. What Little Crow became in the eyes of historians, Indians, and the public at large fails to convey any sense of the man as a leader and an Indian. Neither aspect of the dual image that exists is accurate. More importantly, myths have developed in an effort to make these images seem real. Despite the efforts of many writers to prove the contrary, Little Crow did not initiate the uprising, nor did he lead the Indian forces into it. He was not a brutal person and, according to all the available evidence, never killed anyone during the fighting. Yet he played a major role in the war and worked diligently to expand the fighting to include other Sioux tribes once the war began.

In addition to these enumerated shortcomings, previous accounts of Little Crow have totally failed to assess his political role. Little Crow's understanding of the nature of the Indian-white relationship was far superior to that of his contemporaries. He developed a rational policy for dealing with whites, based it upon negotiation and accommodation rather than war, and thus preserved Indian identity and peace. His attempt to implement such a policy may by itself warrant a study of his life.

In order to accept such revisionist theories, one must first discard the myths that have surrounded Little Crow for so many years and attempt to view him in a new light. Little Crow's life must be assessed in relation to his tribal and familial obligations, elements that were important in his culture and to his people. Such a quest leads in many different directions. It requires an understanding of Dakota culture, especially social systems, Dakota leadership, and Dakota religion, as well as some basic knowledge of government policy and the dynamics of interethnic relations. In a word, this book is an attempt at ethno-biography, or the writing of biography from the perspective of a minority culture. Such an approach is the only way to escape the Little Crow that myth has created.

The setting for Little Crow's life is the world of the Mdewakanton Sioux tribe — approximately two thousand people — who selected Little Crow to "speak" for them in 1851. The Mdewakantons were part of a seven tribe nation, generally identified as the Sioux people. They occupied lands in the eastern section of the Sioux domain, congregating during the summer in villages along the upper Mississippi and lower Minnesota rivers. This location put them within reach of early French and British traders who reached their lands in the late-seventeenth century. By 1800 the Mdewakantons had become part of an extensive trade system, but one that was to last only a few decades. Little Crow's life spans a controversial and tumultuous period in the history of Indian-white relations. He witnessed the demise of the fur trade, the development of an Indian policy based upon removal and acculturation, and finally the inauguration of the wars with the Plains Indians. A study of his life contributes considerable information regarding the nature of Indian politics and the nearly impossible task faced by most tribal leaders in the period—preserving tribal identity and some degree of independence at a time when government officials were developing policies of acculturation.

Throughout this period, Little Crow worked as a power broker, trying to obtain the best possible bargain for his people while simultaneously attempting to satisfy an insatiable personal hunger for power. In short, Little Crow was a politician who happened to be an Indian, a man who used his persuasive ability as a speaker in tribal councils to mediate the difficult transition from a traditional tribal world to one increasingly dominated by the white majority. He realized early in his career that resisting such a change was futile, and he actively assisted in the negotiation of multi-million-dollar treaties that resulted in the surrender of eastern Sioux lands. He knew that taking a positive view of such negotiations would gain him prestige among the government administrators of the newly created reservations and among the native peoples who would benefit from the annuities distributed as a result of the treaties. After many of his own people went one step farther and adopted farming on the reservations, Little Crow finally turned to wearing white man's clothing when it became obvious that such a supposed cultural transformation would gain favor with government officials. Little Crow realistically saw accommodation as a viable and necessary alternative to resistance.

Even so, he believed that such accommodation did not have to include massive cultural change, and he continued to maintain traditional ways, especially in regard to his religion—a gesture that made him popular with more militant Indians on the Minnesota reservations who increasingly found fault with the government's acculturation programs and resisted them, ultimately bringing a war in 1862. Although Little Crow did his best to prevent the war, he was left with little choice but to join the fighting in hopes of bringing the war to a successful conclusion for his people.

Little Crow's life also provides an opportunity to examine the nature and limitations of Indian leadership, a topic of some confusion to students of the American Indian. The term "chief" is inherently authoritarian in tone, and most writers of Indian history have characteristically given Indian leaders strong roles, whether deserved or not. But traditionally, Indian groups such as the Sioux did not place decision-making powers in the hands of one individual. Rather, men gained reputations as leaders through example, by showing promise as a man of war, through demonstrating important spiritual powers, or from an ability to mold societal consensus through speaking.

Despite the plebian nature of Sioux society, it was much easier for some individuals to assume the rank of "chief," or tribal spokesman, than others. Oftentimes, rank at birth influenced such decisions. Polygamy was common, and a Sioux man might have several sons from several wives. Probably for reasons of age and experience, the first son of the oldest wife usually was regarded as a candidate for leadership. Moreover, certain families simply were larger and more important than others, and thus a dynastic political system evolved among the Mdewakantons whereby the eldest son of an important leader was automatically considered a candidate for chieftainship. Little Crow benefited from both of these conditions, being the eldest of the sons of a band chief who briefly served as speaker of the Mdewakanton tribe.

Sioux leadership functioned within a societal context, individual chiefs building consensus by manipulating close kinsmen. Although seemingly superficial in concept, kinship obligation is essential to understanding leadership. The Sioux were a communal people who placed a strong emphasis on tribal or familial identity and the need of individuals to be productive in order to promote the well-being of the band or society. Material possessions were important only to the degree to which they benefited society at large, and chiefs functioned within this communal world in part giving away material goods as quickly as they came to possess them. The more generous a leader was, the more the people respected him and the more influence he gained.

For Little Crow, kinship manipulation took on new meaning as federal authorities moved up the Mississippi River and rewarded the Sioux initially with presents and later with annuities, thus creating and maintaining obligations. The young Mdewakanton chief quickly realized that the whites possessed the means with which to secure influence and power, and he turned to working with them. While the acceptance of large amounts of annuities offset the decline of game, such changes also affected the traditional nature of Sioux leadership. Little Crow became a broker, and his role as a leader was increasingly marred by the basic dilemma that most Indian leaders would ultimately face in the nineteenth century; economic dependency and the political implications of it benefited chiefs who were willing to accommodate themselves to whites, but it damaged their credibility with their own people.

Considering the constraints inherent in Sioux politics as well as the growing meddling of whites, it is truly a wonder that any native politician could function at all. Of course, this is what makes Little Crow uniquely interesting as an individual, for not only did he continue to work within this framework, but also he became increasingly important as a leader as the 1850s drew to a close. It is ironic that he should be remembered only as the leader of an Indian outbreak. Although not a "patriot chief," Little Crow should be remembered as a leader who struggled to shape a realistic alternative to warfare in the cultural confrontation that took place between whites and Indians.

After beginning this project, I quickly discovered that writing Indian biography is a task that can only be fully appreciated by those among us who have made a like effort. Sources play out at times, making it necessary to use the context of the times rather than the main character as a thread in holding the story together. It is difficult to understand what the main character is thinking in the absence of letters or diaries. Although I take full responsibility for the shortcomings of the book and realize that some critics may wish to retitle the study, "Little Crow and the Mdewakanton Sioux," I still believe that such difficulties should not hinder scholars from similar undertakings.

A second problem arises in the use of basic terms. Historically non-Indians have identified the Mdewakantons as being one of the seven tribes of the "Sioux confederacy," which included the Mdewakantons, Wahpetons, Wahpekutes, Sissetons, Yanktons, Yanktonais, and Tetons. Unfortunately, the term "Sioux" is Algonquin in origin, roughly meaning "enemy." Yet the term, derivative "Siouan," is used consistently by modern linguists, appears in virtually all documents in the nineteenth century, and is unavoidable when referring to the seven tribes of the confederacy. While many Mdewakantons today prefer the more accurate "Dakota," a term meaning "league" or "ally," in this study "Dakota" is used specifically in reference to the four "eastern Sioux" tribes, namely Mdewakanton, Sisseton, Wahpeton, and Wahpekute, and Sioux is employed in a generic sense to identify the members of the confederacy.

In order to convey the intonation of the Sioux language, linguistic markings have been used on Dakota names and terms. These appear as the letters *n*, *ś*, *ź*, and *ħ* in such words as wicaśta wakan, Unktehi, and Peźutazi.

Prelude:
Incident in a Raspberry Patch

ON THE MORNING of July 3, 1863, sixty-three-year-old Nathan Lamson and his son, Chauncey, left the town of Hutchinson on the Minnesota frontier to return to their farm. About six miles north of the city, they encountered Indians. The white settlers of Hutchinson had been in a constant state of alert since the eastern Sioux, or Dakota, Indians had begun a war eleven months earlier. Lamson's thoughts turned to the many whites who had been killed in the fighting, and he immediately stalked the two adversaries he saw plucking raspberries near a poplar grove. When in range, Lamson fired, wounding the larger man in the groin. Other shots quickly rang out as Chauncey, his father, and the wounded Indian maneuvered through the brush straining to get nearer to each other. When the gunshots ceased, Lamson lay wounded in the brush, and the larger of the two Indians was close by, shot mortally in the chest. Young Chauncey, without ammunition and under the belief that his father had been killed, raced back to Hutchinson for help, leaving the wounded men alone in the raspberry patch that had suddenly become a battlefield.[1]

Nathan Lamson lay hidden in the brush, fearful of moving, as he listened to the larger Indian gasp for breath in a sequence that foreordained an agonizing death. Soon, another human voice broke the rhythm. A young Indian boy, about sixteen years old, moved forward and knelt beside the wounded Indian, who addressed him in a subdued voice. It was a strange scene to Lamson, and his thoughts turned from the excitement of the skirmish to an interest in what was being said. It seemed as though this dying, middle-aged man was giving what final instructions he could, telling the boy that he would now have to continue alone. Then, the still unidentified Indian died, and the boy quietly took new moccasins from a bag, dressed the man's feet, covered his body with a blanket, and left. The battle had ended and so had the life of Taoyateduta, better known to

Lamson and his fellow settlers as the Dakota chief Little Crow, the man who had led the so-called "Great Sioux War." Lamson failed to recognize the man he had shot or the symbolism surrounding his death.

The inglorious death of an unidentified Indian was greeted with jubilation in the frontier settlements of western Minnesota. The eastern Sioux, architects of conflagration that had resulted in the deaths of at least four hundred civilians, had become incarnations of the devil.[2] The frenzied Hutchinson townspeople celebrated the killing by moving the body of the Indian to town, where it was left lying in the main street. Boys, in a festive mood, spent the Fourth of July placing firecrackers in the ears and nostrils of the corpse. A few people speculated about the identity of the man, one or two suggesting that the corpse resembled Little Crow, but others who claimed to have known the notorious chief challenged this assertion. The head had been scalped by the time the body reached town and nearly all of the hair removed, making any identification based upon facial features dubious. Lamson had wanted the trophy in order to collect the seventy-five-dollars-a-head offered by the state for the scalps of hostile Sioux Indians.[3]

Toward evening, when the desecration ceased to be amusing, Dr. John Benjamin convinced others to help him move the corpse to a refuse pit outside of town. Dr. Benjamin covered the body with some dirt, but a cavalry officer dug it up and severed the head from the torso. The doctor managed later to retrieve the skull, but then the torso disappeared from the garbage pit. By that time most of the flesh had fallen from the bones, making it possible to verify that it was Little Crow. The severe breaks in Little Crow's wrists, his double teeth, coupled with the testimony of his son Wowinape, who had been with him at his death and had been captured in August, verified the earlier speculation of the Hutchinson townspeople.[4] The notorious chief, leader of one of the bloodiest frontier wars in American history, had been killed while picking raspberries.

1

A Dakota Childhood

At the turn of the eighteenth century, the upper Mississippi River possessed the aura of a fresh, new land, at least to the naked eye of early European fur traders and explorers. The rivers sparkled with blue water, the forests seemed untrampled, and the vast prairies to the west of the giant Mississippi rolled before the eye in an endless fashion reminiscent of the solitude existing on the open sea. But the apparent virgin atmosphere was an illusion; in 1800 these lands belonged to the eastern Sioux, or Dakota, people—hunters and gatherers whose villages extended from Prairie du Chien, the farthest northern European outpost along the Mississippi, into the eastern prairies of what are today North and South Dakota.

Europeans had been among the Dakota people for well over a hundred years. The French came first, followed after 1760 by the British. These foreigners came to trade, quickly intermarried with the Sioux, and became permanent, though numerically small, fixtures in the sparsely populated Sioux domain. For the most part, the early European traders did little to disturb the native world, not wanting to change the Indians or their ways. For a time, whites and Indians lived side by side, each party profiting from the knowledge and abilities of the other. The mutually beneficial relationship even failed to change during the War of 1812 when more than a hundred Dakota warriors joined the British against the Americans. Only after the United States Army moved up the Mississippi and established Fort Snelling at the mouth of the Minnesota River in 1819 did it seem apparent that a new era had begun for the Dakota people. While the Americans would continue the old patterns of trade and intermarriage, they also sought to control the upper Mississippi River and eventually would attempt to change the Sioux and their way of life.

Into this culturally stable but politically changing world Little Crow was born in about 1810.[1] His proud parents lived in a village named Kaposia. The name, which meant "not encumbered with much baggage," was significant, since the Kaposia people were always on the move.[2] The band spent much of the summer at the village, which was located just north of the junction of the St. Croix and Mississippi rivers, and hunted and gathered food during the remainder of the year. The spot selected for Kaposia allowed the men of the village to participate in the economic growth that occurred along the upper Mississippi in the late eighteenth and early nineteenth centuries. Accordingly, young Little Crow seldom if ever suffered from want, game being plentiful and the traders generous with powder and lead. It was in this stable environment that Little Crow learned what was expected of him in order to be a Sioux Indian, as well as of life's joys and obligations.

The Mdewakantons demanded little of boys such as Little Crow, their childhood being dominated by play and the hunting of small animals. Sioux boys learned a few important lessons, especially regarding the responsibilities of being Sioux. The Dakota people's history emphasized important leaders whose sacrifices and direction had helped the nation remain strong. Indeed, the name that the people called themselves, the "Dakota," implied strength through unity, roughly translating as the "allies" or the "league." This unity evolved from an intricate social or kinship structure. Little Crow received a position in this group and was prepared early in life to meet basic societal responsibilities. Symbolic of this preparation was the selection of a permanent Indian name when entering adulthood. While whites would always use the generic title Little Crow, the young Kaposia warrior took his place in Dakota society as Taoyateduta, meaning "His Red Nation." Although the name itself had a significant connotation, everything Little Crow was taught as a child and adolescent reinforced the basic notion that Dakota men existed for the benefit of the band and the tribe.[3]

The history of the Sioux and Taoyateduta's place in the community surely must have interested the youngster. There always seemed to be a sense of destiny in his life, as well as an overriding interest in politics. Taoyateduta would have learned that the mighty Sioux nation had spread over much of present Minnesota and North and South Dakota by 1800. The western branches of the nation consisted of seven large bands known collectively as the Teton people. Little Crow probably knew little about them other than what he had heard, but at one time they had lived on the lower Minnesota River not far from Kaposia and a generation or so before had migrated to the Missouri River region. Closer but still somewhat removed from Little Crow's Dakota people lived the Yankton and Yanktonai Sioux tribes. They occupied the James River valley and regions west and north of Big Stone Lake, frequently moving to the Missouri.

Taoyateduta's contact with these people came no doubt during buffalo hunts in the west and during the trade fairs along the James River, when his Dakota relatives bartered manufactured goods for the fine buffalo robes taken by the Yanktons and Yanktonais.[4]

Such hunts more frequently brought the young Kaposia boy into contact with other Dakota or eastern Sioux people—Sissetons, Wahpetons, Wahpekutes, and other bands of Little Crow's own Mdewakanton tribe. The largest contingent of the Sisseton tribe inhabited the headwaters of the Minnesota River, occupying villages on the shores and islands of Big Stone Lake. Smaller bands could be found southwest of the lake as well as near the mouth of the Blue Earth River, a tributary of the Minnesota. Wahpetons intermingled with the Sissetons along the upper Minnesota River, their lowest villages not more than forty miles upriver from what would one day be Minneapolis, and other larger groups congregated between the Blue Earth River and Lac qui Parle Lake. The Wahpekutes lived a rather isolated existence along the headwaters of the Blue Earth and Cannon rivers. In all, these three eastern Sioux tribes numbered perhaps four thousand people. The Sissetons were the most numerous with a population of more than two thousand and the Wahpekutes the least at about five hundred.[5]

Little Crow's own Mdewakanton tribe totaled at least two thousand people and may have been larger in the century before his birth. But the tribe remained vital in 1810, with five other semisedentary villages besides Kaposia located along the Mississippi and Minnesota rivers. The largest and perhaps most important village at this early date was under chief Wabasha, a middle-aged man who had strong attachments to the British. Wabasha's village moved from time to time, but it was most frequently found just north of present-day Prairie du Chien at the mouth of the Upper Iowa River or below Lake Pepin, a thirty-mile-long enlargement of the Mississippi. At the north end of the lake another smaller Mdewakanton band under Red Wing congregated. The movement of Wabasha's and Red Wing's bands south of Kaposia illustrates a pattern of tribal diffusion that also involved the three other Mdewakanton bands. The smallest, under Penetion, had moved up the Minnesota River, locating roughly nine miles from the river's mouth. It was joined on the lower Minnesota by a second only slightly larger village under Black Dog. This village came into existence shortly after the War of 1812, when Black Dog's people, a division of Little Crow's band, settled halfway between Penetion's village and the mouth of the Minnesota. Fully twenty miles beyond Penetion's village, on the western frontier of the Mdewakanton domain, was

Shakopee's village, the largest Indian encampment on the Minnesota River. Although populations fluctuated, Shakopee's village rivaled Wabasha's camp in size, having at least five hundred people. Penetion's, Black Dog's, and Red Wing's bands seldom reached two hundred. Kaposia held roughly four hundred and was able to field some eighty warriors.[6]

The village that Little Crow grew up in was designed to fit the climate and the hunting and gathering needs of the people. Kaposia was located on the east bank of the Mississippi, about five miles south of present-day St. Paul. This location, virtually in the center of Mdewakanton occupation, gave the men immediate access to river transportation along the Mississippi as well as the St. Croix River, which could be reached either by a short hike overland or by canoe. The village served as a staging area for the many hunting and food-gathering trips that occurred during the year. The only extended period of occupation occurred during summer when hunters periodically rested and the women planted and harvested sparse corn crops. Travelers who passed the village observed about a dozen permanent, bark houses at Kaposia. The bark structures were made of an elm frame with elm-bark walls and roofs. Although the structures varied in size, most could house more than two dozen people. At their entrances, large wood platforms were constructed for food drying and for sleeping during hot summer nights.[7]

While bark houses were suitable permanent summer abodes, they lacked the mobility of the standard Sioux living structure made of buffalo hides. As families left Kaposia to hunt and gather food, they carried along the skins necessary to build a tepee. These houses could be put up in minutes after a few saplings of fifteen feet in length were cut and assembled into a cone. An opening was left at the top to allow smoke from the cook fire to escape. During the harshest portion of the winter, women gathered dry swamp grass to bank against the tepee walls and to use on the floors. Tepees provided highly mobile and reasonably warm housing for the Mdewakantons.[8] No doubt most of Taoyateduta's earliest remembrances included the hustle and bustle involved in breaking camp and moving. It was most likely an exciting life for a youth, filled with new adventure, extensive travel, and many different sights.

Mobility allowed the Sioux of Little Crow's boyhood to live a cyclical existence, exploiting various resources at particular times of the year. The fall deer hunt, beginning after the first killing frost, was perhaps the most ordered of these events. The Kaposia Mdewakantons generally moved up the St. Croix River for this hunt, exploiting the river's many tributaries. The soldiers' lodge—a group of men experienced in the hunt—set down boundaries for each day's excursion in order to give every man a fair chance; they also directed the movement of the village from one locale to another. The deer taken during the hunt were always shared, the successful hunter keeping some meat and the hide. These were exciting times for the children as they waited all day in camp for the men to return. Once the hunters arrived, the children sought out those who had been successful and shouted "Oo-koo-hoo! Oo-koo-hoo!" They announced the names of each hunter who had killed a deer to the entire camp and continued until well after dark. The deer hunt continued until midwinter when the animals were past prime condition. The women dried excess meat over a fire for later use.[9]

After a brief rest at the Kaposia village, the people were off again in early March, dividing forces into sugar-making and hunting parties. The women collected sugar following an age-old process, an ax being used to open the tree and a birch-bark tap employed to direct the sap into containers. The men sought smaller game animals, especially muskrats and beavers. The hunters walked out onto the ice of sloughs to spear them in their houses. The thaw ended muskrat hunting and prompted yet another migration back to the main village where preparations began for planting cornfields. A few Mdewakantons, under the direction of the soldiers' lodge, struck out for the west to trade and hunt buffalo. But since buffalo had already become scarce in the lands adjacent to Kaposia, more often than not the late spring was spent fishing, chasing small game or waterfowl, or fasting. The period of scarcity characteristic of the spring was generally alleviated in the summer when berries, wild turnips, and other food plants matured.[10]

Hunting was the most important means of obtaining food, but gathering provided significant supplements, especially when the hunt failed. The Mdewakantons harvested a variety of seeds, roots, berries, and plants. They watched specific regions of the countryside, knowing that at regular intervals edible plants would be ready. Perhaps the most important gathered food was wild rice. Parties generally found wild rice abundant in the upper Rum River region below Mille Lacs Lake. Along with the meager corn crop, which could feed a Dakota family for upwards of a month, gathered foods provided an important part of the Sioux diet.[11] Children, such as Little Crow, often assisted in gathering food, a task that gave them an opportunity to contribute to the village sustenance.

Political institutions mirrored this loosely structured, cyclical pattern. The village council offered the standard forum for political debate. At one time, the elders carried more important issues on to a tribal council, but that had become a rarity by the nineteenth century because of the distances between villages. Councils operated under a set of unwritten rules; nearly anyone could speak who felt he or she possessed the societal stature necessary. Even so, a generational barrier existed in council; young men in their twenties generally listened to the advice of older, more experienced leaders. The purpose of debate was to arrive at a consensus, a state of affairs where the vast majority of elders agreed upon a particular course of action. When a consensus failed to form, individuals were free to go their own way and do whatever they felt was best.

Individual chiefs had no special privileges in councils, although they generally announced decisions. They developed influence—indeed, they became recognized as important leaders—proportional to the success they had in helping to form a consensus. Individual chiefs who demonstrated good sense and oratorical ability rose to the position of "speaker," a rank of high importance in the tribe. Such men often opened councils and focused attention on the issues at hand. Although in the historic sense the influence of speakers is unclear, they played important roles in council by the mid-nineteenth century and appear to have obtained the honor through a process of election.[12]

While tribal spokesmen went through a process of evaluation and eventual election, village chiefs usually inherited their positions, a son being selected by the outgoing or dying village leader. Taoyateduta came from a dynasty of Mdewakanton village chiefs, there being at least four men identified in early records as "Petit Corbeau," or Little Crow, before him. The European name apparently was derived from the tendency of these men to carry the wings or skin of a crow on their backs or dangling from their belts. The Little Crows served the Mdewakanton people for many decades. Taoyateduta's grandfather, Cetanwakanmani, became an important Sioux leader in the last decades of the eighteenth century. His leadership brought the dynasty to prominence. His son, Big Thunder, or Little Crow IV, increased the influence of the line, often by working with whites who migrated up the Mississippi River during the 1830s and 1840s. Each of these men held his position by being an aggressive warrior and by giving wise advice in council. Even so, leadership was closely tied to the notion of relatedness. Put simply, the Kaposia people followed the Little Crows and listened to them in part because they represented the most important family in the band. Indeed, virtually every member of the band was a relative in some degree of the Little Crow family.[13]

Such relatedness, or kinship ties, was crucially important to the Sioux. The training a child received stressed relatedness, and from the beginning of his life, Taoyateduta was taught to consider all individuals in the village as kin, or in the rough European equivalent, close relatives. The Sioux kinship system had a well-understood structure, with a division existing along sexual lines. The Dakota term for father, for example, could apply to the biological progenitor, his brothers, his parallel male cousins and his male cross-cousins. The term for mother followed a similar pattern, applying to the females of the birth mother's generation. In addition, when the Dakotas used the term children, they were referring to their own offspring, as well as those of parallel cousins; thus when a Dakota spoke of a niece or a nephew, he or she generally meant a cross-cousin of the opposite sex. The Sioux people placed a great amount of importance on relationships. Those whom Europeans generally identify as uncles or cousins were usually as important to a Sioux boy as his biological parents. People customarily addressed each other by their kinship identification, which served to reinforce familial notions of obligation. More importantly, since nearly all the people in the Little Crow village were related to each other, kinship imparted a strong sense of community, of belonging to what the Sioux called a tiyośpaye or lodge group.[14]

Kinship structures provided a place in the society for everyone, regardless of sex or age. Elders were expected to help around the village, keep the story of the people alive, and give good advice. Women and girls took care of the lodge, prepared hides, and did most of the food gathering. Young and middle-aged men defended the people and hunted. No wonder that a discerning youth such as Taoyateduta would begin to understand his role at an early age. He was the son of a chief, and he was expected to be a leader one day. Yet as a boy he also realized the importance of listening—the importance of his place. He knew everyone in the village and where each belonged, what family ties existed, and how those kinship connections were linked to his own. Such things were important to the Sioux, for they lived and survived, or perished, together as one people.

Perhaps the most important aspect of kinship was the sense of loyalty that evolved from it. Taoyateduta quickly realized that loyalty had important political implications, for it was impossible for any one man to assume a leadership position without the support of an extensive kinship network. Of course, Little Crow benefited from having a large, important family, yet from the very beginning of his career, he sought to expand his relationships with people of other Mdewakanton and eastern Sioux bands. He took as wives four daughters of a Sisseton Sioux chief, offering substantial bride prices to demonstrate his generosity and testify to the fact that they were his social equals. He constantly courted his many uncles (fathers in the Dakota equivalent), cousins, and nephews who were added to his kinship network via marriage. One reason for Taoyateduta's eventual success as a chief was the extensive kinship network that he inherited and further developed.

The value of this kinship network came from the way in which it culturally functioned in Sioux society. Depending upon degree of relatedness, kinsmen were expected to be kind, generous, and loyal to other kin, especially elders and close kin. Children were taught to respect the wisdom of grandparents and parents, regardless of the number, and to seek their approval for actions. The praise that hunters received upon returning from a successful hunt only exemplified a much broader, and more expansive, system of societal reinforcement. Young people also realized that communal hunting and protection of the village necessitated complete cooperation with brothers, cousins, and lesser relatives. Accordingly, Sioux men never denied the requests of such relatives—particularly fathers and brothers—and were willing to die when necessary to demonstrate familial loyalty. Reinforcement of kinship relationships also occurred through the constant exchange of presents. Gifts became a vehicle for proving one's fidelity as well as noting degrees of relatedness. It was an ordered social world that Taoyateduta grew up in, one which provided him with a strong sense of identity and pride. Ideally, young Dakota men knew their obligations, their place in the village, and that they could count on relatives to assist them in the common struggle for survival.[15]

Religion played a primary role in the upbringing of Sioux children such as Taoyateduta. For the Sioux, religion encompassed a reverence for the mysteries surrounding daily life and death. At the center of their understanding was taku-wakan, or that which is mysterious. As an early observer noted, while whites made reference to medicine men, medicine feasts, and the medicine dance, to the Dakota people these always had been wakan-men, wakan-feasts, and the wakan-dance. Numerous dieties took shape under this umbrella of wakan. There was Unktehi, the god of water, who had helped produce man and earth, and Wakinyan, the great mysterious bird, who was responsible for thunder, and even the Great Wakan, or Spirit, a neutral diety who also played a role in creation. But principally the Sioux believed that these supreme beings were neither good nor evil. Along with many others, these spirits existed in the rocks and water of the land, helping at times to make life easy, but more frequently causing the people difficulty by casting spells and bewitching the animal life that brought sustenance.[16]

The Dakota also bestowed anthropomorphic characteristics on most animals and believed that animals could affect the good fortune of the unborn. Once an infant like Little Crow came into the world, animals filled the verses of lullabies and became the subjects of late-night story-telling in the lodges. Those animals who were thought to represent good omens were spoken of in tones of deep reverence as if the animals them-selves could hear and under the belief that they were actual kin. Story-telling also emphasized the powers of animal spirits and how they had been responsible for certain selected ancestors becoming great men. The crow, the animal that Taoyateduta identified with, had special meaning for him in the stories he heard. But constant references were made to a variety of animals, particularly those that demonstrated great wisdom, like śunktokeća, the wolf. He was cunning and always watched his prey carefully. When pursued, the wolf kept his head and took one last look at his pursuer before disappearing.[17]

Part of religious upbringing included learning that religion, hunting, and tribal responsibilities, or sacrifices, went hand in hand. Taoyateduta faced the realities of tribal life at an early age. While hunting initially was projected as sport and game to male children, elder relatives constantly reinforced the communal contributions necessary of young hunters by congratulating them on their success at killing small birds and animals. Small game added to the village larder, and children had to be convinced that by sharing it they were doing what was just and right. Yet animals possessed spirits that needed to be placated. These spirits could and often did cause sickness for villagers. It was common for young hunters to learn how to make sacrifices to animals and to respect them for their wisdom, so that the animals would continue to aid the people.[18] After reaching adulthood, a Sioux hunter would take only part of a deer carcass, leaving the remainder to others in the village, and thank the spirit of the deer for his success.

Such lessons of sacrifice and sharing often became difficult for young children, even though appeasing the spirits was essential. Children fre-quently were told that ancestors became great hunters and providers because of the power and strength gained from the Great Mystery, or Great Spirit. Boys were taught to surrender their most prized possessions to this power; some gave up bows and arrows while others sacrificed a favorite pet, such as a dog. The more important the item, the better one would stand with his creator and other villagers. Sacrifice was essential to the survival of the village, for the small items that were given would soon be replaced by much larger contributions of the kind that would keep relatives alive. Successful hunters also gave many feasts, earning much respect in the village, and were looked upon as important men. But acquiring such success meant giving up all thoughts of material possession. The more important young men in Sioux villages were always the poorest, the most reckless in pursuit of game or war, and the most generous.[19]

For any young man of Taoyateduta's stature, the lessons regarding sharing must have had special meaning. It was crucially important for men who wished to lead to give of their time, energy, and prized possessions in order to secure a reputation as a generous person. One of Little Crow's first opportunities to demonstrate such dedication came as a child of twelve when a companion broke through the ice of a river. Recklessly abandoning concerns for his own safety, he crawled out onto the thin ice and saved his companion's life. Yet another good example of this generosity came not long after Taoyateduta had assumed the chieftainship of his band in 1851. Shortly after posing for a portrait done by a young artist, Taoyateduta rose and took off the magnificent headdress of seventeen eagle feathers that he had worn. He promptly gave it to a group of dancers who had performed in front of his tent. Generosity and swift action in support of the village was often spontaneous, a learned cultural trait that brought praise to the individual and honor to his family. The village, in turn, reinforced such generosity by sending criers out to proclaim good deeds and make them known to all.[20]

The emphasis upon hunting productivity inherent in the society created a necessity for the keen observation of nature. To Taoyateduta the woods became a classroom where elders taught nature lore. Elders encouraged the young Little Crow to observe animals and their habits, the weather, and on what side of the tree the moss grew thickest. The lessons continued at night in the lodge where elders asked what had been learned that day and occasionally cross-examined young hunters.[21] Always these lessons were tied to a reverence for the Great Mystery, for it was this power that directed events and controlled the lives of the people.

Appropriately, the lessons in nature lore and the societal emphasis upon spiritualism had the most meaning to a young Dakota boy when he first prepared to go to war. This process began when a shaman, or wicaśta wakan, decided that the time was right. Shamans, powerful people in Sioux camps, were always listened to and even feared. Nevertheless, the record of the shaman had much to do with whether others accepted his invitation. For adolescent boys the forming of a war party created great anticipation, most being hopeful that the warriors would ask them to join the party. When the offer came, as it would inevitably, a boy had reached the point where he was about to enter manhood.[22]

As a young man such as Taoyateduta prepared for war, he underwent a spiritual cleansing. The ceremony, or rite of passage, was meant to produce a vision, and thus personal power. The young warrior who sought such power placed himself under the control of a zuya-wakan, or a shaman who specialized in war. This man directed the purification, which included fasting and the spending of three days and nights in the inipi, or steam bath. During this period the inductee symbolically left life as an adolescent and re-emerged as a new person—a young adult. Upon completion of purification, the young man received sacred armor from the zuya-wakan, represented by a spear, an arrow, and a sacred bundle of paints. These objects possessed sacred, life-saving properties. He was also told by the shaman to which animal the armor was dedicated—the crow in the case of Little Crow. Thereafter, he was never to slay this animal, for its spirit would have a direct impact upon the warrior's life and his destiny. The completion of the ceremony brought the freshly created warrior a new name to go with his new identity.[23]

The entry into manhood offered one other major opportunity not enjoyed by all Dakota men and women. Within each village a society existed, called by whites the medicine society, which performed the wakan dance or medicine dance. It had been given to the Dakota people by Unktehi. It did not exist among all Sioux groups, but the society possessed extreme power in Mdewakanton villages, where perhaps half the adults were admitted. The secrecy of the society enhanced its influence. Those who joined were guaranteed supernatural power, invitations to frequent feasts, long life, and the companionship of the most influential people in the village. Indeed, virtually every member of the society was recognized as a wicaśta wakan.[24]

Just when it occurred has escaped the chroniclers of the age, but Taoyateduta entered the medicine society sometime in early adulthood. Most inductees remained unaware of their selection until just before the great medicine dance, at which point they were called into the main lodge and told of their good fortune. The secrets of the society were revealed, and the new members were presented with a medicine sack, the contents of which varied but generally held the skins of an otter, a raccoon, a weasel, a squirrel, a loon, and a snake and several varieties of fish bones. While often dismissed by whites as a foolish collection of unimportant items, these objects, according to Sioux belief, worked in harmony to bring great spiritual power to their owners. The sack had often belonged to a close relative who had recently died, and the new owner temporarily took his identity in order to ensure the transfer of the spiritual strength.[25] The dance that followed was the highlight of all village events, with old members lining up on one side, their medicine sacks held high, and occasionally "shooting" new members with their sacks. This consisted of touching them at the breast, which supposedly forced a small shell into their hearts. The inductees fell lifeless to the ground, rising minutes later after they coughed up the shell to show to the assembled crowd. The dance went on all day, being interrupted only by occasional displays of sleight of hand.

In the course of his upbringing, Little Crow also learned about death. The Dakotas believed in an afterlife, but they spent little time contemplating its nature. Some of their number believed that the body possessed four souls; one died with the body at death, the second remained near the grave, the third lingered in the swatches of hair kept by relatives, and the fourth proceeded to the land in the south to live with departed relatives. What existed in this land of spirits to the south never seemed overly important, other than that it was a place where ties with departed family members would be renewed. Such a view precluded the notion of accountability and suggested a passage from one life into another unencumbered by moral barriers. As Little Crow would often say in later life, he feared not death for he knew what it brought.[26] Such apparent security in life speaks well of the learning process that welcomed every Sioux male at birth.

This strong sense of identity and purpose both complicated and facilitated the way in which the Dakota people viewed strangers. For some outsiders—particularly the Ojibway to the north and east and the Iowa, Sac, and Fox to the south—it could mean suffering instant death. They were not of the Dakota people, who often thought them to be unworthy of life. These outsiders had no regard for helping the tiyospaye or lodge group. Yet to others, especially the growing number of Americans who came to Sioux lands with goods that made life easier, the Dakota would offer friendship and alliance. Processes of kinship adoption had existed for centuries, allowing the Mdewakantons to bring into their bands people from alien societies. Various villages began incorporating whites through adoption after their arrival in Sioux lands in the seventeenth century, thereby cementing trade through intermarriage. Taoyateduta grew up fully aware that such traders as Jean Baptiste Faribault, Joseph Renville, and the Campbell brothers, Scott, Duncan, and Colin, were all his relatives.[27] The founding of Fort Snelling in 1819 at the mouth of the Minnesota River continued this process of miscegenation, as white men lived thereafter within about ten miles of the Little Crow village.

Thus, as this man Little Crow reached maturity in the 1820s, he found that the world of his youth was on the verge of change. The forests and plains no longer held the numbers of game animals that had historically been the basis of the eastern Sioux economy, and white men had an increasing impact on the Dakota ecosystem. Being a young man, Taoyateduta had yet to reach the stage in life where change had to be taken seriously. Dakota young men had traditionally lived for the excitement of the hunt and for the glories of war. Nevertheless, the changes that occurred in the eastern Sioux domain did affect the thinking of Taoyateduta's father, Big Thunder, who assumed the chieftainship of his people during the winter of 1833–34. How would the eastern Sioux respond to the growing presence of the whites? Would the building of Fort Snelling, less than a dozen miles from Kaposia, be the final chapter in the unfolding story of Sioux-white relations, or would it be the beginning? Certainly these questions were important ones for a chief to consider. And time would ultimately show that such issues would not go away. Rather, they would one day be inherited with the mantle of Mdewakanton leadership.

2

The Formula for Leadership

FOR the Little Crow dynasty, the early decades of the nineteenth century proved both rewarding, in terms of enhanced prominence, and perplexing, in respect to the growing economic dependency that the Dakota people faced. The increased infiltration of Sioux lands by white Americans brought more prestige to the Kaposia band. Fort Snelling was built near the band's village, and the fort quickly became a commercial center. Taoyateduta's grandfather, Cetanwakanmani, and his father, Big Thunder, sought peaceful coexistence and friendly ties with the whites near the fort, being aware of the benefits that they could provide for the Dakota people. Nevertheless, such benefits came at a cost; increased trade with whites soon depleted resources and ultimately made it impossible for the eastern Sioux to live without assistance from fur traders and United States government officials. Even so, the Kaposia people did not blame whites for their predicament, nor did they view economic dependency as a threat to their existence. Cetanwakanmani and Big Thunder embraced the whites who ascended the Mississippi River and came to view some of them as kinsmen. This unique relationship had a significant impact on young Taoyateduta as it helped shape his evolving notions of politics.

Kinship institutions molded Sioux perceptions of whites. Ordinarily, the Dakota people feared strangers, who had no inherent reason to do what was best for a Dakota kinship group. But when outsiders offered advantages—such as trade goods—to the native community, the Sioux often adopted the newcomers, using an age-old process that gave the person a Dakota identity, or name, and a place in tribal society. For example, the Dakota people quickly adopted traders, who in a traditional fashion took Indian wives. Much like young Dakota hunters, traders assumed a family responsibility by providing relatives with the trade goods necessary for survival and, in turn, received pelts from relatives. Thus the fur trade was not just a capitalistic venture; it was a communal enterprise, rooted in the kinship system. Nineteenth-century traders worked hard to overcome this communal mentality, but they were unable to wipe out completely the patterns that had evolved in the early years and continued to hand out presents, or what they called "credits," to their Indian customers in the fall and collect furs as payments in the spring.[1]

This unique relationship did not change appreciably even in 1819 when a military garrison and a government Indian agent moved into the neighborhood near Kaposia. Lawrence Taliaferro, a Virginian, represented the government to the Indians. He realized that through the use of presents and the creation of kinship ties his Dakota charges would be easier to handle. Accordingly Taliaferro took a young Sioux woman from Black Dog's small village (a faction of the Little Crow band), and a daughter was born to the union in August 1828. Such an "affine" relationship, or one deriving from blood ties, gave Taliaferro important leverage with the Little Crow band at the same time that it placed pressure on Taliaferro to assist his new kinsmen. Taliaferro's father-in-law was Cloud Man, a Little Crow villager who was related to Taoyateduta. Cloud Man's son, Smokey Day, was a close companion of the young, future Mdewakanton chief.[2]

The young son of Big Thunder no doubt watched Taliaferro carefully as the agent formed a working relationship with the Sioux Indians near his agency. Taliaferro's position gave him the opportunity to hand out presents at his council house, as the government annually allotted a small amount of money to use in pacifying the Indians. Thus the agent's influence with Dakota leaders evolved both from "affine," or blood ties, as well as from "fictive" relationships, or those coming purely from ceremonial adoption and gift-giving. Indians living close to Fort Snelling had constant contact with the agent, received presents regularly, and fit Taliaferro closely into their kinship structure. With him they smoked the pipe of peace, a symbol in itself of kinship ties, and addressed him in Dakota as "Father." He accordingly developed a kinship network based upon his own biological relationship with the Sioux and the presents that he used to reinforce it.[3] Other Dakota leaders from the Sisseton, Wahpeton, and Wahpekute tribes were also prone to listen to Taliaferro, since they were related to the Mdewakantons and to other white traders, who often reinforced the government's position.

Such interrelated ethnic ties had an important impact on the life of young Taoyateduta, and he learned much from them. His grandfather, Cetanwakanmani, who apparently was killed by Ojibway during the winter of 1833–34, and his father, Big Thunder, chief until 1845, became two of the most frequent visitors to Taliaferro's council house. They acted as strong advocates of the American occupation, working with the agent both to resolve difficulties and to maintain peace by implementing a form of consensus political rule that had been handed down to them by their ancestors. In council, with tribal representatives present, spokesmen for the Sioux would address the agent regarding a problem, striving for resolution through the force of argument. Taliaferro, as well, would join in the discussion and offer his "good offices" to bring about consensus. Sometimes discussions went on for days, and a consensus did not form. But all Indian leaders left fully aware of the position of the government and usually convinced that it was in their best interests to respect it.[4]

Taliaferro especially seemed to rely on Cetanwakanmani's support and assistance. When, for example, Taliaferro was leading a peace delegation of eastern Sioux to Washington, D.C., in 1824 and he found many chiefs unwilling to go beyond Prairie du Chien, Cetanwakanmani rose and said: "My friends. . . . We are here, and should go on. . . . I have taken our father [Taliaferro] here by the coat-tail and will follow him."[5] The delegation then decided to follow Taliaferro to the capital. Three years later, when the Siouan-speaking Winnebago threatened American occupation of the upper Mississippi, Cetanwakanmani and others from his village kept Taliaferro informed of a contemplated alliance between the Winnebago and Wabasha's village. "I am your friend," the chief told the agent, "and will tell things that I hear." In leaving Taliaferro, he invariably concluded his speech with, "My father I take you by the hand."[6]

For his part, Taliaferro rewarded this loyalty with presents and moral support. He refused to see other lesser politicians from the Little Crow village—such as the aggressive Grand Partisan, a war chief—unless Cetanwakanmani was present. He also rewarded Cetanwakanmani with a presidential medal that was equal in size to Wabasha's and larger than those held by Black Dog, Penetion, and Grand Partisan. The medal became a symbol of power in that the holder would receive a yearly allotment of presents and be allowed to distribute them to his followers. Cetanwakanmani thus acquired considerable status simply through being recognized as an important man by the agent.[7] Finally, as a reward for loyalty, Taliaferro recognized Big Thunder in the mid-1830s as the heir to his father's position. Although Taliaferro may have regretted this decision when the new Little Crow IV succumbed to strong drink, the chieftainship was passed down without mishap.

Taliaferro's political assistance, however, failed to alleviate the growing discontent in Little Crow's village with the leadership of Cetanwakanmani and his son. Younger men, led by Grand Partisan and Medicine Bottle, slowly began to leave the village after 1825.[8] Some perhaps were angry with the way government soldiers treated their people, especially women, and with the failure of Cetanwakanmani or Taliaferro to do anything about it. Cetanwakanmani himself had been knocked down by two drunken soldiers in 1826—one example of the kinds of problems that attended living close to Americans. But the majority were probably discontented with the growing anarchy that came with Cetanwakanmani's increased use of alcohol and the meddling in Sioux affairs by the government.[9]

The government's efforts to prevent intertribal war no doubt prompted the most debate in the Little Crow village as well as among other Sioux Indians. Warfare hindered the fur trade and made it more difficult for the government to control Indians. While it was obviously a humane policy to stop intertribal fighting, the fur companies found that Indian warfare prevented the exploitation of the regions being fought over. Such lands usually held the best fur reserves. In addition, the growing popularity of the removal policy in the United States during the 1820s created pressure to stop Indian warfare. Eastern tribes simply would not be removed into regions that were hotly contested by other Indians. Taliaferro tried to end the fighting in a series of treaties negotiated in the early 1820s. Other more formal councils followed at Prairie du Chien in 1825 and 1830.[10]

Opposition to the peace policy existed at Kaposia. Young Sioux men gained prestige in war; indeed, it was uncommon for a man to take a wife until he had proven himself in war. While Cetanwakanmani admitted on numerous occasions that peace was best for his people and he tried to argue in its behalf, he also pointed out that once the wars with such aggressive neighbors as the Ojibway and the Sac and Fox ended, these other Indians would encroach upon Sioux hunting ground. Warfare resulted in the loss of one or two men each year, but the old chief wondered if such losses were not justified. Consequently, the issue was never resolved; Taliaferro continued to pressure the eastern Sioux to give up intertribal raiding, and Cetanwakanmani, although often holding a different view, felt obliged to listen to the agent's advice.[11]

The growing availability of liquor created as many difficulties for the Little Crow chiefs as warfare. By the late 1820s, Cetanwakanmani drank heavily as did many of his people. Fights regularly broke out in his village with many people being injured. Grand Partisan, the rebel, used the disorder as a rationale for abandoning his chief; nevertheless, he soon became involved in the liquor traffic himself, using his new village at "Pine Turn," located eight miles south of Kaposia, as a transfer point for traders who wished to ship liquor overland to the Minnesota River and avoid detection at Fort Snelling. As Pine Turn grew, Kaposia declined from several hundred people to a mere sixty at one point. By 1834 Kaposia had regained a few of its discontented inhabitants, showing a population of 183 people, but the struggles cost Cetanwakanmani considerable prestige in the eyes of his people.[12]

Certainly the severity of Cetanwakanmani's troubles would have lessened had the economic base at Kaposia remained stable. As late as 1820 the Little Crow villagers still enjoyed a diversified economy, with hunting, gathering, and a small amount of farming providing an abundant food supply. Although the number and quality of furs available for trade had declined from the peak years of the late eighteenth century, the American Fur Company still maintained outfits at the mouth of the Minnesota River, as well as on the St. Croix, Rock, Chippewa, and Black rivers. The company's records show that these traders took in considerable numbers of deer, raccoon, fisher, beaver, and bear skins.[13]

A dramatic decline shook the Dakota trade economy by the late 1820s. As the numbers of deer and beavers thinned, the Mdewakantons resorted to hunting muskrats in late winter in the sloughs of southwestern Minnesota. Traditionally the Sioux had taken few muskrats; the Indians preferred venison as a food source, and the fur traders had little use for "rats," as they were called, when beavers were plentiful. The rat hunts had become so important by the late 1820s, however, that fully three-fourths of the pelts taken by the Mdewakantons were muskrat. By the time of Cetanwakanmani's death in the mid-1830s, muskrats constituted 95 percent of the skins harvested. Obviously, such numbers brought a reorientation in hunting and dietary patterns. Many Mdewakantons turned away from the woodlands and looked to the western prairie for skins to support themselves. Unfortunately, a rat pelt was worth ten cents, or less, in comparison to three dollars for a beaver skin.[14]

As both the take of prime peltry and trade profits declined, the American Fur Company was able to drive out most competition and cut back on credits given to hunters. Several of their traders working with Cetanwakanmani's people even began to repossess items issued in the fall as "credits" but not fully paid for in the spring. By the early 1830s, company employees commonly gave credits only to the better hunters and ignored the older men, who could not participate as effectively in the chase. This retrenchment strained long-standing kinship alliances between traders and Indians, and several company employees, including Jean Baptiste Faribault, who traded with the Little Crow band, were assaulted. Only the most important leaders and hunters received supplies at the Kaposia village, among them the sons of Big Thunder. (Unfortunately the records do not reveal which sons were involved in these transactions.)[15]

Cetanwakanmani and Big Thunder turned to Taliaferro for aid during the economic crises. "Our people suffered much last spring," Cetanwakanmani noted in council with the agent in 1829. "Our traders deprived us of our guns and our traps. I felt ashamed of this . . . had it not been for your kind assistance we must have starved."[16] Dakota warriors surely became distressed when traders deprived them of the weapons that they needed to feed their families, thereby forcing them to rely on the government for food. Taliaferro aided the Little Crow people by purchasing and distributing some rations every year thereafter. He also handed out fishhooks, lines, rat spears, and other items. But the repossession of goods only increased, and Cetanwakanmani as chief continued to voice complaints. "It would be better to knock us on the head," he said in 1831, "than to starve us to death."[17] Men, women, and children suffered alike from the traders' actions.

Both Indians and agents saw farming and increased gathering as the solution to these economic difficulties. Taliaferro especially encouraged the Sioux to fish in order to supplement other foods usually gathered, such as wild rice, berries, and roots. But gathering could not fill the void created by the loss of game herds, forcing even the Indians to consider farming as a means to alleviate their economic problems. Cetanwakanmani seemed less opposed to increased farming than most chiefs, for he had spent many hours watching the soldiers at Fort Snelling plow. He went so far as to ask Taliaferro for a plow in 1828, but the agent failed to fill the request immediately. When he did so in 1834, Cetanwakanmani's son, Big Thunder, had assumed his father's political position. Members of Big Thunder's band loaded the plow into a canoe and ferried it down to the village. That spring the first furrows were plowed by Sioux Indians at Kaposia.[18]

The plowing failed to produce much change, even though Big Thunder and his war chief, Big Iron, stuck with the work for an entire week. Fortunately they received some assistance from Samuel W. Pond, a young Connecticut missionary who had just arrived on the upper Mississippi. Pond held the oxen as the two Indians tried to manage the plow. The handling of the plow caused the most difficulty, as Pond noted that the Indians labored "like men wrestling."[19] The experiment marked the last time that Big Thunder tried to plow; he seemed to think that plowing was worthwhile in general but not something that an Indian warrior ought to attempt. Whether Taoyateduta witnessed this spectacle is impossible to determine, but later in life he resisted becoming a farmer.

Big Thunder's frustrating attempt at becoming a husbandman illustrates the enormous economic difficulties facing the Dakota people by the mid-1830s. Strong cultural prohibitions existed in the Sioux world against men doing "woman's work," in this case farming, but some change was essential, since the old hunting grounds along the St. Croix and Cannon rivers were virtually exhausted. Deer could no longer be found in herds anywhere east of the Mississippi. In increasing numbers men and their families were leaving to hunt muskrats along the upper tributaries of the Minnesota River. Even Big Thunder's young son, Taoyateduta, turned to the prairies, leaving Kaposia sometime in the early 1830s. The departure of such groups signaled the eventual dissolution of Kaposia.

Taliaferro spent many hours with Big Thunder discussing these problems. The Kaposia chief's role in finding solutions expanded considerably after a smallpox epidemic carried off old Wabasha and many of his people in 1835.[20] From Taliaferro's viewpoint, there was only one solution: the Mdewakantons had to sell a portion of their land in order to buy food annuities and receive instruction in farming. The agent became convinced by 1836 that Big Thunder, as well as several other Mdewakanton leaders, would accept such a solution, providing they did not have to leave their homeland. The land that the agent had in mind lay east of the Mississippi, and Taliaferro cautiously broached the question of a land sale to Sioux leaders. While notes of his council with them have not survived, the agent reported that leaders were receptive to the idea. Big Thunder, clearly a key figure in Taliaferro's plans, gave implied support by his actions. He asked that a plow and yoke of oxen be permanently placed at his village.[21]

The next year Taliaferro convinced the government and the Indians to negotiate. A delegation of twenty-six eastern Sioux chiefs journeyed to Washington in September 1837 and quickly went into council with Secretary of War Joel R. Poinsett. The government soon proposed to purchase approximately five million acres of land from the Mdewakantons—all of the territory the tribe held east of the Mississippi River. Poinsett offered one million dollars as compensation. The money was to provide food annuities and farm equipment for each Mdewakanton village.[22]

Big Thunder rose to speak first for the Mdewakantons, indicating that he had been selected as the primary spokesman for the tribe. "We have listened to the talk you have made us," he told Poinsett, but in accepted Indian custom the chief concluded that further discussion would be necessary before any agreement could be reached. Consensus on such an important issue would take time. Over the next few days, various leaders addressed Poinsett, expressing concern over the amount of land to be purchased and suggesting that more money would be appropriate. Nevertheless, a consensus supporting the sale finally evolved after five days of discussion. Afloat, a Mdewakanton of minor importance, probably best represented the sentiments of the delegation when he told Poinsett: "What you have said is all very true . . . we hope that you will assist us so that we can live another day—we did not come to go home empty." A day or so later, Big Thunder, again speaking for the tribe, finally provided the answer that Poinsett had been waiting for: "I consent to the offer you have made us." The chief only wished to be consulted on how the money was to be divided up.[23]

In the aftermath of the negotiation, the Sioux delegation went sightseeing in Washington, and a few leaders, including Big Thunder, apparently had their portraits painted by Charles Bird King. Taliaferro made certain that Big Thunder was included on the list since he obviously had been helpful in the negotiation. But since Wabasha's death in 1835, Big Thunder also was the most influential chief.[24] The delegation evidently appreciated the agent's thoughtfulness and the many presents because, when the Indians returned to the upper Mississippi in November, Big Thunder asked the interpreter, Scott Campbell, who also happened to be his relative, to write Taliaferro and tell him "Not to undo any part of the Treaty."[25] He and most other leaders were quite satisfied with it.

The Treaty of 1837 brought important changes to Mdewakanton landholdings. Big Thunder's camp, the only Mdewakanton village then located on the ceded land, moved across the river to the west bank of the Mississippi in 1838. Within days whites occupied the east bank of the river. In the months and years that followed, the white population steadily increased on the ceded lands, bringing many more of them into direct contact with the Indians. Moreover, while the delegates had prepared to depart for Washington, Methodist missionaries, under the leadership of Alfred Brunson, arrived and began to survey the region near Kaposia. They soon opened a school for Sioux children near the new Kaposia village, plowed a hundred acres of land, to the delight of the Indians, and harvested a large crop of corn.[26] Finally, when the annuities arrived in October 1838, the fruits of the treaty negotiation became obvious; in all, the Little Crow band received eighty-five barrels of flour, three barrels of pork, three barrels of salt, and nearly two hundred barrels of corn. Taliaferro also distributed goods, although the Indians received these coolly. Even

Taliaferro realized that most items, especially beads, ribbons, and silk cloth, were useless. This disappointment hardly matched the anger that erupted when tribal leaders were told that they would have to wait until 1839 to receive the fifteen thousand dollars in cash annuity, because it was interest on an investment that had to mature.[27]

In the decade following the Treaty of 1837, Mdewakanton dependency on the federal government increased. Traders gave liberal credit once again after they realized that the government would repay losses from annuity money. Thus more and more food each year came from the government or by purchase from the traders rather than from hunting. Diets changed in the Mdewakanton villages as larger quantities of pork and wheat bread were consumed each year. Chiefs, such as Big Thunder, were pressured to send their children either to mission schools or to the new government schools that agent Taliaferro attempted to build. Moreover, the government was for the first time actively involved in trying to make farmers of Sioux warriors. Taliaferro hired a white man to work in each village, plowing and instructing the Indians in husbandry. In the case of Kaposia, Thomas W. Pope became the government farmer. He also operated a school over the winter.[28]

While teaching agriculture as a means of establishing economic independence had been the primary goal of the treaty, the program that Taliaferro designed never achieved any degree of success. The agent first sought competent instructors who would work with the Indians. But there were few such men to choose from on the frontier, and those selected generally accomplished little. As soon as the Indians saw that whites would plow for them, they avoided this task. In addition, when Big Thunder realized that Thomas Pope received an annual salary of four hundred dollars, he pressured Taliaferro to remove Pope and hire one of his relatives. His choice was Alexander Faribault. Taliaferro considered Faribault to be unqualified and denied the request. This social rebuff prompted Big Thunder's men to kill the oxen issued for the farming program. Their anger apparently convinced Pope to resign. Taliaferro then chose John Holton to be the next farmer. Big Thunder only continued to conspire against Holton, driving off cattle and disrupting the planting process. Big Thunder's actions were typical of Sioux behavior. When a kinsman, such as Taliaferro, denied a request, the accepted response was to vent anger through destruction.[29]

The schools likewise enjoyed little success. Taliaferro had envisioned that each village would have a government-financed school, but by 1841 the only such school in operation among the Mdewakantons was at Kaposia.

31

Although it was in the largest Sioux village on the Mississippi, the school had few pupils, and all the teaching was done in English. The Methodist mission school at Kaposia and a second mission school at Red Wing also received some financial aid from the government, but the private institutions did no better than the government school. The Methodist mission director, Alfred Brunson, petitioned the commissioner of Indian affairs to direct the army to force children into the classroom, but the government refused. The next year, the mission and government schools at Kaposia closed.[30]

The increased haggling between government officials and Sioux leaders over the implementation of the treaty seemed uncharacteristic when compared with past interethnic relations and suggested the beginning of a new era. Indeed, whites such as Taliaferro and the traders in the past had been incorporated into villages and often had Indian families. The bickering with Indians and lack of support for the treaty by government officials convinced Taliaferro to resign in 1839. While traders remained and even became more liberal with credit, the treaty formalized interethnic relations to the extent that kinship reinforcement became less personal. Government clerks automatically handed out rations by the 1840s, and the agents who followed Taliaferro correspondingly placed less emphasis upon individual councils with chiefs such as Big Thunder.

In addition, white populations on lands adjacent to the Sioux domain increased, changing the landscape of the upper Mississippi River valley. Settlers moved onto the east bank of the Mississippi in small numbers in the late 1830s and early 1840s, planting a few crops on what once had been the Mdewakanton hunting domain. Big Thunder's old village site east of the Mississippi was occupied by Pierre Parrant, who, to the dismay of Taliaferro, often made his living selling whiskey. Parrant, who was called Pig's Eye because of a peculiar facial characteristic, had initially settled upriver closer to the fort, but Taliaferro had ordered him to leave, and he built a new whiskey shop across from Kaposia in the late 1830s. The location soon attracted a small group of French-Canadian farmers who called their village "Pig's Eye." Many of Big Thunder's men regularly frequented Parrant's establishment. A few of them, including the chief's son, Taoyateduta, realized that Parrant's liquor could be sold in the west to Sisseton and Wahpeton relatives. By the mid-1840s, traders on the Missouri River were finding that competition from these Mdewakanton men was ruining their business.[31] The liquor trade had become an important commercial endeavor on the Mississippi River and inland from it.

Despite the increased white population, Big Thunder tried to maintain traditional activities. In May 1841 he led a large war party up the St. Croix River and attacked the Ojibway at Lake Pokegama. He realized that this action was in clear defiance of government policy, but his old friend Taliaferro no longer represented the United States at the eastern Sioux agency, and the chief had never agreed to support the new one. Missionary Samuel Pond spoke against the plan and warned Big Thunder that such a course would bring evil to his family and village. Big Thunder smiled and replied: "The Great Spirit is very friendly to me; see how many children he has given me [pointing to several sons present]; I am not afraid of his displeasure." Unfortunately the raid failed, and his two eldest sons, Tamazawakan and Dowan, were killed. He dressed them in new garb, placed them in sitting positions against a tree, and returned to his village, seemingly convinced that while the Great Spirit would take care of his sons, he had at least temporarily forsaken the Kaposia band and its chief.[32]

The next year, the Ojibway retaliated and attacked the Little Crow village near Pig's Eye. The Sioux warriors, who had been drinking all day, were unprepared for the battle and suffered a dozen casualties. The fighting prompted the government to host a major peace negotiation in 1843 at Fort Snelling. Big Thunder and his subchiefs agreed to turn over to the government those young men who broke the peace. They also accepted the agent's argument that the bands ought to be compensated for losses through the transfer of annuities. Some observers noted that the two serious setbacks experienced by Big Thunder's people had helped to produce a more pacifistic mood, a far cry from the way the villagers had acted a few decades before.[33]

The intertribal fighting and the fiasco of the farming and educational programs strongly suggested that the Treaty of 1837 had been an utter failure. After the land sale, whites moved ever closer, and alcohol availability increased substantially. The Mdewakantons had rejected farming and often killed the stock sent by the government to work their fields. Yet Mdewakanton leaders did not seem overly distressed at their condition or angry with the government. Indeed, most councils with agency officials in the 1840s reveal only minor complaints. The most common was the failure of the government to distribute a five thousand dollar fund set aside for education, a minor portion of the money available under the 1837 treaty.[34] The friendly nature of interethnic relations can only be explained by the success of the annuity program that came with the treaty.

The annuities had rejuvenated the Mdewakanton tribe. Starvation, a fear during the 1830s, had been averted, and relatives from the west began to return to their eastern villages in order to benefit from food and goods handed out annually by the government. Their numbers included Big Thunder's son, Taoyateduta, whose name appeared on the 1843 annuity roll after he went back to Kaposia temporarily to receive his annuities. In addition, death rates declined after the treaty, due to vaccinations and the consistent food supply. Infants could digest wheat bread more easily than boiled corn. Some children even cried for "bread," refusing to eat corn. As a result of the in-migration and the dietary changes, the Mdewakanton population nearly doubled in the decade after the treaty, surpassing two thousand people by 1849.[35] The distribution of food had also taken pressure off hunters, who could now go about their occupation or roam in the west—as Taoyateduta did—under the realization that if the hunt failed, the government would supplement food supplies and feed their families. Mdewakanton hunters had more time on their hands to feast, lounge in the lodges, and, unfortunately, to drink whiskey.

The treaty also offered men like Big Thunder political benefits. Chiefs in Mdewakanton villages lost power in the 1830s, as traders rewarded individual hunters, disrupted older political patterns based upon consensus, and meddled in tribal political affairs, using their relatives to influence the council meetings. But as the fur trade declined and the government programs increased during the next decade, chiefs regained some influence. Their role as mediator increased appreciably in two ways. First they listened to the views of tribal members in councils or shaped those views through oratory; then they represented the village or tribe in larger councils with government officials. More importantly, chiefs provided advice about the types of annuities that were to be given out, and once the goods and food arrived, chiefs distributed them to individuals. Annuities, in other words, offered an opportunity for chiefs to reinforce kinship obligations and regain lost influence.[36]

Just as Big Thunder's role in the new political order seemed to be on the rise, he accidentally shot himself in the chest while grasping a firearm in a moving wagon. The accident occurred in October 1845 as the chief was assisting in the harvest. The government doctor, called to the chief's bedside from Fort Snelling, confirmed what Big Thunder already knew— the wound was mortal. In the last few days of his life, Big Thunder sent for one of his sons then living at Kaposia. This son was fourth in line to the chieftainship after Taoyateduta, who was at Lac qui Parle, and the two brothers who had been killed in 1841 by the Ojibway. According to one account, Big Thunder forthrightly told this young son that he had not been pleased with his heavy drinking and bad habits. Even so, he declared him to be his favorite and gave him his chief's medals, symbols of the descent of leadership. He then advised the young man to do his best to adopt the positive aspects of white culture and to learn to live with the increasingly populous and powerful Americans. Big Thunder died the next day, supposedly convinced that he had settled any debate over who would lead the Kaposia band after his death. His actions, however, only prompted a controversy. One of Taoyateduta's half-brothers had been selected to be chief, and he—the eldest—had been passed over.[37]

Big Thunder left a legacy of accommodation and compromise. He believed that government officials were trying to help, and he saw nothing wrong in incorporating Americans—traders and government officials—into the Sioux consensus political system when they assisted his people. To some extent, Big Thunder had become a "government chief," and he encouraged his sons and his people to follow in his footsteps. Such politics had brought the Mdewakantons, especially those at Kaposia, back to a position of prominence among the eastern Sioux. Despite the advantages offered by such policies, however, Big Thunder left a host of problems. Alcohol use, economic dependency, and the numbers of whites on adjoining lands increased during the 1840s. More importantly, accommodation placed demands upon Dakota leaders that could not easily be met. Soon after Big Thunder's death, this policy would expose a central dilemma: chiefs who accepted the advice of whites and incorporated them became dependent upon these new kinsmen to act in the best interest of the Sioux people.

Few Indian leaders demonstrated more awareness of the growing complexities of interethnic relationships than Big Thunder, and this understanding apparently influenced his selection of a successor. Big Thunder probably came to believe that the son who had lived with him at Kaposia was best prepared to adopt and implement his policies. The new formula for leadership necessitated residence at Kaposia and learning to work with the whites who now played a pivotal role in Mdewakanton affairs. This belief obviously led Big Thunder to reject Taoyateduta, who had spent so much time in the west and was seemingly not prepared for such a compromising role.

Surely those familiar with Taoyateduta's personality, including his father, must have realized that he expected to be chief. Taoyateduta began planning his return to Kaposia within hours of hearing of his father's death. He had supporters the length of the Minnesota River. While his return would precipitate a leadership crisis, such was the destiny of the man who would one day speak for the Mdewakantons.

3

The Price of Leadership

TAOYATEDUTA'S eventual return to Kaposia and his
challenge to the right of his half-brother to the chieftainship was anticipated
by many Mdewakantons. Yet some village members, including his own
father, considered him to be unfit for leadership, for he had been less
than an exemplary youth and had departed at an early age for the west.
Taoyateduta, then, had a threefold problem as he considered how best
to go about securing what he considered to be his birthright. He had to
depose his half-brother, gain the respect of his more important relatives
at Kaposia, and maintain and perhaps expand upon the close relationship
that his father had fashioned with the Americans at the nearby fort.

Considering Little Crow's determined character and his strong sense
of destiny, it seemed certain that he would either meet these challenges
or perish in the attempt. Taoyateduta, however, had made mistakes as a
youth and had a bad reputation to overcome. Many Mdewakantons believed that he had abandoned his home village in the early 1830s just
when economic difficulties along the Mississippi River became acute.
Despite his traditional upbringing, young Little Crow had failed to take
seriously all of the rules of Dakota society. He had sought the affections
of women who belonged to other men at Kaposia, and he had gained a
reputation as a lothario. Some evidence even suggests that he was
threatened by men in the village because of this immoral activity.[1]

As a young man, Taoyateduta associated with rather disreputable fellows. Certainly his friendship with Jack Frazer, a Dakota mixed-blood
who was in all likelihood a relative of the Little Crow family, failed to
enhance his reputation. Frazer was sacrilegious, constantly poking fun at
Dakota customs, and even mimicking Dakota spirits. Taoyateduta frequently hunted with Frazer in the Blue Earth River valley in the 1830s,
and on one such outing, both men attempted to move ahead of the main
body of hunters and gain an advantage. Their efforts produced a warning
from several men in the party, who told them that such activity scared
off the game and hindered the success of the larger body. Nevertheless,

Taoyateduta and Frazer took these warnings lightly, forcing the hunting party to form a soldiers' lodge and punish them. The soldiers ultimately destroyed all of Frazer's belongings, even cutting up his mother's tepee, and both Taoyateduta and Frazer received stern lectures.[2]

The tendency of Taoyateduta and his friends to acquire buffalo robes from western Sioux Indians through gambling or the use of liquor also did much to damage the future chief's reputation. During the 1840s, Taoyateduta often spent the spring months in the west, along the James River, bartering for robes. More respected eastern Sioux leaders frowned upon this activity. The Indians who traded with Taoyateduta were unable to pay off debts to traders and oftentimes were refused credits the next spring. But Taoyateduta saw nothing wrong with the practice, and many traders concluded that he was a more destructive influence upon their commerce than were white competitors.[3]

The actions of Taoyateduta and his friends were hardly criminal, but they demonstrate the reckless and entrepreneurial behavior that characterized the young chief's early life. Like his friend Frazer, whose cultural rebellion was severely criticized by his peers, Taoyateduta seemed at times to enjoy challenging, or ignoring, established authority. On the other hand, all young Dakota men yearned for adventure, and it was common for them to be rash: to go to war without seeking the advice of elders or to defy traders. And many elders expected young men like Taoyateduta to show independence and to be nonconformist. While Little Crow may have gone too far, his actions were not entirely unexpected of an individual of his age or lineage. Young Dakota men were encouraged to be more energetic and impulsive than those men entering middle age.

In addition to his impetuosity, Taoyateduta possessed a reservoir of strength and energy that was unmatched among his people. Nearly every observer who knew him emphasized both traits. Asa W. Daniels, for example, wrote of Little Crow: "He was of a nervous temperament, restless and active, intelligent, of strong personality, [and] of great physical vigor." Both his energy and strength surface during another hunting incident that occurred when the future chief was about thirty years of age. Dakota hunters frequently ran down animal herds by foot, trotting for days at a fast pace—perhaps seven or eight miles an hour. Henry Hastings Sibley, the American Fur Company factor for Minnesota, and trader Alexander Faribault spent time hunting with Taoyateduta in 1841. Sibley and his friends, mounted on horses, discovered a large herd of more than a thousand elk, a rarity by this late date, which they pursued. The chase went on at a steady pace for five days, the party traveling about twenty-five miles over each twenty-four-hour period. Taoyateduta trotted along "on foot, keeping up and conversing with them" as they went. Needless to say, the fur traders came away from the enterprise impressed with Taoyateduta's stamina.[4] The incident also showed that Taoyateduta was a man who, when he chose to participate in an event, was willing to exert whatever effort was required to impress others.

Taoyateduta's exhausting efforts as a hunter illustrate his psychological need to overachieve, a desire that was especially evident when it came to political matters. Little Crow never missed an important council, and not long after gaining prominence as a leader, he dominated important discussions. His people's need for his political energy and talent increased after they moved to new reservations along the upper Minnesota River in the 1850s. He regularly rode from reservation to reservation, even in snowstorms, carrying letters for government officials, collecting gossip, and participating in political discussions along the way. Indeed, Taoyateduta became so notorious as an instigator of debate that whenever he appeared at the agency, government officials cringed at the thought of what he might say and what new issues would evolve from his actions.[5]

Confrontation on Taoyateduta's part, however, was tempered by the fact that he had many white friends and possessed a strong curiosity about their foreign culture. He showed a particular interest in books and the written word, especially after missionaries arrived in Minnesota in the 1830s and designed an alphabet for the Dakota language. Taoyateduta enrolled in mission school and learned the mechanics of reading and writing his own language as well as a smattering of English and arithmetic.[6] His interest in numbers probably came as a result of his early contact with fur traders. In the trade of the 1830s, Indians received credits according to numbers and types of skins, and they paid these debts in the spring with furs. Obviously it became more difficult to cheat Indian hunters who had some knowledge of Arabic numerals, and all sources strongly suggest that Taoyateduta grasped very rapidly the rudiments of Euro-American arithmetic computation.

The future chief's interest in numbers also evolved from his fondness for playing cards, a skill for which he had few equals, white or Indian. The Sioux loved to gamble, and Taoyateduta was no exception. He played all games of poker and apparently had a system for winning. He probably counted discarded cards, since he could correctly determine what possibilities existed in his opponents' hands. One particular story amply demonstrates his skills. At annuity payment time in the mid-1850s, it was common for a number of gamblers to invade the reservations, one group of professional poker players hiring a liveryman to transport them the sixty-odd miles from St. Peter. They wore diamonds and fine clothes, signs of success in their trade, but they made the mistake of engaging Taoyateduta in a long poker game, from which they emerged a couple of days later literally destitute of everything. They were reduced to asking reservation officials for a ration of bread and coffee to tide them over on their long trip back to St. Paul.[7]

Taoyateduta's skills at the game of politics were no less adept than his facility with a deck of cards. James W. Lynd, a trader's clerk and an early student of his political acumen, noted: "He possesses a shrewd judgment, great foresight, and a comprehensive mind, together with that greatest of requisites in a statesman, caution." He dressed meticulously for every political event, and at virtually every council for which accounts exist, Little Crow's appearance was noted. He demonstrated a further commitment to politics by the orchestration of a series of marriages, the matches serving as a means of securing political allies. Like all good politicians, he told constituents what they wanted to hear, and occasionally whites concluded that he was undependable. One missionary went so far as to write of Taoyateduta that "popularity is his God."[8] But such activity, even in the Indian world, was astute politics. Taoyateduta was wise enough to realize that consistency of argument was not as important as poise, or even generosity—a trait that all successful Indian leaders had to demonstrate.

The best evidence of his political acumen surfaced in dealing with whites. Taoyateduta was a master of the offhanded comment and the sarcastic turn of phrase, and he frequently gained the sympathies of whites by such methods. He freely granted interviews to newspaper editors—one of the reasons why he became so well known—and on at least one occasion, he used the press as a means to demonstrate his own worth as a politician.[9] This is not to say that he lacked conviction, for he did see certain issues as being crucial to the preservation of his people. But he was a politician of the first order, shrewd in the extreme, and capable of compromise when he was unable to get his way.

Taoyateduta's early life obviously helped shape his personality. He was one of at least ten boys born to Big Thunder and his three wives. The available evidence strongly suggests that the first wife, Miniokadawin, was his mother. Although age thirty-six when his father died in 1846, Taoyateduta spent at least a decade in the west prior to assuming a leadership role. He first lived on the Des Moines and Cannon rivers with the Wahpekute people. Later he left them and moved to the upper Minnesota

River where considerable numbers of Wahpetons and Sissetons lived. It is impossible to date these early movements, but at least one source suggests that he had already left Kaposia by his twentieth birthday.[10]

Sometime in the 1830s, Taoyateduta took as wives two Wahpekute women from the Cannon River valley. The two women were daughters of a noted Wahpekute chief, suggesting that Taoyateduta had made a good match. Most likely, Taoyateduta's father-in-law was Tasagye, or The Cane, an important tribal leader who met frequently with Lawrence Taliaferro. Perhaps Taoyateduta met his future wives during one of these visits, since Kaposia was so close to the agency. Although he had one child by his first Wahpekute wife and two children by the second, later offspring never knew what happened to these children. Taoyateduta's ties with the Wahpekute were not long lasting.[11]

Taoyateduta had abandoned his wives among the Wahpekute by 1838. He undoubtedly surmised at the time that warfare with the Sac and Fox Indians, who were expanding into northern Iowa from the Mississippi River, was seriously depleting the Wahpekute population and that this decline would limit their political role in future tribal affairs. If this were not enough, factionalism within the Wahpekute tribe also broke out in the 1830s, and several murders occurred, including the killing of Tasagye.[12] Since divorce occurred frequently among the eastern Sioux—biological fathers were simply less necessary in an extended family environment— few Indians held anything against the young Mdewakanton for his decision to leave. Taoyateduta was free to find new mates, presumably with a band not destined for virtual annihilation by outsiders or through self-destruction.

Taoyateduta looked farther west for a second family, taking a new wife in the summer of 1838. She was Mazaiyaġewin, the eldest daughter of Inyangmani, a Wahpeton who rose to the leadership of an important Sisseton band at Lac qui Parle.[13] Taoyateduta returned briefly to Kaposia in the fall, apparently to show off his new acquisition, but the chief-to-be increasingly spent more time at his new Lac qui Parle home.[14] During the 1840s, he bartered for and received Inyangmani's second daughter, Saiceyewin, she being but ten years of age when purchased. Some years later, in separate transactions Taoyateduta convinced Inyangmani to give up his two remaining daughters, the last one being acquired with some difficulty as Inyangmani thought that he had been more than generous with Taoyateduta. Polygyny was a common practice among the Sioux, and the acquisition of sisters occurred regularly. Indeed, Taoyateduta's domestic life was quite harmonious as the sisters always got along well.[15] Taoyateduta's marriage into the Inyangmani family was also a wise political choice; his father-in-law was an important man with several other children. These bonds helped Taoyateduta gain influence in the west.

Settling at Lac qui Parle also had advantages because of the considerable Mdewakanton community that had moved to that vicinity. The Mdewakanton migration west began in 1825 when game herds in the east started to dwindle.[16] The selection of Lac qui Parle as a trade site in 1826 by the important Sioux, mixed-blood trader, Joseph Renville, contributed markedly to its growth. This man, a descendant of a French voyageur and a Sioux woman named Miniyuhe of Little Crow's family, had taken as a wife a niece of Big Thunder's and created an extensive kinship network with his Mdewakanton relatives. Using his relatives as hunters and laborers, Renville developed a small commercial empire at Lac qui Parle. Major figures in this socioeconomic system were Left Hand, a brother of Renville's Dakota wife Mary, Joseph Napeśniduta, a nephew of Mary and Left Hand's, Renville's four sons, his younger brother Victor, and the chief of the local Sisseton band, Inyangmani, who had to be consulted on most matters. Many of these men worked in Renville's soldiers' lodge, an organization that normally existed for the purpose of controlling the hunt but could be easily adapted to working in a kinship-oriented commercial network.[17] Taoyateduta was related closely to all of them, since Left Hand and Mary Renville were his cross-cousins, Joseph Napeśniduta, a cross-cousin once removed, and Inyangmani, his father-in-law. These relationships entitled Taoyateduta to the constant respect and assistance of the Lac qui Parle people, and he, of course, was required to reciprocate.

In addition to these people, the Lac qui Parle community contained a large number of children who were either offspring of Renville's or of various members of the Little Crow family. Among the more important were the four surviving sons of Old Eve, who were distant cousins of Renville's. The father of the boys was a brother-in-law of Renville's father. The four sons included Paul Mazakutemani, Eagle Help, Abel Fearful Face, and Cloud Man. The last mentioned married a Sisseton woman and became a subchief of that tribe, and a sister of the brothers married a nephew of Wakanmani, a minor Wahpeton chief.[18] In addition, two sons of Left Hand's, Lorenzo Lawrence and Joseph Kawanke (they were both full-bloods who, in part, took English names), lived at Lac qui Parle and were frequently connected to Taoyateduta. After one adds to this list Renville's large number of children—four boys and four girls—as well as the offspring and relatives of Inyangmani, it becomes evident that Taoyateduta was related to nearly every person of importance, trader or chief, in and about Lac qui Parle.[19]

The fictive and family ties that Taoyateduta nurtured at Lac qui Parle naturally would have had an impact on his life. Yet they loomed all the more important after missionaries arrived in 1835 and converted Renville and several of his relatives to Protestantism. Thomas S. Williamson and Alexander Huggins were sent by the American Board of Commissioners for Foreign Missions; Stephen Return Riggs and Gideon H. Pond joined them a few years later. Renville allowed the missionaries to use the tepee headquarters of the soldiers' lodge as a church. By 1846 they had converted almost forty people, the majority of whom were women. The missionaries opened a school and, with Renville's assistance, translated books of the Bible into the Dakota language. Once the language had a written form, missionaries were able to teach Sioux men, women, and children how to read and write in their own language.[20]

Nearly all the converts—or those sympathetic to Christianity—came from the Renville, Inyangmani, or Wakanmani families. Joseph Napeś-niduta, from the Little Crow village, became one of the first full-blood male converts in 1841, and young Joseph Renville, Eagle Help, Paul Mazakutemani, and Lorenzo Lawrence all joined a short time thereafter. Men such as Inyangmani, Left Hand, and Wakanmani became so closely connected to the missionaries that they were practically church members and attended services regularly. (All three were polygamists, and in a classic example of nineteenth-century Protestant zeal, the missionaries refused the men full membership until they accepted monogamy.) In addition, most of these men attended school in the late 1830s, and a few learned to read and write to some degree in the Dakota language. Eagle Help was considered the premier scholar, learning arithmetic as well as how to write cogent letters in the Dakota language. Riggs convinced him to teach school for the mission after the Indian moved to Lake Traverse in 1841.[21]

The success did have its limitations, however, and the missionaries remained unsure of whether their converts actually grasped the full meaning of Christian doctrine. Typical of their concern was a problem that developed with Eagle Help after his wife of many years died. Although lacking cause, he immediately thought of seeking revenge for his loss and planned a raid on the Ojibway. It mattered little that the Ojibway had nothing to do with his wife's death; Dakota men and women typically sought to ease their grief by causing either themselves or others to suffer.

When the missionaries objected to the plans of their star pupil and refused to grind corn for the warriors who wanted to join him—a social insult of the highest order—Eagle Help killed two of the oxen belonging to the mission. He viewed his mission friends as allies and kinsmen who had an obligation to support him in his time of need. Eagle Help's conversion, then, clearly fell short of missionary expectations, and the same was true of other Christian Indians. Of the nearly twenty men who professed the Protestant faith by the end of the 1840s, over half received suspensions at one time or another and a few, such as Renville, had died.[22]

Despite the backsliding, the conversions had a dramatic effect on Taoyateduta. Many of the most adamant Christians were his relatives, and he learned much about white Americans from them and the missionaries. Although the young chief-to-be did not give up his native ways at Lac qui Parle, he did study intently with Gideon Pond in 1837, and the school records show that he attended classes throughout the year 1844–45. Riggs, who later taught him, commented that he made "some progress in the knowledge of letters." But most important of all, Taoyateduta attended church and, according to Riggs, "became considerably acquainted with the truths of the Christian religion." Two of his wives converted, although he later forced them to leave the church, and Riggs was convinced that Taoyateduta himself showed promise of being saved.[23]

Besides learning from his missionary friends at Lac qui Parle, Taoyateduta also emulated the commercial efforts of his in-law, Renville, carrying alcohol into the west to trade for furs or horses. Just when Taoyateduta realized how lucrative such an exchange could be the records fail to show, but trader Martin McLeod, who ran the post at Lac qui Parle, suggested that Taoyateduta worked in the liquor trade at about the same time that he attended classes at the mission school.[24] Taoyateduta's attempts to work in the trade and his interest in schooling and Christianity underscore the fact that, like his grandfather and his father, he was interested in adapting white ways and values if they suited his needs. He quickly discovered, for example, that being a capitalist rather than an exploited hunter provided a better opportunity for making a living. In addition, there was something mystical about learning to read and write. Taoyateduta's actions even suggest a willingness to supplement his religion with Christianity. He probably failed to understand the sacrifices necessary to satisfy the missionaries, but he had nothing against new religious dogmas. Like most Indians, he viewed religion as an extension of one's personal self. In a sense, the new Little Crow who emerged from the years at Lac qui Parle was a man of considerable worldly experience, well suited to take the place of Big Thunder in the fall of 1845.

Taoyateduta's father and his two half-brothers felt otherwise. Big Thunder had passed his medals down to one of the half-brothers, and immediately after Big Thunder's death, the half-brothers declared that since their elder brother had departed for the west and had lived at Lac qui Parle for at least a decade, he had no right to return and claim the chieftainship. When word of this succession reached Taoyateduta, he began to plot his return to Kaposia, waiting until the spring of 1846 when the ice had cleared from the rivers. He had organized a large following of people to go with him, mostly friends and relatives from Lac qui Parle, including Lorenzo Lawrence. Other men from the Shakopee and Black Dog villages joined the party as it descended the Minnesota River and turned into the Mississippi.[25]

As the canoes carrying Taoyateduta and his party approached Kaposia, hundreds of people poured out of the bark and buffalo-skin lodges that were haphazardly clustered along the riverbank. News of Taoyateduta's approach had been carried overland, and when he arrived, his half-brothers, weapons in hand, warned him not to land. "If you do you shall die," their supporters shouted. "You are not wanted here," one of the half-brothers finally stated. "Go and live at Lac qui Parle." Taoyateduta, sensing that death was near, stepped into the middle of the throng, folded his arms, and said, "Shoot then, where all can see." A shot rang out, knocking Taoyateduta into the arms of his chief soldier, Talking Sacred Stone. Supporters rushed to his side as the half-brothers fled, and his Sisseton wives burst into wails. The ball had passed through both his forearms, breaking the bones, and after shattering, had continued on to make less serious wounds in his breast and face. Placed in a canoe, Taoyateduta was quickly moved upriver to Fort Snelling. At the post, the surgeon examined the wounded man and recommended that both hands be amputated. When informed, Taoyateduta refused, believing that a chief without hands could not lead. He returned to his village to be attended by his own shamans. The wounds slowly healed, but for the remainder of his life, Taoyateduta carried the ghastly scars of this attempted assassination. His wrists remained deformed, his hands hung awkwardly from them, and he always covered them. He never regained the total use of his fingers.[26]

Soon after this skirmish, the village elders decided to throw their support behind Taoyateduta. He had shown great courage, and many villagers felt that if he lived the Great Spirit had clearly destined him to be chief. The elders sanctioned the execution of his half-brothers, both of whom were killed by supporters of the new chief. One reliable report suggested that they were shot while lying drunk in a lodge, no chance being given them to escape. Another indicates that Taoyateduta had them bound and shot. One of the executioners was Lorenzo Lawrence, who shortly thereafter took as a wife one of the widows of the men he helped to kill. Another was Little Dog, another half-brother of Taoyateduta's. The deaths of these two aspirants left the way open for Taoyateduta to assume complete control at Kaposia as band chief and adopt the name "Little Crow."[27]

With the elimination of his half-brothers, the elevation of Little Crow to the position of band chief was inevitable. He naturally had the proper family background and kinship connection, and he had courted support among the Mdewakantons both at Lac qui Parle and Kaposia. He possessed extraordinary oratorical skills and had demonstrated unusual courage in front of the entire village. These qualities and his selection, however, only gave him an opportunity to help form consensus in the village council and to speak for the Kaposia band when it needed representation in the larger Mdewakanton tribal forum or in negotiations with whites. Such a position did not guarantee the continued support of the village populace. Taoyateduta surely remembered the desertions from the band that had occurred during his grandfather's years as chief in the 1820s and his father's in the 1830s.

Even so, the young chief understood that his ascendancy was to some extent a steppingstone to the speakership of the entire tribe. While Wabasha generally had been recognized as the tribal spokesman until his death in 1835, Big Thunder then became spokesman and played a major role in the 1837 treaty. After Big Thunder's death eight years later, the position went to Bad Hail, a man of little talent who was closely tied to the fur traders, especially Sibley. Bad Hail had gained a reputation as a warrior, but he demonstrated little speaking ability and failed to grasp the issues that would determine the future of the tribe.[28] Thus Taoyateduta, still only thirty-six years old, became an immediate contender for the tribal speakership. The only other candidate of the same intellectual ability was the young Wabasha, who had begun to demonstrate some of the same boldness that had gained prestige for his father many years earlier.

Taoyateduta's difficulties in ascending to the village chieftainship must have suggested to him the many dangers and sacrifices attendant on tribal leadership. Nevertheless, the actions of his half-brothers fit a pattern that plagued the Little Crow family after 1841. The killing of his two brothers by the Ojibway in that year, followed by the accidental death of his father four years later, must have brought Taoyateduta to question his own purpose in life. In addition, two brothers and two sisters committed suicide during these years of trial. The sisters did so because they were promised to men whom they did not want to marry. Why the two brothers took their lives remains a mystery.[29]

Family catastrophe of this sort helped to account for a dramatic change of attitude that became apparent in Taoyateduta after becoming chief. His reputation as a whiskeyseller, a womanizer, and mischiefmaker was simply unbecoming of a chief, and the new Little Crow realized the need for his own reformation. When reminded of his past in the fall of 1846, the new chief promised to change: "I was only a brave then; I am a chief now." Imbued with a new sense of responsibility, Taoyateduta set out to reform his village, asking the Indian agent Amos Bruce for assistance. Bruce responded by organizing a series of temperance pledges—an old idea that had first been used in the early 1840s—and Little Crow became a strong spokesman for sobriety, taking the pledge for seven months. Although drinking did not cease entirely, the pledges brought an immediate decrease in the consumption of alcohol, much to the wonderment of many white observers. The success of the program attracted the attention of government authorities, who took notice of Little Crow's increased influence.[30]

The chief quickly followed this reform by announcing that he wished to have missionaries return to Kaposia. The Methodists had abandoned their station near the village some years before, due to the opposition of the village people. They had failed to attract a single convert, and their school, taught in English, had benefited the Indians very little. Yet Taoyateduta obviously saw some advantages in missions and discovered that Thomas S. Williamson, still at Lac qui Parle, was willing to answer his call. As the chief told agent Bruce, "He [Little Crow] wishes a preacher to take charge of it, so that he can give good advice to his people." Williamson, who arrived in November and soon established both a church and a Dakota school, seemed convinced that with Little Crow's assistance he would have a much better chance of winning the souls of the Mdewakanton people. Never before had a chief of such importance encouraged missionaries to settle in a village.[31]

Yet a few American Board missionaries remained cautious. Riggs, for example, pointed out that the Mdewakantons had shown little inclination for missionaries in the past. He seemed convinced that the call for missionaries by Little Crow was orchestrated by the dozen or so converts

Frank Blackwell Mayer visited Kaposia in 1851 and sketched the village, showing summer bark houses and winter tepees made from hides.

"Pounding Hominy—The Chief's Children," a Mayer painting, shows youngsters who were probably part of Little Crow's family. Mayer painted most of his village scenes at Kaposia.

Mayer sketched Little Crow at Traverse des Sioux in 1851. Guided by notes on the sketch, the artist later executed a formal portrait. Probably the on-site rendering, which shows more rugged facial features, is an accurate representation of the chief's appearance.

"Leaving for a Hunt, Kaposia," by Mayer shows a shaman (right, center) and mounted, armed hunters. The pointed head coverings and ankle-length robes were made from heavy blankets.

Mayer witnessed a lacrosse game played during the Traverse des Sioux negotiations and probably sketched the action. He produced this painting in 1898, a year before his death. Mayer observed that "the Kaposia Indians are noted for their proficiency in this game" (With Pen and Pencil on the Minnesota Frontier, 150).

who had moved from Lac qui Parle to Kaposia in the 1840s. Among the more important church members then at Kaposia were Joseph Napeśniduta, his wife, and four of Joseph Renville's children. Two of Taoyateduta's wives probably lent support, since they had once professed to be Christians.[32] Williamson discovered shortly after arriving that Taoyateduta had convinced the village elders to accept a mission because of the assistance Williamson, a physician, could offer. Smallpox, in particular, had been a constant worry throughout the 1830s and 1840s, and the Sioux understood and valued vaccination. Finally, after arriving on the scene, Williamson questioned the commitment of Taoyateduta, suspecting that the chief may have wanted to use him as a means by which to increase his own prestige.[33]

Taoyateduta supported the school program over the winters of 1846–47 and 1847–48. Both he and two younger half-brothers attended classes with some regularity. The whole number of pupils who enrolled at Kaposia the first year totaled fifty-four, and the average daily attendance was about a dozen. The next year, the average daily attendance grew to nearly thirty students. Marguerite Renville taught most of the classes; although some students learned to read and write in their own language, others did not attend classes regularly enough to make much progress. The church received less support, however, and only six members were allowed to take communion regularly. At this point in his life Taoyateduta showed no interest in attending church, and for this reason, Williamson soon began to doubt that the chief would lead the hoped-for reformation.[34]

Williamson's pessimism only increased as conflicts over acculturation programs erupted among Indians, government officials, and traders late in the decade. The problems began when agent Bruce recommended that the government offer educational programs of its own at the Mdewakanton villages in 1847, and Commissioner of Indian Affairs William Medill quickly sanctioned such a project. Bickering soon occurred over the appropriation of money from the educational fund, which had been created in the 1837 treaty.[35] This fund set aside five thousand dollars a year, but only a very small portion of the money had been spent by the 1840s. As word leaked out that new schools were to be constructed at all the Mdewakanton villages, traders encouraged the Indians to oppose them. The traders concluded that if the Sioux complained loudly enough, the government might be forced to distribute the fund rather than invest it in education, and they believed that most of this money would accordingly fall into their hands.[36]

A government school should have had little effect on the American

Board effort at Kaposia. But the Sioux found it difficult to see any difference between church-supported and government-funded institutions, in part because the missionaries previously had been recipients of small grants from the school fund. Williamson had at times showed an interest in the money, pointing out that if the Protestants did not get the fund the Catholics surely would. When queried by the Indians, however, Williamson denied that he had received government support and said plainly that he did not want it. This apparently satisfied Taoyateduta, who again gave his support to the village school program in January 1849.[37] But by spring even the chief and his supporters neglected to attend classes. Instead, they gambled in their lodges and occasionally traded for whiskey east of the Mississippi River.[38]

Since day schools were dependent on the interests of the Indians, Williamson and his assistants continually looked for ways to neutralize societal pressure. Their difficulties invariably led to some discussion of the use of boarding schools. While such schools had been established with mixed success some years before by the American Board, it was not until the spring of 1848 that the missionaries at Kaposia asked the government for permission to board Sioux children in their homes. Commissioner Medill supported the effort, providing an annual contribution of fifty dollars per student. Williamson concluded that the amount was hardly sufficient to feed and clothe the children, yet he and his wife, other station workers, and a few government employees who worked for the Office of Indian Affairs agreed to try the experiment.[39]

Little Crow once again threw his support behind the boarding schools. He sent two of his children to live at Williamson's home. Wowinape, whom Williamson renamed Albert, was a two- or three-year-old when he entered the school in 1849. His father soon claimed that villagers intended to poison his son if he were allowed to stay with the mission family, however, and this opposition to education convinced Taoyateduta to withdraw him temporarily. By 1850–51 Wowinape was back in the makeshift Williamson boarding school along with Little Crow's second child, a girl the missionaries called Emma. "She learned to read and speak English beautifully," Williamson later claimed. Both children were removed after a year and soon forgot most of what they had learned at the school.[40]

Little Crow's support for education evolved primarily from his experiences at Lac qui Parle. He had found education useful, and he wanted his children to have some measure of learning. His support also stemmed from the fact that many of his Lac qui Parle, Mdewakanton relatives had moved with him to Kaposia. A few of them, including Lorenzo Lawrence, lobbied for schools even though the Kaposia villagers as a whole had often opposed education in the past. Little Crow was never able to win over the opponents to education in his village, and as the debate over schools brought threats to his children's safety, the Kaposia chief began to vacillate in his support of education.[41]

Interestingly, as opposition to schools escalated, Taoyateduta turned increasingly to trading and gambling for furs in the west. By 1848 this activity grew to such an extent that traders, such as Henry Sibley and Martin McLeod, attempted to patrol rivers and stop the illegal traffic. Eventually the army got involved, sending patrols out to halt native canoes that headed west with contraband. No one knew how many Indians participated in the venture, which had been made illegal by federal statute, but in 1848 McLeod listed those he considered to be the ringleaders. They included Black Tomahawk, Whistling Wind, Smokey Day, Little Crow, and all members of Little Crow's Kaposia village.[42] Sibley's trader at Traverse des Sioux, Joseph La Framboise, indicated at one point that Smokey Day had been so successful in his efforts that he had accumulated 130 undressed buffalo robes. La Framboise wanted Sibley to "have him snatched" once he reached St. Paul and the robes forcefully taken from him.[43]

When trading whiskey for skins failed, the ringleaders often obtained them through gambling or theft. McLeod identified Little Crow and his brother Tapateduta as being the most successful at acquiring skins by these methods. Their hunting, the trader exclaimed, was almost always done "in the lodges among my Indians," at Lac qui Parle. McLeod believed that the kinship connections held by both men at Lac qui Parle made it possible for them to get robes and pelts that even he could not acquire. Yet another stratagem employed was theft. At one point, Taoyateduta and several Mdewakanton relatives surprised a lodge of Ojibway who were hunting on Sioux lands. They killed the occupants of the lodge and made off with sixty raccoon skins and a number of otter pelts. Supposedly, Little Crow counted coup on the enemy and gained several eagle feathers for his headdress on that day.[44]

The commercial activities of Little Crow and his relatives afforded an opportunity for these men to avoid the awful prospect of farming. Despite the 1837 treaty that had provided farm instructors for the Mdewakanton villages, and despite Big Thunder's attempts to farm in the 1830s, the agricultural program at Kaposia had failed to effect any meaningful cultural change. Instead, the assistance from the government allowed men like

Taoyateduta to continue living a fluid life, hunting occasionally and trading and gambling for pelts. The farming program and the food annuities combined to provide a considerable supplement to the traditional hunter-gatherer economy of the eastern Sioux.[45]

The sense of security provided by the treaty ended abruptly in September 1849, however, when word reached the chief that the government wished to negotiate once again for a land sale.[46] While some support existed in Mdewakanton villages for another treaty, since it certainly would have meant more annuities, many Dakota leaders realized that a sale would force them out of the Mississippi valley forever.

The passage of a statehood bill for Wisconsin in 1848 was followed by the creation of the Minnesota Territory the next year. A new territorial governor, Alexander Ramsey, arrived in St. Paul, the new capital, with the express intent of ending Sioux ownership of lands within the bounds of the new territory. By summer 1849, the commissioner of Indian affairs had given Ramsey and John Chambers, an Iowa politician, permission to negotiate with the Sioux, instructing them to pay approximately two to two and one-half cents an acre for land. Ramsey and Chambers hoped to convince all four eastern Sioux tribes—the Mdewakantons, Wahpekutes, Wahpetons, and Sissetons—to relinquish their claims to lands as far west as Big Stone Lake.[47]

A treaty negotiation had been in the discussion stage for some time, and interested traders and missionaries were prepared for the news. The missionaries felt that any future treaties should include clauses calling for the construction of boarding schools, institutions that would at least offer the opportunity to save Sioux children. They believed that earlier support by the Office of Indian Affairs for such schools had been inadequate and that boarding schools built at some distance from Sioux villages would separate Indian children from the obtrusive influence of their parents. Their experiments with Little Crow's children offered a prime example of the problems that they faced insofar as Little Crow, so they believed, should not have been able to withdraw his children from their school once so much time and effort had been invested in them.[48]

The traders, on the other hand, saw the treaty as a chance to acquire payment for the debts of Indian hunters. Although Congress had recently enacted a law prohibiting the direct payment of such debts through a treaty, Henry Sibley, who had been elected to Congress, told Ramsey in blunt terms that a treaty could not be successfully negotiated without a payment. Sibley further noted that the price suggested by Washington was scandalously low; traders wanted the Sioux to receive at least ten cents an acre, which would provide more money to pay debts and to stimulate the local economy.[49]

Ramsey and Chambers opened negotiations in the fall despite Sibley's advice. The commissioners soon discovered that rumors had been circulated among the upper Indians, or Wahpetons and Sissetons, suggesting that if they came to St. Paul, their chiefs would be deposed from their positions. Riggs later notified the governor that traders started the rumors and that the Indians accordingly would not come to St. Paul even though many of them favored a treaty.[50] Meanwhile, the commissioners met briefly with the Mdewakantons. Young Wabasha, rather than Bad Hail or Taoyateduta, spoke for the tribe. He quickly noted that his people had already sold a large segment of land to the Great Father and that several promises had been made during and after that negotiation that had yet to be fulfilled. Wabasha then produced a list of demands which Sibley had written for him. The list included payment of the education fund, now totaling about fifty thousand dollars, compensation for wood taken from Sioux lands by the soldiers at Fort Snelling, and the delivery of a herd of horses.[51]

Ramsey, considering everything on the list to be trivial, quickly agreed to each point. But the Indians refused to discuss another treaty until the promises had been fulfilled. Not having the authority to purchase horses or hand over fifty thousand dollars, Ramsey elected to distribute presents and end the council. In his report to Washington, Ramsey noted that traders and mixed-bloods had more influence over the Sioux than he had anticipated.[52] By December the governor had decided to work with Sibley to effect the treaty. In substance, he had agreed to support trader claims and assist them in obtaining payment in order to open Minnesota to settlement.[53]

Sibley, McLeod, La Framboise, and others in the trade worked hard throughout 1849 and 1850 to bring as many Indian leaders under their control as possible. While Sibley had been pushing austerity in the trade for years, urging his traders to end the practice of handing out presents and even credits, he now reversed these orders. McLeod began dispensing goods on a liberal scale near Lake Traverse, reaffirming ties that had been allowed to lapse during the 1830s. The Sissetons and Wahpetons wanted a treaty and the annuities that it would bring, which made McLeod's job much easier. Therefore, most attention was given to the lower Indians, or the Mdewakantons and Wahpekutes. Sibley opened his store near St. Paul to them, handing out credits and presents on a large scale. He employed many of their mixed-blood relatives, even though they were not needed in the trade. These tactics succeeded, as Henry Sibley's brother Fred reported that chiefs Wakute, Grey Iron, and Shakopee were considered to be safe on the treaty issue. Sibley's father-in-law, Bad Hail, who was a sometime speaker for the Mdewakantons, also would support a treaty.[54]

Nevertheless, these men did not have sufficient influence to ensure tribal consensus, and at least two leaders remained undecided. Wabasha had seemed hostile in negotiating with Ramsey in 1849, and his views were unchanged the next year. Wabasha correctly concluded that the treaty was an attempt to force the Sioux out of the Mississippi valley. But the traders especially worried about Taoyateduta. Fred Sibley reported that he appeared "very fair" when at Sibley's store, but he talked "badly" when among other Indians. It seemed as though Little Crow had yet to make up his mind on the treaty and wanted to remain on friendly terms with all parties before exercising his influence on negotiations.[55] Undoubtedly, Little Crow judged that the upcoming debate over the treaty would be the first major test of his political skills.

Yet Taoyateduta's mixed signals regarding a land sale may have evolved from the sober realization that the eastern Sioux could not long continue to stand in the path of white settlement. By 1850 the missionary clique, which included many of his relatives, was arguing strongly for the development of boarding schools and the concentration of Indians on farming reserves. Riggs and Williamson led the campaign, detailing their ideas in a document entitled "Outline of a Plan for Civilizing the Dakotas." Specifically, the plan called for the abolition of the "community property system," or large villages, among the Sioux and the adoption of settlement patterns designed around nuclear family units.[56] Once the proposal reached the hands of government officials, they argued for the need to "restrict" and "confine" the Sioux. The Indians, they now felt, had to be "concentrated" on a small section of land and persuaded to pursue "worthwhile" subsistence endeavors.[57]

Little Crow's proximity to St. Paul and the missionaries made it possible for him to sense more clearly the tenor of these discussions. A real estate boom along the east bank of the Mississippi River in 1849–51 added meaning to talk of "civilization" programs and possible removal. Little Crow must have wondered how long the whites would allow his people to stay under such circumstances. St. Paul had become a bustling town of 142 buildings virtually overnight, and two frame houses existed alongside the skin and bark lodges at Kaposia. Across the river from

Kaposia, Parrant's settlement of Pig's Eye showed a population of at least a dozen French-Canadian families, who had established prosperous farms.[58] While Little Crow's people went out of their way to get along with their new white neighbors, selling them firewood and trading game for supplies, they also realized that Kaposia was now on the outskirts of a growing urban center, and Anglo-Americans looked ever so jealously at the lands and resources on the opposite side of the river.

Some Indians near St. Paul responded to these changes by becoming adamant in their desire to sustain the ways of the past. Hunting east of the Mississippi River remained possible, even though it was not very rewarding, and some of Little Crow's people stubbornly returned to the St. Croix valley each fall. While there, they competed with the Ojibway for the few remaining animals of the region and, much like in years past, fought over game resources. Just such an encounter occurred in 1850 when the Dakotas killed fourteen Ojibway. Governor Ramsey was appalled by this event, occurring so near white population centers, and he reluctantly ordered the imprisonment of twelve of Little Crow's warriors, knowing full well that it would hinder the contemplated treaty. When Little Crow made it clear that he wished to remain with his men, Ramsey had him incarcerated as well.[59]

In an attempt to negotiate a settlement for the losses, Little Crow agreed to pay money out of the Mdewakanton annuity to cover the deaths. Initially, Ramsey was reluctant to accept the offer, but he desperately wanted a treaty, and Indians in prison were unlikely to negotiate. Subsequently, Ramsey agreed to Taoyateduta's offer, and the government freed the Kaposia Mdewakantons. To prevent further fighting, Ramsey held yet another peace council at Fort Snelling in June 1850. About three hundred Sioux attended the gathering along with approximately a hundred Ojibway. After Hole-in-the-Day, the noted Ojibway chief, told the assemblage of the large number of his men who had been killed by the Sioux, Bad Hail questioned his figures, contradicting them with numbers of his own. Ramsey convinced both sides that the Great Father was best suited to decide what the reparations should be, and the government ultimately took five thousand dollars from the Mdewakanton annuity. Soon after the settlement was reached, Ramsey distributed among the Sioux a substantial number of horses and presents, thus bringing the council to a close on a positive note.[60] By fall, most Mdewakantons went off on their hunts in a good mood, convinced that Ramsey did indeed care for them and keep his promises.

Taoyateduta decided to lead his people back up the St. Croix River onto lands that his ancestors had hunted. He had heard that the buffalo had remained near the Missouri River, making it difficult to survive in the west or to trade for robes near Lac qui Parle. In addition, game animals on the St. Croix were more abundant than in previous seasons, deer being in sufficient numbers to feed his people.[61] But he must have realized that such hunts east of the Mississippi River would soon be impossible. Lumbermen had been at work for some time clearing much of the forest near the river, and Ramsey would certainly not wait long before once again broaching the question of a treaty.

The winter of 1850–51 was surely a period of reflection for Taoyateduta and his people. Chiefs such as Wabasha seemed convinced that the Great Father had become greedy and wanted to push the Sioux out of their homeland. Others, including several close relatives of Taoyateduta such as Lorenzo Lawrence, considered the white man to be the Indians' friend and ally. They advocated farming and even questioned the value of Sioux customs and religion.[62] Little Crow vacillated. Surely the whites could not all be wrong, as Wabasha believed. They had provided food and assistance for years. They had taken seriously their responsibilities as kinsmen to help the Sioux. More importantly, did an alternative to negotiation exist? Wabasha showed no signs of having one. Little Crow realized that the expanding white population could not be held off forever, and, having lived in the west, he was less concerned about the emotional impact of removal than many other Mdewakantons. Perhaps now was the time to seek the mantle of tribal leadership that seemed to be no one's preserve and support a treaty negotiation. He still had many relatives on the upper Minnesota River, and working with whites had brought power and influence to Taoyateduta's grandfather. Indeed, his own father had served as tribal speaker during the last important negotiation in 1837.

While waiting out the cold Minnesota winter, Little Crow undoubtedly considered the alternative to cooperation with the whites. He had watched the process for years. Prestige and influence would flow from being able to work at compromise with the Americans and convince fellow tribesmen to follow a reasonable course. The alternative was to remain in the shadow of Wabasha—hardly a rewarding choice for an energetic man like Little Crow. But the price of such recognition was enormous—the loss of a homeland. These were trying times for any Mdewakanton leader, especially one who had a keen awareness of what the future held.

4

Sale of a Homeland

As the snow cleared from the banks of the St. Croix River in the spring of 1851, speculation regarding the upcoming treaty negotiation reached a fever pitch. Many Mdewakantons showed considerable apprehension, as well they might, since almost any sale would result in the loss of the Mississippi valley, their homeland from time immemorial. But most Mdewakanton chiefs were realists, aware that treaties meant annuities and that there would be support for a negotiation in the Indian camps. More importantly, a small group of people at Kaposia, including Joseph Napeśniduta and White Dog, had already turned to farming and were about to form a "farmers' society." A treaty would provide funds for plows, oxen, and agricultural assistance.[1]

Little Crow realized that many other factions were urging the eastern Sioux to negotiate, especially the traders who frequently had pressed the Indians for the payment of debts. Many of Taoyateduta's people felt obligated to help their commercially minded friends and relatives, but the kinship bonds connecting Indians, mixed-bloods, and traders provided whites with a powerful lever to use in the negotiation. Missionaries, knowing that the benefits of a treaty would outweigh negative aspects, used their ties with influential men to push for a sale.[2] It almost seemed as if preventing a land sale had become an impossibility. The only openly hostile figure in the entire scenario was Wabasha, who had spoken against the agreement from the start. It remained to be seen whether Little Crow, now about forty years old, somewhat impetuous, but gaining prestige among his people with each passing year, would join this Mdewakanton chief in defiance of the government or show a willingness to negotiate as men such as Black Dog, Bad Hail, and Shakopee had already done.[3]

Traders were cognizant of the danger inherent in the vacillation of men like Little Crow. Sibley and others had worried about him from the start; the Kaposia chief had said nothing to alleviate those concerns during the winter of 1850–51. Indeed, by spring, the tone of Sibley's letters became more guarded, and perhaps for this reason, both he and Ramsey ultimately endorsed an idea offered by Martin McLeod.[4] The Lac qui Parle trader suggested that Ramsey and Luke Lea, the man picked to replace John Chambers as treaty commissioner, purchase land from the Sissetons and Wahpetons first and then face the more cautious and sophisticated Mdewakantons with a *fait accompli*. McLeod stated flatly that the Sissetons and Wahpetons wanted a treaty and its attending annuities so badly that they would sign almost anything.[5]

With this crucial decision made, Lea, Ramsey, and a host of newspaper editors, traders, and missionaries congregated on board the steamboat *Excelsior* in late June for the trip up the winding Minnesota River to the treaty grounds at Traverse des Sioux to meet the Sissetons and Wahpetons. The commissioners were pleased with the site because it had the advantage of being accessible by riverboat, thus facilitating the transportation of the large amounts of food necessary for the successful negotiation of a treaty; feasting made the Sioux obligated to listen to the offers of the commissioners. As a courtesy, the commissioners invited Little Crow to travel with them, no doubt hoping to impress him with the ride, and he arrived at St. Paul on June 29 with a delegation of his principal men.[6] While Traverse des Sioux was outside the territorial limits of the Mdewakanton people, Little Crow knew the region well since he had spent so much time on the upper Minnesota River in his youth. He also expected to visit with many of his Sisseton relatives at the council.

When the commissioners arrived in late June, however, most Sisseton and Wahpeton Indians were still at their buffalo hunting grounds. After nearly two weeks, Ramsey became anxious about getting the discussions underway, and on July 12, he asked a Sisseton, Walking Thunder, how long it would be before the treaty negotiations could begin. Walking Thunder cavalierly said: "If our Great Father wants to buy our land, we will talk with him about it at a proper time. Our Great Father has several cattle left yet. There is no hurry."[7] In other words, the consensus process took time; Ramsey would have to have patience if he wished to deal with the Sioux.

While the commissioners waited, the camp at Traverse des Sioux quickly took on a carnival atmosphere, with young Dakota men and women playing games, such as lacrosse, and everyone feasting on the government-supplied food. A frontier wedding took place between two mixed-bloods—trader David Faribault marrying the young and strikingly beautiful Nancy McClure.[8] All the events made interesting subjects for the artist Frank Blackwell Mayer, who had accompanied the party up the river on the *Excelsior*, but Mayer continued to return to the subject that interested him most—Chief Little Crow. He had been introduced to Taoyateduta by Captain Seth Eastman, another artist of note, and the missionary Williamson. Mayer described Little Crow as a man of "some forty five years of age," with a "very determined & ambitious nature, but withall exceedingly gentle and dignified in his deportment." His face showed "intelligence" when he talked, and "his whole bearing" was "that of a gentleman." On July 2, Mayer finally convinced Little Crow to sit for him and executed one of the more spectacular examples of Indian portraiture.[9]

Little Crow's role in the Traverse des Sioux negotiations was limited to that of an observer. Even so, Mayer noted that the Kaposia chief and his band seemed to be "considered as especially our friends." Their tents occupied ground close to the commissioners' encampment, facilitating daily contact between the two groups, and Little Crow appeared to be supportive of what the traders and the government were attempting to do. Other lower Indians, particularly Shakopee and his band, were viewed differently. Shakopee begged for something nearly every day, exasperating the commissioners, and most whites seemed pleased when he left. On July 12 a report reached Traverse des Sioux that Ojibway Indians had killed two Dakotas near St. Paul, precipitating his departure. Although evidence is lacking, Little Crow apparently returned home at about the same time.[10]

Initially the councils with the Sissetons and Wahpetons, which began on July 18, failed to produce a treaty, and at one point the negotiation almost broke down. A lacrosse match caused a misunderstanding on the afternoon of July 19 when chief Sleepy Eyes and many companions abruptly left the council to attend the scheduled event. The commissioners thought the Indian delegation was walking out and, already frustrated, they prepared to leave.[11] But the missionaries and the traders brought the politicians from both sides back together two days later. At that point, Curley Head, the principal spokesman for the Indians, finally declared: "I meant to have said before that we wish to sell . . . our country if we are satisfied with your offer."[12]

Two days later agreement was reached on a compromise treaty, and the missionaries promptly had it translated into Dakota and given to the Indians. Riggs read it several times to the chiefs and explained each article. In brief the government gave the Sissetons and Wahpetons $1,665,000 for their claim to lands extending from the Des Moines watershed to Otter Tail Lake, and from Traverse des Sioux to Lake Traverse. Most of the money was to remain in a trust and draw interest, but the remainder was earmarked for immediate reservation development, to finance the removal of the Indians from their lands, and to pay trade debts. The commissioners agreed that $275,000 would cover debts and removal.[13] Despite the fact that former Commissioner of Indian Affairs A. H. H. Stuart had warned Ramsey and Lea against providing the Indians with a reservation within the land purchase, a concept then in disfavor with many senators who would have to ratify the treaty, one was mapped out, extending ten miles on either side of the Minnesota River from the Yellow Medicine tributary to Lake Traverse.[14]

The news of the signing at Traverse des Sioux reached St. Paul within a few days. The *Minnesota Pioneer* heralded it as the "greatest event by far in the history of the Territory," and its editor went on to exclaim poetically that he could now behold the "red savage, with his tepees, their horses, and their famished dogs, fading, vanishing, dissolving away."[15] This attitude of self-congratulation was presumptive since the government had yet to deal with the Mdewakantons and Wahpekutes, who held the land from Traverse des Sioux to the Mississippi River and had fewer reasons for selling since they already received annuities. Ramsey and Lea were confident of success with them, approaching this last leg of their task as though it were a mere formality. On July 29 they called the Mdewakanton and Wahpekute chiefs together in a warehouse at Mendota, smoked the peace pipe to symbolize the good will and strong bonds of friendship that existed between the eastern Sioux and the Americans, and offered eight hundred thousand dollars for the lands held by these people, half the amount given to the upper bands. The treaty commissioners, Ramsey and Lea, argued that this money would buy large amounts of annuity goods, hire farmers to grow crops, and generally secure for the Mdewakantons a life of ease. The commissioners also noted that since the Sissetons and Wahpetons had sold their lands, the Mdewakantons could not expect to keep their hunting grounds. "You would not only have the whites along the river in front but all around you," Ramsey logically argued. "You should pass away from the river and go farther west." The Minnesota territorial governor expected an immediate answer to the proposition or, at the very least, a counteroffer. He got neither.[16]

To Ramsey's discomfort, Wabasha, acting as spokesman, asked what had become of the money from the 1837 treaty education fund. The commissioners countered by telling him that the money would be included in the future treaty, Lea even suggesting that a substantial portion—thirty thousand dollars—could be paid when the treaty was signed. Since federal officials had not agreed to provide this money, Sibley had made certain that such a sum was available, having it shipped from his company's St.

Louis office.[17] The somewhat masked attempt at bribery failed, however, and the Indians took the treaty offer back to their lodges without comment. The next day, Wabasha returned the document unsigned. Although the commissioners at the request of Wabasha had moved the council outside to Pilot Knob overlooking the Minnesota River, the airy atmosphere did not provide a more congenial setting. As the Indian leaders wished neither to criticize the proposed treaty nor to speak for it, an awkward silence fell over the council.[18]

The undaunted commissioners opened a third round of discussions on July 31. Little Crow, dressed impressively in a white shirt and collar, a bright neckerchief, a red belt with a silver buckle, and a pair of intricately beaded trousers, was among those attending. The Indians were unwilling to negotiate, but after a protracted period of silence Little Crow finally rose to speak. He began slowly, discoursing on the past and on the wisdom and experience of the other men around him, some of whom were older than he and had made the trip to Washington in 1837. He noted that despite his inexperience the Mdewakanton leadership had "put it upon me to speak—although I feel as if my mouth was tied" and proceeded to discuss the fairness with which the government had treated his people during past negotiations. He impressed his audience, especially the reporters present who later commented on his shrewdness and intelligence. Finally Little Crow got to the point—the Treaty of 1837 had not been administered as promised. "These men [the Mdewakanton and Wahpekute chiefs] sit still and say nothing; and you [the commissioners] perhaps are ashamed of us," Little Crow stated, "but you, fathers, are the cause of its being so. They [the chiefs] speak of some money that is due them . . . we do not want to talk about a new treaty until it is all paid." When Ramsey again tried to sidestep the issue, saying he needed time to get the money ready and negotiations for the treaty should proceed, Little Crow sternly retorted, "We will talk of nothing else but that money if it is until next spring. That lies in the way of a treaty." Although a brief meeting occurred the next day, the formal negotiations temporarily broke off, with the commissioners now angry and the Indians firmly entrenched.[19]

Private meetings took place over the next four days. For the most part, traders and mixed-bloods conducted these talks, but the missionary Gideon Pond was present most of the time. Throughout these discussions, Little Crow showed the greatest degree of flexibility, and Wabasha continued to oppose a sale. Little Crow had accepted the inevitability of a land sale and focused his attention instead on establishing reservation boundaries. He obviously knew the terms of the Sisseton and Wahpeton treaty and wanted to have his reservation located farther to the east, as close as possible to the woodlands. Ramsey and Lea had originally suggested that the southeastern boundary of a proposed reserve be drawn where the Redwood River enters the Minnesota. While the commissioners could not agree over the boundary line, they substantially increased the price offered for Mdewakanton and Wahpekute lands.[20]

When negotiations recommenced on August 5, the most important question remaining to be settled was the size and location of the reservation. Little Crow continued to haggle over the southeastern boundary, demonstrating the concern shared by many chiefs that the Mdewakantons would be forced to live on the open prairie, and argued strongly for placing it at Traverse des Sioux. At this crucial point, a soldier from Shakopee's band rose to support Little Crow's argument, and others, including Wakute, followed. Consensus was forming; if the boundary were moved farther east, then the treaty would be signed. Sensing the mood, Ramsey and Lea agreed to bring the boundary down the Minnesota River, nearly half the distance to Traverse des Sioux, and place the line at the mouth of the Little Rock River. Ramsey then called upon the Mdewakantons and Wahpekutes to sign. Wabasha, tired of the whole affair, finally turned to a crowd of warriors who had gathered behind the chiefs. He awkwardly asked if any of them intended to kill the first chief who signed, a threat that had been made a few days before, apparently while the private discussions took place. Shakopee's brother, Red Middle Voice, responded that this rumor was not true and that the warriors wanted the treaty. Ramsey then turned to Medicine Bottle, one of Little Crow's relatives and his chief soldier, and asked him who should have the honor of signing first. He symbolically pointed to his own chief.[21]

Before Little Crow picked up the quill pen, he addressed the warriors. "I am willing to be the first," he began, "but I am not afraid that you will kill me. If you do, it will be all right." A man must die sometime, Little Crow concluded, and he could be killed only once. Then, as he turned to the table that held the document, he made one final statement. "I believe this treaty will be best for the Dakotas, and I will sign it, even if a dog kills me before I lay down the goose quill." At that, he approached the treaty table, was handed a chair, and sat down and wrote out his name—Taoyateduta—in big, bold letters. With this stroke, Little Crow symbolically had assumed the mantle of leadership for the Mdewakantons. He had also formally committed himself to a policy of accommodation with whites.

The Mdewakantons and Wahpekutes received $1,410,000 for their lands, or nearly as much as the Sissetons and Wahpetons were awarded. The bulk of this money was to yield an annual interest of $58,000, approximately half of which would be used for annuities with the remainder being earmarked for reservation development. Of the funds not deposited, $220,000 went to pay debts and remove the Indians, and another $30,000 was reserved for immediate construction on the reservation. Old funds from the 1837 treaty were to be shared with the small Wahpekute tribe. Finally, as the Indians signed the treaty, $30,000 from the old education fund was handed to them. The money hit the streets of St. Paul nearly as fast as it went into the hands of the Indians, being spent mostly on horses and liquor.[22]

Despite the obvious opposition of some Mdewakanton leaders, the majority of Dakotas were pleased with the many benefits expected from the treaty.[23] The terms had been discussed openly for two years, and many Indians had come to see annuities as the solution to nagging economic problems. Moreover, the commissioners had frequently promised that the treaties would result in the full development of reservations, complete with farms, warehouses, and every necessity of life. Nonetheless, virtually before the ink had dried on both documents, a controversy erupted, leading historians later to condemn the treaties as a "Monstrous Conspiracy."

As the Sisseton and Wahpeton delegates at Traverse des Sioux lined up and signed the treaty, traders also had them place marks on a separate document, or "traders' paper." This agreement called upon the Indians to hand over to the traders a large sum—$210,000—from their removal and subsistence money to cover the cost of lost credits. Although many Indians agreed that such a payment should be made, few if any knew of the amount assigned to traders, and they wanted to control the distribution of the money themselves.[24] White merchants, such as Sibley, also asked the Mdewakantons and Wahpekutes to sign a traders' paper. While the Wahpekutes agreed to these demands—setting aside ninety thousand dollars for their debts—the Mdewakantons promptly refused to initial any documents. They had no doubt learned what went on at Traverse des Sioux, probably being informed by mixed-bloods, and even though several of their leaders agreed in principle to pay past debts, the majority of Mdewakanton chiefs wanted more control over the payment. Sibley then attempted to force the Mdewakantons to acknowledge their debts by cutting off credit at his store, but this stratagem failed.[25]

Other whites soon saw the debt controversy as a golden opportunity by which to gain access to the funds pledged for debt payment. Chief among them was Madison Sweetzer, an opportunist from Pennsylvania with political connections, who suddenly appeared at St. Paul. Sweetzer applied for a trade license and by early fall had opened a post at Traverse des Sioux where he convinced a considerable number of upper Indians to sign a petition protesting the traders' paper. The document requested that he be empowered to act legally in their behalf. Despite the fact that Little Crow and Shakopee had not signed a traders' paper, Sweetzer acquired their support of his cause, obviously because they wanted an ally in what was shaping up as a struggle over control of a sizable portion of the treaty money.[26]

Meanwhile, another problem temporarily overshadowed the debt controversy. After whites heard of the treaty signing, many moved west of the Mississippi River and began to claim townsites and to build farms. The Mdewakantons still owned the land and protested vigorously to agent Nathaniel McLean. The agent, in turn, asked Colonel Francis Lee at Fort Snelling to stop the invasion, but the colonel only wrote to Washington for orders that never came. Thus, as the Senate began to debate the Sioux treaties in the spring of 1852, considerable areas of Mdewakanton land had already been occupied by whites. Fortunately, as the hungry and discontented Sioux returned from winter hunts, they found the trespassers willing to feed them, rather than chance a violent outburst.[27]

The influx of whites and the difficulties in procuring food prompted Little Crow to seek out Governor Ramsey. In late April, he had a long talk with the governor, discussing a variety of subjects. The chief reiterated his support for the treaty and, according to Ramsey, said that he would "cheerfully accede to all the requests" of the Great Father. Ramsey saw no duplicity in these comments and concluded that Little Crow "has ever been favorably disposed to the whites." Ramsey felt it was now time for the government to court Little Crow and recommended that the chief be placed at the head of an Indian delegation that would be sent to Washington, D.C. Little Crow had requested such a trip, and Ramsey thought the chief deserved this reward.[28]

Little Crow's cooperation seemed to have its limits, however, especially when he spoke in front of a mixed crowd of Indians and whites at Kaposia on May 22. The treaty had not been ratified, and settlers were rapidly staking out land claims and even hunting game. On this occasion, the Kaposia chief, dressed in a striking, full suit of otterskin and with a raccoon tail dangling on each leg, talked very pointedly about the unratified treaty. Obviously playing on the emotions of the audience, Little Crow said that back in August, "Our Father" had patiently sat down "to talk with us." But rather than negotiate, he "whittle[d] a stick and then whistle[d], and he kept on in that way for almost two moons [months]." The Mdewakantons, Little Crow said, "got very tired" and raised no corn. Finally, after "Our Father," or Ramsey, had eaten all the cattle that he had brought, "he got up . . . and belched up some wind from his great belly and poked his treaty at us, saying, I will give you so much for your land." While Little Crow admitted that Ramsey had informed the Mdewakantons that the Senate must ratify the treaty and the chief also agreed that the white settlers, who "showered down" homes on Sioux lands, had assisted them, he wondered what had happened to the money and annuities promised for their homeland. He concluded by asking the assemblage: "Now what have we? Why, we have neither our lands, where our fathers' bones are bleaching, nor have we anything."[29]

The difficulties appeared to be resolved a month later when news of the Senate ratification of the treaties reached the upper Mississippi. The senators had shown little interest in the issue of Indian debt and only briefly debated Sweetzer's petition. But the cautious relief in Indian camps soon turned to outrage when it became known that during the ratification process the Senate had removed the clause that allowed the Dakotas to have reservations in Minnesota. This act must have seemed like a betrayal to Little Crow, since he had become a supporter of the treaty after convincing Ramsey to move the reservation boundary farther east, back into the woodlands of the lower Minnesota River valley.[30]

Traders, politicians, and missionaries alike condemned the actions of the Senate, but they could do little about them. While the upper Sioux might have been convinced to accept their treaty without reserves, the Mdewakantons would never have done so.[31] Wabasha's reaction testifies to the Indians' opposition to the Senate "amendments." When asked about them he simply replied: "There is one thing more which our great father can do, that is, gather us all together on the prairie and surround us with soldiers and shoot us down."[32] Ramsey finally asked the Mdewakantons to accept the amendments on August 27, but they adamantly refused to do so. They were sullen and dejected and had begun to quarrel with the white settlers now living near them. Some compromise had to be worked out, for the Treaty of Mendota was in jeopardy.[33]

Ramsey realized that the Mdewakantons would consent to the amendments only if he could obtain a temporary permit for them to occupy the reservations. Whites would not want the lands set aside for reservations for some time—Ramsey thought twenty-five years—and the Senate had left the final determination of what was to be done with the reservation lands to the discretion of the president, who had the option of assigning the lands to the Indians. In such circumstances, Ramsey and Lea asked Office of Indian Affairs officials in late August if the president would agree to let the Sioux use the lands formerly designated as reservations for twenty to twenty-five years. While they waited for an answer, however, Ramsey decided to use the promise of occupancy as a means to acquire Sioux agreement to the Senate amendments.[34]

Rather than attempt such a delicate negotiation himself, Ramsey hired Henry M. Rice, a St. Paul trader, to parlay with the Mdewakantons and persuade them to accept the amendments. The councils between Rice and the Indian leaders were never recorded, perhaps because of the promises made to the Indians. At any rate, Little Crow later testified that Rice had agreed to his demands regarding the easternmost boundary of the proposed reservation—the Kaposia chief still wanted it moved closer to the woodlands, at least to the mouth of the Cottonwood River. In addition, some evidence suggests that the Mdewakanton leaders were left with the impression that they might stay on their reservation forever. Feeling as though they had received a better deal from Rice than Ramsey would have given them, the Mdewakanton chiefs signed the amendments on September 4, and the Sissetons and Wahpetons agreed to the changes a few days later.[35]

After the councils, Ramsey left for Washington to pick up the money needed to implement the treaty. Upon returning in November, he prepared to pay off the debts owed to traders. A large number of Wahpeton and Sisseton leaders, as well as all of the Mdewakanton chiefs, wanted the governor to turn over to them the funds designated in the treaty for debts, in contravention of the traders' paper signed by the Sissetons, Wahpetons, and Wahpekutes which had been designed for the express purpose of avoiding giving the money to the Indians. Ramsey, therefore, refused the requests of the Indian leaders and proposed instead that the representatives of each tribe sign a "receipt" for their money and allow him to distribute the funds. The governor pompously argued that it was "proper" that they should pay their traders, but he refused to indicate how much he intended to give to the traders and made no attempt to determine what the Indians actually owed.[36]

The Mdewakantons balked at the governor's proposal. Wabasha and Wakute, a minor chief from Red Wing's village, defiantly said that they wanted to distribute the money themselves, thereby paying only legitimate debts. Various rumors suggested that the mixed-bloods, including Wakute's nephew Jack Frazer, were becoming jealous over the large amounts of money that traders expected to receive and were urging the Indians to stand fast against Ramsey's actions. On the other hand, chiefs Good Road and Bad Hail supported the governor's position. Furthermore, Bad Hail had a son who had been imprisoned at Fort Snelling for killing an Ojibway, and Ramsey had promised to release him in exchange for the chief's support.[37]

With sides clearly drawn, many Indian leaders and whites turned to Little Crow. He had yet to speak out on the debt issue, and the traders had no idea what he would eventually say. After what must have been considerable soul-searching, the Kaposia chief elected to support Ramsey. His decision was probably influenced by Alexander Faribault, one of Sibley's men, who appealed to the chief's sense of kinship obligation. Faribault had a long talk with Little Crow, called him "brother," and promised to pay nearly three thousand dollars to him in return for signing the needed receipt. Faribault had been Little Crow's trader, and the Kaposia band was obligated to him for past assistance. Such bonds, anchored by friendship, blood, and assistance in the daily struggle for survival, made it difficult for Taoyateduta to refuse Faribault's request. Once Little Crow agreed to the deal, other chiefs followed, Wabasha and Wakute signing the receipt on the evening of November 9. Little Crow and the other band chiefs received nearly three thousand dollars apiece upon signing the receipt. These payments, which totaled twenty thousand dollars, were subtracted from the ninety thousand dollars set aside by Ramsey for debts. Most of the money given the chiefs was turned over to mixed-blood relatives, including Frazer, who then supported the debt distribution. The majority of the cash quickly reached St. Paul merchants. While the payments to traders and chiefs stimulated the local economy, the withdrawal so seriously depleted the debt and removal funds that the government soon found itself unable to finance the upriver journey of the Mdewakantons.[38]

After obtaining the consent of the Mdewakantons, Ramsey went to Traverse des Sioux to acquire a "receipt" from the Sissetons and Wahpetons. He carried along money to be distributed as annuities for 1852, which he promised to pay as soon as the Indians signed the receipt, but the Sisseton and Wahpeton chiefs refused his offer. Red Iron, the chief at Traverse des Sioux, resisted so strongly that Ramsey jailed him. With Red Iron out of the way, the governor worked with other band members, some of whom were not even chiefs. They finally signed the receipt that allowed Ramsey to distribute $210,000 of the Sisseton and Wahpeton removal and subsistence money to the traders. By mid-December, the entire process was over. The eastern Sioux had watched most of the $495,000 designated for removal and subsistence go to traders and mixed-bloods. Later testimony showed that Ramsey and his secretary, Hugh Tyler, deducted a 10 to 15 percent fee for handling the money.[39]

Soon after these complex negotiations had been completed, Willis A. Gorman replaced Ramsey as territorial governor in Minnesota, and it became Gorman's job, as Indian superintendent, to implement the two treaties. He quickly discovered major difficulties, as Ramsey had used up most of the money earmarked for removal; besides the funds distributed for debt, money had been spent to feast the Indians when they signed the various receipts and amendments, and other removal funds had been committed to flour and pork contracts that had yet to be fulfilled. Perhaps the most obvious problem, however, was the former governor's failure to prepare the reservations for their new occupants.[40] Thus when Gorman assumed his duties in spring 1853, the Mdewakantons still occupied their old villages. In late May, Little Crow asked Gorman if his people could stay at Kaposia until the reservations were ready. Taoyateduta and other leaders argued that they would suffer on the prairie without food or fields from which to harvest a crop. Gorman reluctantly agreed, telling the Mdewakantons that they would have to migrate to the reservations as soon as occupancy was possible.[41]

Meanwhile, settlers began to seize the old village sites from the Indians. Surveyors laid out town lots at Kaposia in the spring, forcing the Indians to look elsewhere for fields in which to plant. Little Crow did not resist these incursions, but other tribal leaders were less amenable.[42] Clashes occurred at Black Dog's, Wabasha's, and Wakute's (Red Wing's) villages. Gorman encouraged the emigration process by providing food for groups that reached Shakopee's old village and by warning traders that he would refuse them licenses if they did not support removal. Nevertheless, the undertaking did not go smoothly, and many Mdewakantons still remained as near to the Mississippi River as possible at summer's end, subsisting on ducks and begging for food.[43] Although the Indians were understandably reluctant to give up old homes, the lack of progress on the new reservations further hindered removal. Whereas a beautiful location had been selected for the new Lower Sioux Agency (for the Mdewakantons and Wahpekutes) near the junction of the Redwood and Minnesota rivers, government promises of ripening fields and stocked warehouses at that place went unfulfilled. The agent, Richard Murphy, a likable but disorganized person, lacked any sense of planning. His poor administrative skills, the difficulty of getting building materials into the region, and the lack of a motivated labor force impeded the development of farms.[44]

While the majority of Indians could easily see that governmental officials were failing to fulfill their promises, a few Mdewakanton leaders also berated Gorman for the obvious inconsistencies in the entire reservation program. Why should the Sioux settle on their reservation and turn to farming, the chiefs argued, if the government still possessed the option of pushing them off the land at some future date? Acting Commissioner of Indian Affairs Charles Mix had obtained a pledge from the president giving the eastern Sioux "full and complete" title to their upper Minnesota River reservations for five years, but this commitment was substantially less than what Ramsey had recommended. Gorman pointed to the difficulties involved with such a tenuous title and even went so far as to suggest in his 1853 annual report that the Senate had erred in taking the reservation clauses out of the treaties. Gorman asked if it were not possible for the Sioux to receive some guarantee of fixed tenure on the lands designated for reservations, concluding in his report that the Indians were, in fact, correct: it was foolhardy to invest treaty money in farms, mills, buildings, and other improvements and then abandon them.[45]

Convinced of the need to obtain a permanent title to the reservation land and acutely aware of the growing criticism of the treaties among the Indians, Gorman asked eastern Sioux leaders in the fall if they would like to visit the nation's capital and place their grievances before the Great Father. The Indians still had confidence in their Great Father in Washington, and Little Crow, in particular, had already expressed an interest in seeing him. In exchange for such a trip, however, Gorman asked Mdewakanton leaders, represented by Little Crow, to move to their reservation. Most agreed to do so, provided Gorman handed out food and presents. The superintendent distributed fifteen hundred dollars worth of provisions in November 1853, prompting most of the Mdewakantons to bring their families to the upper Minnesota.[46] But they would not stay all winter, since there was insufficient food for them, and the Mdewakantons had traditionally wintered in the protected, eastern river valleys. Nevertheless, as the Mdewakantons slowly migrated up the Minnesota River, they came to realize that, because their old villages in the Mississippi valley had been overrun by whites, the reservation was all that remained for them.[47]

Unfortunately the political climate in Washington, D.C., late in the fall of 1853 made the Sioux delegation's trip impossible. Local newspapers had printed accounts of the distribution of treaty funds that openly accused commissioners Ramsey and Lea of fraud in their negotiations. Several politicians, including Sibley, who was territorial delegate at the time, called upon the Senate to investigate the charges. During the subsequent hearings, which went on throughout the fall and early winter, Ramsey defended himself by simply arguing that the Indians were incapable of handling such large sums as those earmarked for debt. The testimony of witnesses showed evidence of wrongdoing, but in February 1854 the Senate exonerated the former governor.[48]

At this point, Gorman invited Little Crow to accompany him to Washington. Why other chiefs were excluded is a mystery, although it is possible that due to the wintertime dispersal many could not be contacted. Yet both Ramsey and Gorman had specifically wanted to reward Little Crow for his role in the 1851 treaty negotiations, and the Kaposia chief was now a principal figure in the Mdewakanton hierarchy and was also the first major chief to give up his old village for the new reservation. Thus Little Crow, Gorman, and Henry Belland, who had married into the Kaposia band, left for Washington on April 1. The trip was to have a profound impact on Little Crow and the destiny of the Mdewakanton people.[49]

The journey by rail and steamboat undoubtedly both thrilled and frightened Taoyateduta, who had never been east of Wisconsin. Yet he had certainly spent many evening hours listening to his grandfather describe his 1824 trip to the capital. Taoyateduta's father, Big Thunder, had been to Washington in 1837 and had no doubt vividly retold his experiences in the capital.[50] Thus Little Crow had some idea of what to expect.

Although the particulars of the trip are sketchy, it is known that Little Crow had a chance meeting with a delegation of six Chickasaw Indians in a Pittsburgh hotel on April 7. He apparently was so interested in these more sophisticated Indians that he elected to stay an extra day in Pittsburgh and travel on with them to the capital. This arrangement necessitated letting Gorman, who had business obligations, travel on ahead of Little Crow and Belland. The governor reached Washington on the evening of April 7, Little Crow and Belland arriving the next evening. Once in the capital, Little Crow and Belland checked into "Mr. Maher's" Western Hotel. Since Gorman was staying in the National Hotel, unquestionably a more elegant establishment, Little Crow and the governor saw little of each other. The separation may be explained by the fact that Little Crow was in the capital "on his own responsibility," a circumstance reported in two newspapers. Either Little Crow was not allowed to register at the National Hotel, or he could not afford its elegance.[51]

Despite Little Crow's advent, more or less, uninvited, he soon gained access to George Manypenny, the commissioner of Indian affairs, and even to President Franklin Pierce. The discussions with these men centered on the issue of Sioux ownership of lands designated but not confirmed as reservations. Nevertheless, Little Crow's advice had little to do with solving the eastern Sioux reservation problem, since the secretary of the interior had recommended on April 5, 1854—three days before Little Crow's arrival—that the eastern Sioux be allowed to remain on their earlier prescribed reservations "until the Executive [president] shall deem it expedient otherwise to direct."[52] On April 13, the president agreed to this executive decree. Although several senators concluded at the time that a congressional act granting the eastern Sioux permanent tenure was necessary, such a bill, passed by the Senate in late April, did not clear the House. When this latter body acted in regard to Sioux reservation lands in July, it still left the decision on permanent occupation to the president. Unfortunately, Pierce failed to issue any more executive decrees, and the Dakotas kept their reservations wholly at the discretion of the chief executive.[53]

Although Little Crow played an undetermined role in all these maneuvers, he was in Washington during the discussions and claimed credit for the change.[54] He was convinced that his people had been granted the original reservations forever and their title confirmed to lands extending down the Minnesota River to the mouth of the Big Cottonwood River. Little Crow had argued vehemently for this boundary in 1851 and came away from Washington in 1854 believing that the Big Cottonwood fell within the Mdewakanton reservation. Upon returning to Minnesota, Little Crow declared that the commissioner had agreed to distribute $20,035 of the annuity funds owing the Sioux from their 1837 treaty as an act of good faith. In all, Little Crow understandably felt that his trip had been a thorough success, an exercise in statesmanship that would certainly enhance his position in the Dakota hierarchy, and that ties that he, his father, and his grandfather had nurtured with the Great Father in Washington had been reinforced.[55]

Like most Indian leaders who visited Washington, Little Crow retained vivid impressions of the city and its many attractions. Art galleries, theaters, government buildings, and monuments were everywhere. He watched, for example, as workers laid marble in the ongoing project to build a monument honoring George Washington. The stone obelisk was then at the 152-foot mark, or one-third complete. Little Crow also undoubtedly visited the Hippodrome, a massive tent structure that could seat five thousand people for plays, gymnastics acts, and animal shows. The rage of the spring 1854 season was "Franconi" and his troupe of performers, many of whom were comely young women.[56] Certainly, Little Crow strolled along the many boulevards of the city and visited its many arcades. He even observed the famous western painter John Mix Stanley at his studio-arcade, often called "Stanley's Western Wilds." Coincidentally, Stanley was just then finishing a landscape of Kaposia, complete with bark and hide lodges, women dressing hides, and men carrying canoes to the river. Little Crow was delighted and gazed for a long time at the scene, pointing to familiar sights. But Stanley also had completed a painting of the burial ground near Kaposia, and this picture produced in the chief a more sullen mood. He looked for a long time at the depiction of the dead being mounted on scaffolds, then raised his hands above his head, clasped them, and stalked out of the room. No one watching his reaction even attempted to fathom what had been racing through his mind. No doubt he lamented the fact that he would never again return to that village so poignantly portrayed by Stanley.[57]

True to his nature, Little Crow gave several interviews while in the capital. Reporters from the Washington *Daily Union* spoke with him twice, using Belland as interpreter. Little Crow was said to be "delighted with the city," and the chief was in turn described as "commending," his countenance was seen as an indication of "firmness and intelligence." Although the reporter questioned whether he ought to have been allowed alone on the streets, there was no doubt that Little Crow was able to convince everyone he met of his "high position" and importance.[58]

Once back on the upper Mississippi, Little Crow faced realities that he had been able to avoid in Washington. While he had won a battle in the capital, or so he thought, the victory meant accepting removal and reservation life and convincing his people to do likewise. Such massive change posed a serious challenge to Little Crow's leadership; even he had become nostalgic when confronting the issue of removal at Stanley's studio in Washington. Nevertheless, he, more than the other leaders, also understood that resisting the wave of whites rather than settling west of the Mississippi was futile. This had become even more obvious after Little Crow witnessed firsthand the immense resources that the Great Father could draw upon. Negotiation and compromise remained the only rational alternatives. By the spring of 1854, the men in charge of Indian affairs in Minnesota automatically turned to Little Crow for assistance. They were fully aware that he was now the premier spokesman for his tribe and for a policy of peaceful coexistence.

5

Spokesman for the Sioux

LITTLE CROW'S RETURN from Washington marked a new era for the Mdewakanton people. Thereafter, the reservation along the upper Minnesota River increasingly became the focal point of the tribe's existence, and the interaction with government officials reached levels never before seen. This new way of life—more confining, more agriculturally oriented—provided Little Crow with an opportunity to demonstrate his value as a leader. Commissioner Manypenny had agreed to let Little Crow distribute $20,035 in annuity money, and Gorman later praised the Kaposia chief for his diplomatic acumen in council.[1] Thus Little Crow faced the challenge on the reservation fully convinced that he had touched the heart of the Great Father and that he would now be looked to as the man to lead the Mdewakantons and perhaps even the other three eastern Sioux tribes.

Once in St. Paul, the chief encountered other people who were interested in his trip. Newspapermen interviewed him, and he boasted of his services while in Washington. "He has many marvellous tales to tell of what he saw and done [sic] during his absence," a reporter noted in the *Minnesota Pioneer*. "He claims to have arrived in Washington just in the nick of time to prevent the removal of the Sioux to the Missouri." Such attention fueled Little Crow's sense of importance, and the reporter intimated that the chief truly enjoyed his new celebrity status. Further evidence of his increasing prominence came when he demanded supplies of Gorman in order to facilitate his tribe's removal to the new reservation, and Gorman agreed to his request.[2] No wonder, then, that in late May, as Little Crow slowly traveled up the Minnesota River, he successfully convinced many reluctant Mdewakantons encamped along the way to gather their belongings together and to follow him to Redwood. Government officials had made many promises that he now used to convince the Mdewakantons to try reservation life. Little Crow seemed convinced that his people would be well taken care of in their new reservation homes.[3]

The removal under Little Crow's charge proceeded gradually, due to the unwillingness of some Mdewakantons to leave their old woodland homes and the logistic difficulties involved in moving so many people. Asa W. Daniels, a physician who watched the process from an observation point near where Fort Ridgely was being built, described the migration in some detail. "Little Crow and his braves marched ahead with their guns," he recorded, "followed by the rest of the band with their families and household possessions." The caravan of wagons and carts made up a considerable column that proceeded along the trail in casual disorder. Many women and children hopped on and off the loaded wagons as the horses plodded along in the warm June sun. Once the Indians reached the vicinity of the military post, Little Crow again showed his worth by negotiating with the army officers for food supplies. He then returned to the lower Minnesota River and made sure that stragglers were not lingering in the newly opened towns of Shakopee and Mankato. Almost all of the Mdewakantons had reached the reservation by late June.[4]

Unfortunately, on June 27 trouble broke out during one of the last trips when a party of fourteen Ojibway Indians appeared on the banks of the Minnesota River. Little Crow had one last load of possessions to transport from Traverse des Sioux. To accomplish this, the chief had borrowed a wagon and acquired the help of a mixed-blood relative named Russell, as well as two white friends, one of whom was Charles Mitchell. The party headed first to Fort Ridgely where the commanding officer, Lieutenant Lewis Addison Armistead, agreed to give the men provisions for the trip. As the wagon carrying the four men headed south along the river a mere mile or two from the fort, the Ojibway warriors sprang from ambush, firing shots that seriously wounded young Russell and grazed Little Crow's shoulder and cheek. The chief and another companion leaped from the wagon and sought cover in the brush. They watched as the Ojibway rushed the wagon and dispatched Russell, scalping him in front of the astonished onlooker, Charles Mitchell.[5]

The troops at Fort Ridgely, taking a breather from construction, heard the gunshots and quickly investigated. Learning of Russell's death, Lieutenant Armistead and a force of troops pursued the Ojibway. They were soon joined by Gabriel and Joseph Renville, who like Little Crow were relatives of Russell and wanted to avenge his death. Armistead, later to be immortalized by leading Pickett's charge at Gettysburg, followed the trail of the fleeing Ojibway for many hours and finally captured seven of the assailants and bought them back to the fort.[6] The soldiers placed them in a guardhouse to await trial.

While the army pursued the attackers, Little Crow recruited a war party at the reservation. Suddenly on June 30 he raced pellmell into the unfinished fort at the head of nearly two hundred angry warriors. A drum roll brought the soldiers in line and prevented the Sioux from seizing their adversaries. Little Crow then retreated to a position outside the fort and "demanded" the prisoners, saying that he would overrun the garrison unless the army complied. Armistead defiantly refused and challenged the Kaposia chief to execute his threat. Little Crow, realizing that his quarrel was with the Ojibway and not the United States Army, quickly lowered his demands, suggesting that if the army would send him an ox for a feast, he and his warriors would quietly leave. This, too, was refused, and the Mdewakantons left in a "sullen" mood.[7]

True to his character, Little Crow preferred to negotiate an end to the troubles, rather than fight, although at times he could be swept up in events where his impetuous, risk-taking nature temporarily reigned. Once it had become obvious, however, that Armistead would not release the Ojibway men, Little Crow wanted, at the very least, for the fort commander to reaffirm his commitment to the Sioux by giving them a present. When this, too, failed, Little Crow concluded that he had no other choice than to punish Armistead. Over the next year, Taoyateduta lent his support to the numerous war parties who sought revenge on the Ojibway, even though he did not join them. The war parties, in turn, started an intertribal war that raged for the next two years and resulted in staggering Ojibway losses, estimated at fifty people by the end of 1854 and fifty more the next year. The war soon overshadowed Little Crow's failure as well as Armistead's stubbornness and diverted attention from events at Redwood Agency.[8]

Activity at Redwood, as well as at the new agency for the Sissetons and Wahpetons located at Yellow Medicine, had picked up appreciably by spring 1854. Carpenters, farmers, and millwrights were all working at creating a farming community out of the untamed prairie environment. Progress came slowly due to the failure of the commissioner of Indian affairs to release necessary construction funds and the near incompetence of agent Murphy. But after the president agreed to let the eastern Sioux stay on their reservation indefinitely, white laborers plowed several large fields and constructed a few buildings to house supplies and workers.[9]

During this early development, an interesting debate surfaced that had a considerable impact on the pattern of future reservation progress. Murphy believed that it would be best to develop a "model" farm in which large, efficiently managed fields produced an abundance of food. Indians, he felt, could then be "concentrated" around these fields and soon take over the operation of the farms as they learned the trade from their white instructors. Other officials and onlookers, especially missionaries, were convinced that such a system would only encourage the sense of "community" that had hindered the advancement of a "civilizing" process in the past. In other words, the Indians would spend too much time with their relatives, feasting, dancing, and being generally unproductive. Missionaries wanted the agent to settle nuclear families on separate farmsteads. Both Riggs and Williamson had been sponsoring just such a program at their two new missions near Yellow Medicine where a small core of Dakota men, only a few of whom were mixed-bloods, had opened individual farms and begun construction of buildings.[10]

Nevertheless, Murphy ignored the missionaries' pleadings and assigned a seventy- to eighty-acre plot to each band at Redwood. By fall 1854, despite the agent's frequent absences from Redwood, lands had been prepared, and Indian women had planted crops. Some plowed lands remained fallow, however, because Murphy had failed to obtain sufficient seed, and the agency suffered from a deficiency of white laborers. Most Sioux men ignored the opportunity to farm and oftentimes did not even give their women much encouragement. The Mdewakantons believed that the treaties would supply the food they needed to get them through the winter.[11]

Dependence on the government soon proved unwise, as agent Murphy had been unable to develop a transportation system capable of moving food the extra 150 miles beyond St. Paul. Worse, the supplies of pork that did reach Redwood began to spoil while sitting in the hot, July sun awaiting Murphy's return for authorized distribution. Even the Minnesota River failed to cooperate, as low water frequently made it impossible to move supplies quickly and cheaply. These difficulties convinced Mdewakanton leaders to re-examine treaty provisions, some questioning whether farms and annuities would ever sustain them. The Mdewakantons, however, were better off than the Sissetons and Wahpetons, who, Murphy conceded, had received virtually nothing.[12]

By October, the situation on the reservation reached a crisis. Dakota Indians milled about the agency buildings, pilfering items when they could and demanding assistance. The commanding officer at Fort Ridgely, a mere ten miles away, feared trouble and noted that the Indians were "almost in a *starving condition.*" The Mdewakantons complained that they had been forced to wait most of the fall for food and goods, making it impossible for them to hunt, and then the promised items had not arrived. According to an army officer on the scene, one or two children actually died from starvation. Fortunately, forty tons of food and annuity goods arrived by flatboat on October 28, allowing Murphy to hand out some of the supplies needed for the upcoming winter. But the food was not sufficient to feed the nearly two thousand Indians who gathered at Redwood, and throughout November and December, the Dakotas gradually left the reservation to hunt either in the Big Woods to the east or along the Minnesota River below the agency.[13]

Conditions in 1855–56 improved overall as agency officials worked to iron out transportation difficulties. Nevertheless, several patterns had already been set that persisted over the next several years. Following the fall distribution of annuities—food, goods, and money—Mdewakanton men left the reservation with their families to hunt and did not return until late spring. While government farmers opened a few more acres each year and carpenters continued to build houses and barns, these changes benefited the eastern Sioux only marginally. Dakota women continued to plant corn in their small, "community" plots, but agricultural programs languished. Understandably, Dakota leaders constantly complained about the failure of the government to live up to its promises and wondered what had happened to the schools, mills, and substantial amounts of money and goods that Ramsey and Lea had promised in 1851.[14]

The most responsible spokesman and critic during these years of trial was Little Crow. According to Asa Daniels, who knew Taoyateduta well, he very quickly became "the most active and influential" of the Mdewakanton leaders. Unlike many of his colleagues, he exhibited a lively interest in every aspect of operations on the reservations, including the way in which the agent spent money. Little Crow's knowledge of numbers aided him when it came to discussing the multiplicity of funds that existed under the 1837 and 1851 treaties and as he watched the distribution of annuities. He gave careful attention to the efforts of the white farmers, even though he had no intention of becoming a husbandman. He spent many hours in council with the agent and superintendent and seldom missed a debate. Reservation administrators soon realized that while Wabasha was highly esteemed (Gorman ordered a house built for him first), Little Crow had become spokesman for his people, and he brought to that position a dedication that even his critics admired.[15]

Yet Little Crow recognized that leading his people depended to a large extent upon serving their needs. After it became obvious, for example, that there would not be enough food at the reservation to feed the Mdewakantons over the winter of 1854–55, Little Crow suggested to government officials that bands be allowed to return to the eastern wood-

78

lands to hunt. When Gorman learned of this, he ordered that annuities be withheld from bands that left the reservation en masse. Philander Prescott, the government farmer, sought to make them stay by forcing them to sign agreements that denied them annuities if they left the reserve for any length of time. Little Crow shrewdly advised his tribesmen to sign the papers and then leave after the annuities had been handed out. This created difficulties for Prescott, who had to answer to Gorman. Prescott blamed Little Crow, who was "at the head as he generally is" of the entire scheme. By late winter, Gorman gave up on his plans to force the Sioux to remain on the reservation, and many Mdewakanton young men ranged as far east as the St. Croix River in search of game.[16]

Taoyateduta also watched attentively as government administrators and missionaries tried to promote Euro-American civilization at both Redwood and Yellow Medicine. While he supported the efforts of white agency personnel to produce food from reservation lands, he did not accept the notion that Indians should become farmers, believing that the creator made whites to be farmers and Indians to be hunters and warriors. Ironically, while most governmental agricultural development occurred at the Lower Agency, or Redwood, in 1854 two small groups of Indians and mixed-bloods living near Yellow Medicine, many of whom were relatives of Little Crow's, cut their hair, put on white men's clothing, and began to build individual farms. Most were products of the many years of missionary activity near Lac qui Parle. The first group, under Little Crow's father-in-law, Inyangmani, settled near Williamson's new mission at Peźutazi. A second, consisting mostly of Mdewakantons and including several Renvilles, Paul Mazakutemani, Lorenzo Lawrence, and perhaps a dozen others, joined Riggs at his new station on Hazelwood Creek.[17]

Taoyateduta carefully watched the changes that occurred near Yellow Medicine. At one point, he traveled to the agency and harangued officials regarding the efforts of Riggs to build and operate a sawmill. Little Crow's argument against the enterprise hinged not on harvesting of a scarce resource—lumber and firewood—but on Riggs's policy of selling the boards produced at the mill. Sioux people shared their possessions. Inyangmani, his son Henok Appearing Cloud, and Paul Mazakutemani agreed with Taoyateduta's position, speaking out against Riggs, even though all three men had become farmers and were building houses. Being closely related to Little Crow, however, they had a strong cultural obligation to side with the Mdewakanton chief. On the other hand, the government farmer at Yellow Medicine, Andrew Robertson, was also tied through marriage to the Kaposia band and was a close friend of Little Crow's. He

79

supported Riggs in the debate as did several members of Riggs's mission. As with many other issues that he faced in the 1850s, Little Crow found kinsmen on both sides of the argument. Ironically, the increased ties of so many of Little Crow's relatives with whites compromised his position to such an extent that when the chief visited Yellow Medicine Riggs noted that he frequently "talked of becoming a white man." Such a concession was no doubt necessary when surrounded by so many relatives who supported farming.[18]

The debates over resource utilization on the reservations in the 1850s paled in comparison to the attempts made by government officials to stop intertribal war. A crisis over this issue surfaced in June 1856, with Little Crow again playing a major role in the debate. A new superintendent, Francis Huebschmann, replaced Gorman that spring and tried to stop the intertribal fighting that had raged since the 1854 incident at Fort Ridgely. Huebschmann ordered that twenty-one Mdewakantons involved in raids be surrendered and placed in irons before the annuities for the year were distributed. The new superintendent felt that Gorman had been lax in disciplining the Sioux, and he especially deplored the fact that Little Crow had at one point been allowed to break into the agency warehouses and take food without being punished.[19]

Little Crow wanted to avoid a confrontation over the issue of intertribal warfare, as did other Mdewakanton chiefs who supported meeting the superintendent's demands. Nevertheless, Taoyateduta, when being selected to speak for his tribe, rose in council and made a brilliant attempt both to defend the young warriors involved and to appeal to Huebschmann's sense of fairness. Instead of talking of intertribal war, Little Crow slowly shifted the discussion to the many promises made by Murphy and Gorman and noted how most had gone unfulfilled. Finally on June 17, with four hundred young warriors present in "war costume," Little Crow accused agency officials of having "very long pocket[s], into which their [Sioux] funds were slipt."[20] The young men who were listening were obviously heartened by this defense. A newspaper editor present noted that "Little Crow, particularly, was very eloquent in his exposure of the injustice the Indians had met with." Even the stern, teutonic disciplinarian, Huebschmann, paused for a brief moment after hearing Little Crow and agreed to investigate agency affairs, but he quickly recovered and decided to suspend the annuity payments and placed guards at the doors of the warehouses until the twenty-one men were turned over.[21]

At this point, Little Crow turned to diplomacy. He, along with Wabasha, privately told the superintendent after the council broke up that the Indians responsible for the raids ought to be handed over, but it would take time to effect their surrender. The men involved slowly showed signs of giving themselves up, and the cooperation of Little Crow and Wabasha relieved Huebschmann, who seemed to realize that the two chiefs legitimately wanted to resolve the problem. Huebschmann, believing that the charges of mismanagement and corruption were all too true, sympathized with the Mdewakantons, but he felt that discipline had to be restored at the agency.[22]

The corruption that Little Crow mentioned was of the sort found on most reservations in the nineteenth century. Agent Murphy, more honest than most, nevertheless spent much of his time stocking a cattle farm in Illinois and moving the animals to the reservation just prior to the distribution of cash annuities. Murphy then kept the Indians waiting for days, even months, until they had purchased all his cattle, for cash or on credit, at fifteen cents a pound. Traders naturally cooperated with the agent, since they, too, sold the Sioux food. The agent deducted money for these supplies directly from annuities.[23] In addition, observers often characterized the food distributed by Murphy as inedible. At one point, an army officer reported that some flour given to the Indians had been rejected by the military post commissary agent. When the barrel staves were removed, "the mass stood alone and was as hard as a similar lump of mortar." Some of the pork distributed was "so offensive" that one Indian "tired of carrying it and threw it away."[24]

Regardless of mismanagement charges, Huebschmann remained convinced that the Sioux men responsible for the killings had to surrender. Fourteen young Sioux warriors finally did so on June 28; others followed, raising the number of prisoners to nineteen by August. They were confined for two months and then released. The killing of nine Sioux Indians by the Ojibway near Lake Traverse in August made it more difficult for the government to justify holding the men, since it was impossible for the army to punish the Ojibway. Moreover, Huebschmann could not find money with which to finance a trial, and both territorial officials and the army refused to assume authority for judging Sioux warriors.[25]

Convincing the young men to hand themselves over to the army was clearly a difficult job. The act demonstrated the persuasive powers of both Little Crow and Wabasha, who when working together wielded a considerable amount of influence. Yet the incident also showed the growing belligerence of the young men of the tribe. Through the employment of a soldiers' lodge, that quasi-military society organized primarily for the hunt, young men could and did defy recognized chiefs and their councils. Several events, especially during the 1851 treaty negotiation where Mdewakanton soldiers threatened various leaders, had illustrated how militant young Sioux men could be. The combative mood understandably increased during periods of social instability. The migration to the Minnesota River reservation and the influx of whites into the land immediately west of the Mississippi River provoked considerable concern. White settlement of old Sioux hunting grounds, while seen as inevitable by some leaders, was finally becoming a reality to many Dakota men for the first time in the mid-1850s.

Settlers had pushed well up the Minnesota River valley by summer 1855. That fall, large numbers of German immigrants built farms and towns just northwest of where the Big Cottonwood River joins the Minnesota River. They called their settlement New Ulm. This development must have been perplexing to Little Crow, since he had pushed so strongly for establishing the lower boundary of the reservation at the mouth of the Big Cottonwood, and he had received assurances in 1851–52 and again in 1854 that his people would be given the land above that river. Some Sioux men pulled up surveyor stakes near New Ulm and killed several oxen.[26] While not always the case, the men involved were usually young hunters, still economically tied to the chase and unwilling to accept the changes that went on so rapidly about them. As the new Indian agent, Charles Flandrau, said not long after replacing Murphy: "The advance of the whites over the frontiers has been so rapid in Minnesota that the hunting grounds of the Indians has been taken from them before they have had time to become fully domesticated."[27] Leaders such as Little Crow did much to hold these young men in check, even though many chiefs doubtless agreed with their actions and disliked the aggressive Germans.

The frustration of the young warriors, as well as the fact that many eastern Sioux Indians—especially Sissetons, Wahpetons, and Wahpekutes—still remained off the reservation, produced a volatile atmosphere. On several occasions the army warned of a possible "outbreak."[28] Such fears were finally realized in March 1857 when news filtered back to the snowbound Redwood Agency that a group of Wahpekutes had killed more than forty whites near an isolated settlement in northwestern Iowa. The "Spirit Lake massacre," as whites later called it, came after considerable provocation by white settlers and Indians alike and was part of a long-standing, interethnic feud. Three years before, a white man named Henry Lott and his son slaughtered nearly a dozen Wahpekutes—mostly women and children—in an isolated hunting lodge in retaliation for earlier Indian depredations. The army made only a half-hearted effort to bring the Lotts to justice. In addition, some evidence suggests that whites had taken most of the arms possessed by the Wahpekutes just before the outbreak in 1857. Although they found others, the confiscation of arms made it difficult to hunt during the winter. At least one of the causes for the massacre was the shortage of food in the camp of the Indians responsible for the deed.[29]

The Wahpekute Indians involved in the killing, on the other hand, were almost outcasts in their own right. They belonged to a band which had been led by Wamdisapa in the 1840s. Wamdisapa's people had killed the recognized chief of the tribe, Tasagye (probably Little Crow's first father-in-law), and had fled west into the Missouri River valley. Under Inkpaduta's leadership in the 1850s, they returned to Minnesota in order to benefit from the annuity distribution, showing up at Redwood in 1854 and again in 1856. The majority of the reservation Wahpekutes, however, demanded that the Wahpekutes under Inkpaduta be prevented from receiving anything at the annuity payroll table, and the government agency officials involved refused to grant formal recognition to the Inkpaduta band.[30]

While the army pondered a move against the small band of Wahpekute outcasts, who numbered about a dozen men, the news of the killings produced a panic in Minnesota. Hastily organized militia units attacked several Indian bands camped southeast of the reservation. Luckily, no one was killed. Moreover, the event seemed to polarize the Dakota Indians on the reservations, especially at Yellow Medicine, where the Wahpetons and Sissetons showed strong sympathy for Inkpaduta, whose son had taken a Sisseton wife.[31] By May, Colonel E. B. Alexander at Fort Ridgely reported that, if he pursued the Indians responsible, it would be necessary to employ fifty friendly Indians and mixed-bloods to assist him. "Without some aid of this sort," Alexander concluded, "I think the guilty band can successfully elude pursuit, having at their back an immense region for flight."[32] Alexander was acutely aware that trouble could erupt at any time at either of the reservations, and he did not have sufficient troops to police the reservations and to field an expedition.

Alexander's plea for assistance went into the mail at a time when changes were occurring in the administration of Indian affairs at both the national and reservation levels. Consequently, when the new Indian commissioner, James W. Denver, heard of the request, he issued an order that made the distribution of annuities, scheduled for July 1, contingent upon the eastern Sioux tribes effecting the surrender or destruction of Inkpaduta and his band.[33] Before the new and inexperienced Indian superintendent, William J. Cullen, could even approach the Indians on the subject of Inkpaduta, however, trouble broke out at Yellow Medicine. Lieutenant Alexander Murray, stationed at Yellow Medicine, had learned that not more than a dozen miles from his camp Inkpaduta's son was visiting his wife. On July 1, Murray marched to the scene, a cluster of six lodges, and killed the Wahpekute Indian as he attempted to escape and arrested the man's young Sisseton wife. But as he returned to the agency, Sisseton and Wahpeton warriors surrounded his small detachment and plucked the woman from the wagon in which she was riding. Murray never attempted to recapture her, but the incident left many Indians in a hostile mood as Cullen arrived to negotiate with them.[34]

Understandably, the Indians near Yellow Medicine became even more perturbed when the superintendent demanded on July 6 that they catch and punish Inkpaduta before they could receive their annuities. The ultimatum seemed all the more unreasonable since army officers at Fort Ridgely now said that they did not have sufficient troops to accompany any expedition against the Wahpekute murderers. This decision prompted Indian department officials to conclude that the Dakotas ought to assume full responsibility for punishing their own outlaws.[35] Finally, on July 15 as the discussions over who should punish Inkpaduta became hopelessly deadlocked, a young Sisseton stabbed a soldier belonging to Major Thomas W. Sherman's artillery command, and the councils quickly broke up. "We are on the eve of a general war with all these Indians," Sherman concluded in an urgent request for reinforcements written the next day. Many Sisseton and Wahpeton young men, backed by about a thousand Yankton and Yanktonai warriors—the latter tribes had recently clashed with General William S. Harney in the west—were on the verge of assaulting the American position.[36]

At this crucial stage, Little Crow arrived at Yellow Medicine from the Lower Agency to see what he could do. Upon stopping at the agency headquarters, Little Crow was urged by Cullen to go directly to the hostile camp and meet with the leaders. Councils went on day and night, July 16–17, with Little Crow arguing for a more prudent course. Meanwhile, as the Indians debated, Sherman gave orders to attack the hostile Indian camp as soon as further reinforcements, due early in the morning of July 17, reached him from Fort Ridgely. But just after midnight, the Sissetons and Wahpetons, accepting Little Crow's counsel, convinced the Yanktons and Yanktonais to leave their camp and sent a messenger to Sherman indicating that they wished to meet in council.[37] That afternoon, the Sisseton Indian who had stabbed the American soldier surrendered, and by July 20, after three long days of haggling, the Dakotas agreed to send over a hundred men in pursuit of Inkpaduta. The Mdewakantons present, "acting under the advice of Little Crow," as Cullen put it, were the first to agree to this expedition. Little Crow also played a major role in convincing the upper Dakota bands—Sissetons and Wahpetons—to join. Cullen was so pleased with Taoyateduta's assistance that the superintendent implored him to lead the expedition, agreeing to provide ample supplies and horses. The chief accepted and recruited the necessary men. "I cannot speak too highly of the services of the chief 'Little Crow'," the newly tested Indian superintendent noted, "with him I labored night and day in organizing the party [to go against Inkpaduta] riding continuously between the upper and lower agencies, for we scarcely slept until I had the party started after the murderers."[38]

Little Crow's success at resolving the Yellow Medicine crisis showed a significant increase in his political influence. It was the first time that all the major bands at Yellow Medicine had accepted his advice. To what extent Taoyateduta made use of the old friendships and kinship ties that he had developed among these people in the 1830s and 1840s the documents fail to reveal. Such ties were essential in gaining access to councils where leaders listened to his advice about resolving a crisis of this sort. Having such a man as Inyangmani, a major Sisseton chief and leader of the most important band at the agency, as a father-in-law obviously helped. In addition, the Wahpeton chief Wakanmani, his son Grey Foot, and a host of other men, some of whom were Renville descendants and mission Indians, also had kinship ties with Little Crow.[39]

Little Crow's success did not disguise the fact that a group of young warriors at Yellow Medicine still manifested, as one official put it, a "feeling of favoritism" toward Inkpaduta. They sympathized with the difficulties experienced by his people in northern Iowa and realized that Inkpaduta's band had been faced with the same loss of hunting grounds and resources that the reservation Sioux were then experiencing. More importantly, many Sissetons and Wahpetons wished to avenge the death of Inkpaduta's son.[40] Fortunately, a consensus for war failed to develop, and Little Crow defused the tense situation, no doubt promising to intercede with Cullen and get the annuities released. The superintendent quickly delivered some annuities to the Indians after Little Crow's men departed.[41]

Little Crow carefully organized the expedition that went after Inkpaduta's Wahpekutes on July 22. Sherman, who watched the party leave Yellow Medicine, reported the chief to be "sincere," displaying a "fixed determination to bring in the murderers." While Cullen directed that two men be selected from each eastern band to serve with Little Crow, thus distributing the responsibility, Taoyateduta managed to bring along many of his relatives from both agencies. A few members were mixed-bloods, including Little Crow's "cousin" Antoine J. Campbell, and a goodly number were mission Indians. Other men of prominence were Inyangmani, Inyangmani's son, Peter Tapetatanka, and Little Crow's cousin, the Sisseton Cloud Man.[42] Everyone involved expected the trip to be long and arduous, since the Wahpekutes under Inkpaduta had the vast western prairie upon which to hide. Nevertheless, each man had personally pledged to put an end to Inkpaduta before returning home.[43]

Little Crow's force continued west for ten days, searching sloughs and small lakes in their effort to find the Spirit Lake murderers. The commanding officer at Fort Ridgely sent out supply wagons to extend the life of the mission further, but still the party failed to make contact with the hostiles. Finally, in late July, Little Crow and his party stumbled onto seven men and some women and children, all of Inkpaduta's band, encamped on the shores of Lake Herman on the Dakota plains. A mission Indian charged into the group, followed by the remainder of the party. When the skirmish had ended, three Wahpekute men had been killed, and another was mortally wounded. While Little Crow's men tried to spare the noncombatants, women and children rushed into the lake where some drowned. Inkpaduta himself, however, was not among the dead or the captives. The party returned to Redwood with their prisoners.[44]

Little Crow and his men expected that this action would satisfy Cullen and that the remainder of the annuities would be handed out. Colonel John Abercrombie and Captain Alfred Sully, the new commanders of troops at Fort Ridgely, both agreed, noting that since Inkpaduta had fled farther west, any additional expeditions were useless. They suggested that troops from Fort Randall be employed to hunt down the few remaining hostiles.[45] But commissioner Denver, and accordingly Cullen, refused to budge and demanded that the annuity Indians mount another search for Inkpaduta. This garnered an angry response from many of the men who had been with Little Crow. "You told us to go after Inkpaduta, and promised that if we did anything and came back . . . we should get our money," the Sisseton subchief Cloud Man protested in defiance.[46]

Sympathizing with men like Cloud Man, agency officials pleaded with commissioner Denver to lift the ban on annuities. Little Crow, they argued, had fulfilled his part of the bargain, and there was little else that the Dakota men could do, but Denver refused to authorize a distribution. Finally, after the commissioner left Washington and it became obvious that nothing further would be done, the acting commissioner, Charles Mix, granted Cullen permission to hand out annuities in late August. This action calmed the Indians and brought some peace to the reservations.[47]

Inkpaduta remained at large and rumors continued to float about the reservation regarding his whereabouts. In early September, the army finally mounted an expedition of its own to look for the wily Wahpekute leader. For scouts, they turned once again to Little Crow, who agreed to recruit the necessary men. He campaigned willingly for the army, even after the Indian department had been uncooperative regarding the annuity issue. Buttressed by this corps of "friendly Indians," the army expedition explored much of southwestern Minnesota, stopping at Lake Benton and the Pipestone quarry.[48] While he saw no hostile Indians, the commanding officer at Fort Ridgely reported that the troop movement had been a huge success. The expedition "will satisfy the upper Indians that we can penetrate any part of their country, wherever circumstances may render it necessary."[49] This was the last expedition sent in search of Inkpaduta.

The Inkpaduta affair, like so many other events in the 1850s, gave Little Crow a chance to demonstrate his political skills and prove his value as a leader. He, more than other chiefs, seemed to understand that influence and prestige could be secured more easily by working with whites than by resisting them, and he craved the renown and attention that accompanied involvement in events such as the Inkpaduta crisis. It no doubt was a manifestation of a personal wish to be admired and wanted, a need that was exemplified by his own ascension to the chieftainship. Yet his actions also showed an overriding desire to be at the center of pivotal events and debates. Little Crow was simply invigorated by crisis, unlike his rival Wabasha who failed to get involved. Above all, Taoyateduta's efforts clearly left government officials convinced that he was now the most important chief on the upper Minnesota River. He had become the spokesman for the eastern Sioux.

Even so, while Little Crow would use a crisis to further his own political goals, he did little to foster economic advancement at Redwood. The majority of Mdewakanton men still avoided the farm program, and Taoyateduta stood with these traditionalists. There is a certain irony in his stand. Traditionalists were steadily becoming the largest threat to his leadership, since they exhibited belligerence toward a policy of accommodation. Such a situation often forced the chief to straddle the fence between increasingly divergent positions—one pushed by reservation administrators and the other the choice of young warriors. One wonders if Little Crow understood in 1857 what a personal dilemma deciding between the two would become for him.

6

The Broken Promise

THE Inkpaduta massacre prompted a re-evaluation of interethnic relations on the Minnesota Sioux reservations. Leaders such as Little Crow perceived for the first time the division that was taking place in Dakota camps. Many warriors, most of whom were young, sympathized with Inkpaduta and condemned white encroachment upon old Indian hunting grounds. Other Dakota people, including those interested in accommodation and especially those interested in farming, saw nothing to gain in rebellion and much to lose. The problems with Inkpaduta also forced government officials to re-examine policies and look for solutions to the obvious discontent that existed on the reservations. While many Sissetons resisted the government during the summer of 1857 because of their kinship ties with Inkpaduta's people, the troubles at Yellow Medicine also offered a vehicle for displaying pent-up anger. The government needed at the very least to solve the many problems that plagued the administration of the reservations if future disturbances were to be avoided.

This re-evaluation fostered several changes. By fall 1857, reservation officials embarked upon a new course, designed to force immediate acculturation and thus save the eastern Sioux from slow starvation. The plan involved the negotiation of a new treaty, ostensibly necessary in order to allot land on the reservations to individual Indian farmers. Indians looked upon these changes with mixed reactions, most stubbornly refusing to accept the new role of husbandmen demanded of them by the government. Others decided to try the white man's ways, to learn plowing, to cut their hair, and to don pantaloons. The changes slowly but effectively undermined the sense of unity and community that had bonded the Dakotas together as a people for centuries and led to a social and political polarization that made consensus and effective leadership difficult, if not impossible. Little Crow, a talented politician, soon found that the accommodationist tactics of old simply did not work in a new era.

Nothing indicates that Little Crow was aware of the reforms contemplated by the government in 1857, even though a special agent, Kintzing Pritchette, was present at Redwood Agency collecting information throughout the summer. Pritchette's report to Washington that fall analyzed the Inkpaduta affair, assessed conditions on the reservations, and ended on a pessimistic note. The hope of making the Sioux into a "permanent agricultural people," he concluded, "is a vain dream of impracticable philanthrophy." Any agricultural advances they would make, he noted, were an added enticement to "the desire [of whites] for grasping their lands, increased in proportion, as they may have made them valuable by improvement and culture." Equally vain, Pritchette believed, was the attempt of Christian missionaries to convert the Sioux. The situation seemed hopeless, and Pritchette cringed at the contemplation of the Dakotas' "inevitable destruction."[1]

Most of what Pritchette concluded about agricultural progress was certainly true. Missionaries had worked for nearly a quarter of a century with the Dakotas and experienced little success. The more accomplished of their pupils, men such as Little Crow, had learned to read and write and even to speak some English, but more often than not refused to reject their culture or their religion.[2] Earlier agent Taliaferro had introduced the eastern Sioux to intensive agriculture, but they showed little interest in it. Murphy's program of "concentration" had been, for the most part, an utter failure. After three years, most Dakota men continued to leave the reservation in the winter to hunt and send their women into the fields in spring to plant small amounts of corn.

Most agency and territorial officials remained more optimistic than Pritchette and wanted especially to avoid another "Spirit Lake" outbreak. Throughout much of 1856 a debate had occurred in local newspapers on the issue of reservation management. "Give the Sioux of Minnesota land in severalty—let each family possess a farm independent of the rest of his band," was the editorial cry of the *Henderson Democrat,* operated by a former trader, Joseph R. Brown.[3] Missionaries agreed and previously had supported a similar reform. Common fields remained unproductive; Indian lands needed to be fenced so that each nuclear family could take the responsibility of feeding itself. As Brown wrote two months later, the annuity had declined to about "ten dollars to each individual" while the goods and provisions did not "exceed two dollars and thirty cents to each person."[4] The Indians could not live on such sparse fare.

While few radical changes occurred prior to the Inkpaduta massacre, pressure brought upon agent Murphy resulted in minor advancements. At Hazelwood, for example, Riggs helped his Indian farmers form a "republic" that Murphy promptly recognized in August 1856 as a separate "civilized" band. The agent assisted the members with plowing and paid them for farm improvements. The bylaws of the republic, drafted by nearly two dozen mixed- and full-blood members, called upon all participants to discard their medicine sacks that were symbols of traditional religion, reject the "foolish feasts" that were seen as wasteful of resources and time consuming, and adopt white dress. The list of members contained many of Taoyateduta's Mdewakanton relatives, including Lorenzo Lawrence, the man who had defended him against his brothers in 1846, Lorenzo's brother Joseph Kawanke, and several Renvilles. Riggs tried unsuccessfully to have territorial officials bestow citizenship upon his native farmers.[5]

The productivity of the Hazelwood farmers was soon challenged by the followers of Inyangmani, who settled near Williamson's mission, called Pazutazee, or more correctly Peźutazi. Williamson reported that under Inyangmani seventeen families—predominately Wahpetons and Sissetons—had all built either log or frame houses, a few complete with wood stoves and windows. Few had converted to Christianity, but the majority took pride in their fields and seemed at times to be competing agriculturally with the Indians at Hazelwood. The government added prestige to the Peźutazi community by declaring Inyangmani to be chief of the "improvement Sioux," as they were called at Yellow Medicine.[6]

The farming movement made slight inroads at Redwood, too, especially at Little Crow's village. Among the men showing a strong interest in farming was Joseph Napeśniduta, Taoyateduta's in-law, Medicine Bottle, his first soldier and the man who had directed him to sign the 1851 Mendota treaty, and White Dog, yet another Little Crow band member, who soon became the most accomplished farmer at the agency. By fall 1857, the number of husbandmen at Redwood had reached twenty, still a very small minority but a figure that was increasing. More importantly, the few Indian farmers on both reserves plowed their own lands and produced enough food to get themselves and their families through the winter.[7]

Nevertheless, native farmers remained outside the mainstream of Dakota society, and when Indian superintendent William J. Cullen and agent Charles Flandrau took over administration of the agency in summer 1857, they immediately decided upon drastic changes. The vast majority of Mdewakanton Sioux had congregated in six villages, re-creating a band organization similar in structure to what had existed on the Mississippi River. Shakopee's people lived just north of the Redwood River, with

Little Crow's, Big Eagle's, and Mankato's villages located south of the Redwood and just a few miles north of the agency. Below the agency, Wabasha and Wakute settled their people, with a few miles separating the villages. The small Wahpekute village was at the extreme southern point of the reservation.[8] Flandrau, a lawyer by profession, wished to break up this communal life style by assigning private fields to nuclear families. He then intended to give priority, in terms of equipment and assistance, to Indians who would farm. Cullen agreed to ask the commissioner of Indian affairs for permission to develop such a program, a change that would alter, or even end, the general distribution of annuities at the tribal level.[9]

For a program of individualized farming to work, however, most officials felt that the Indians must be granted titles to farms, which necessitated congressional legislation. Unanswered questions also existed regarding the validity of the Sioux title to their reservation lands; could the president simply grant a full title or would it be necessary to negotiate yet another treaty? Since the president had not acted on legislation authorizing him to give Minnesota River lands to the eastern Sioux for reservations in 1854, the only right the Dakota people had to the land was through presidential discretion. As Pritchette pointed out in his fall 1857 report, the issue of reservation development had not been resolved in 1854; it seemed just as foolish for the government to encourage individual Indians to build farms and then have them preempted by white settlers as it was for federal authorities to spend large sums generally on the reservations.[10]

The issue of allotment naturally attracted the attention of traders, because a possible treaty negotiation presented opportunities to acquire payment for Indian debts. For the most part, the traders who now worked the reservations had been among the Sioux only a few years and hardly could justify claims of huge indebtedness. The primary traders included Nathan and Andrew Myrick, Louis Robert, William H. Forbes, and Stuart B. Garvie. These men operated the trade almost wholly on credit, giving the Indians goods and food throughout the year and carrying the debts on their books until the annuity distribution. While a few Sioux still hunted muskrats and other animals and paid their bills with furs, the traders generally expected to get almost all of the eighty thousand dollars distributed annually at each reservation, and it was this payment that kept them in business. To make sure that individual Indians honored their obligations, traders used mixed-bloods and full-bloods in their stores as clerks, many customers trading with a particular store because relatives worked in it. Some traders also hired mixed-bloods to go onto the plains and follow Indian hunting camps to ensure that hunters did not sell their furs to other traders.[11]

Prices for goods remained extraordinarily high on the reservations in the 1850s. Thus many Indians owed debts even after turning over their annuity money—which fluctuated between ten and twenty dollars per person—and their furs to traders. The debts that remained on the books made traders constantly alert for opportunities to force Indian payment. Such a chance came during the winter of 1856–57 when traders convinced a small group of Mdewakantons to sign papers that showed a tribal indebtedness of $54,500. Chiefs Wabasha and Wakute initialed the agreement, no doubt being unaware of the significance of the document. Some evidence suggests that they thought the petition would allow them to come to Washington and renegotiate their 1851 treaty. They wanted to change the location of the reservation from the Minnesota to the Blue Earth River valley.[12]

Agent Murphy immediately opposed the petition and queried other Indian leaders about the issue of debt. Little Crow, as well as several other important chiefs including Shakopee, seemed convinced that Wabasha and Wakute had been victimized by the traders. They agreed that some Indians owed debts, but, as they both said, they were "individual debts, and individuals must pay them." With Murphy's assistance, they composed a petition of their own in which they completely disavowed the acts of Wabasha and Wakute. The manipulation of Wabasha and the open opposition to the traders' scheme voiced by many Mdewakanton leaders damaged Wabasha's influence in tribal affairs and clearly increased the prospects of Little Crow. The proposed trip to Washington never developed, at least that winter.[13]

The campaign by whites to produce a new treaty emerged again shortly, as land speculators coveted the rich, tree-covered Minnesota River bottom where the Indians had been temporarily settled. Two such speculators followed Murphy as agent, Flandrau holding the job for several months during the summer and autumn of 1857 before turning it over to the entrepreneur and sometime-newspaper editor, Joseph R. Brown, in late fall. Flandrau worked closely with former superintendent Gorman on several land investments, while Brown, who had a large mixed-blood family, expected one day to benefit appreciably from the right to file "half-breed" scrip claims along Minnesota's frontier. Flandrau obviously had a land sale in mind when he reported to superiors upon leaving office that large numbers of Indians were willing to divide their tribal holdings and adopt a land severalty program. Flandrau suggested that the old men of the various tribes should be brought to Washington, where they might be "relieved from the influence of their young men," and convinced to sign a treaty.[14] Obviously, Flandrau, who knew the situation well, realized that there would be reservation land left over in the Minnesota valley after such an allotment.

By fall 1857 both reservations were rife with rumors, some Indians anticipating being invited to Washington. To an extent, the rumors evolved from the Inkpaduta affair, which prompted many whites to call upon the government to remove the Sioux from the state. Little Crow feared the consequences of such talk and privately discussed the matter with other chiefs. At one point, the concern he voiced caused trouble at Yellow Medicine.[15] Fears of forced removal abated, however, when superintendent Cullen concluded a very successful annuity distribution in November. The Indian office in Washington had discovered that an additional forty-two thousand dollars was due the Indians under the 1837 treaty, and that sum along with the regular annuities quelled discontent. Cullen and Brown were even able to recruit an Indian police force at Redwood commanded by Red Owl, an important member of the Mdewakanton soldiers' lodge, to patrol the agency grounds and maintain order during the distribution. Most leaders, then, were agreeable when Cullen told them that their Great Father wished to see them and "readjust the treaty." Dakota chiefs assumed logically that their just complaints were finally going to be resolved. The extra annuity money promoted such generous feeling toward the government that the chiefs agreed to pay their own travel expenses to Washington.[16]

The trip to the capital began after Christmas. The twenty-four-man delegation and several mixed-blood assistants sat down with Charles Mix, who was serving as acting commissioner, on March 15, 1858. The Mdewakanton leaders in attendance included the major chiefs—Little Crow, Wabasha, Shakopee, Wakute, Mankato, Traveling Hail, and Black Dog—as well as less important men such as Big Eagle, Whale, Tomahawk, and Iron Elk. Three Dakota men representing the soldiers' lodge, Medicine Bottle, The Thief, and Red Owl, rounded out the delegation. The Wahpekutes sent Red Legs, the son of Tasagye. Finally, the Sissetons and Wahpetons, who would negotiate on their own, had nine men present, several of whom were mission Indians. Due to the troubles the year before, this delegation was not representative of the majority of the Sissetons and Wahpetons, most of whom had tangled with the army in 1857 and were hunting buffalo west of Lake Traverse when the call came to assemble at the agencies.[17]

While government officials expected to negotiate equally with the two different delegations, it soon became obvious that the Mdewakantons had much more business to discuss than their western neighbors. Thus Little Crow, who came dressed in a strikingly attractive "calico hunting shirt," became the central figure in half-a-dozen councils, acting as tribal spokesman for the Mdewakantons. He seemed to want accommodation at the outset, showing appreciation for the opportunity to come to Washington and discuss the problems of his people. "Your good advice has reached our ears," he began, "we listened and heard what you said, and according to promise, you have made the road good." He spoke kindly of Cullen, who clearly had demonstrated more energy and competence in his short tenure as superintendent than his three predecessors combined. Cullen reciprocated by complimenting Little Crow excessively, even saying that the chief had saved his life during the Inkpaduta troubles. In addition, Little Crow indicated that he wanted to observe white society while in Washington to see how his own might evolve, "to walk your streets" and look carefully at the city. Obviously, Taoyeduta knew that Cullen wanted to encourage allotment, and the chief needed to be sure that such a change would be beneficial. The Mdewakanton delegation, faced with an important decision, wished to take its time. Accordingly, the Indian office allowed days and even weeks to transpire between councils.

Substantive debate commenced on March 27. Little Crow, "splendidly dressed," complete with a circle of blue paint around one eye, first told Mix that much of the money due the Mdewakantons and Wahpekutes from the 1837 and 1851 treaties had not reached the Indians. "It takes plenty to enable a person to act like a man [to feed and clothe his wives and children] and not like a poor beggar," Little Crow pointed out. Government officials had promised during both previous treaty negotiations to take care of the Mdewakantons, and Little Crow intended to hold them to it. Mix seemed sympathetic, assuring the chief that the Great Father would send funds very soon. Mix displayed a reluctance to explain to the delegation that they held their lands only at the discretion of the president, thus making it economically unwise to expend all the funds due and possibly lose the improvements resulting from them. Probably sensing an impasse, Little Crow asked for pocket money for the delegation. Mix agreed, although he admonished the Indians not to spend it on liquor. This brought the first sour note in the discussions, as Little Crow sternly reminded Mix that he had mentioned liquor on two other occasions, and he need not bring it up again.

In mid-April, the delegates and the acting commissioner sat down once

Part of the Mdewakanton-Wahpekute delegation in Washington in 1858; standing, Big Eagle, Traveling Hail, and Red Legs; sitting, Medicine Bottle, The Thief, and unidentified

Mdewakantons and Wahpekutes in 1858; standing, Joseph R. Brown, Antoine J. Campbell, Tomahawk (?), Andrew Robertson, Red Owl, Thomas A. Robertson, and Nathaniel R. Brown; sitting, Mankato, Wabasha, and Henry Belland (?)

The Sisseton-Wahpeton delegation in Washington in 1858; standing, Joseph Akipa Renville, Scarlet Plume, Red Iron, John Otherday, Paul Mazakutemani, and Charles R. Crawford (interpreter); sitting, Iron Walker, Stumpy Horn, Sweet Corn, and Extended Tail Feathers

Little Crow in Washington, D.C., 1858

This photograph is probably the one taken in St. Paul in the summer of 1861 and given to Dr. John Benjamin. Little Crow wore a suit donned at the request of Alexander Ramsey. After the war, the photograph went through several generations of copies and was widely sold.

again, and Little Crow immediately spoke of the failures of the government to live up to promises and treaties, specifically mentioning the failure of the government to feed the Mdewakantons during the Inkpaduta affair. "In compliance with your wishes," Little Crow averred, "we went in pursuit of Inkpaduta and neglected our cornfields." The government had also neglected to do sufficient plowing, Little Crow pointed out, and his people accordingly suffered during the winter. The Mdewakanton chief then spoke of specific funds that were due under various articles of the 1837 and 1851 treaties and wondered what had happened to the money. Little Crow even provided the acting commissioner with a list, demonstrating a clear understanding of the complex treaty articles.

Mix responded to the charges by explaining that Mdewakanton funds were "safely kept in the strong box of the treasury," and would be sent when they could be applied properly "to their [the Indians'] benefits." Mix then proposed putting this issue behind them and expressed an interest in negotiating a treaty. Little Crow refused, belaboring the fact that the government had promised to deliver specific amounts of money and goods and had failed to fulfill its obligations. The chief next brought up the matter of the $20,035 that had been promised him in 1854 and which he claimed was never distributed. "You started the money out from your house," Little Crow wryly commented, "for I heard of that with my own ears, but, as I said before, it never reached us." "If I were to give you an account of all the money that was spilled," Taoyateduta noted, "it would take all night." Mix tried to defuse the argument by indicating to Little Crow that his friend Cullen had also mentioned the money and that he had promised to send some of it to the reservation. Additional promises failed to derail Little Crow, who had a long list of complaints and intended to explore each and every one of them in detail.

The chief turned next to land issues and relations with whites both on and off the reservation. He complained especially of the German settlers, who crowded onto the lands near the mouth of the Big Cottonwood River and, in fact, had moved well above its mouth. Little Crow clearly remembered that during his 1854 trip, "you gave me that line . . . the great spirit took pity on me, and made you give it to me." But, he continued, "your Dutchmen [Germans] have settled inside of it."[18] Little Crow could not understand why the government had not removed them. Whites on the reservation also fell under his censure. He was particularly displeased with John Magner, who used his position in charge of the warehouse to exploit Dakota women.

At this point, Mix began pressing the boundary issue, knowing full well that Little Crow had nothing on paper to prove that the government had promised him a reservation boundary line as far south as the Big Cottonwood River. He badgered Little Crow, asking him to point out precisely on Joseph Nicollet's 1838 map what he thought to be the southernmost boundary line of that reserve. Little Crow, taking a pen, approached the strange document cautiously, but he had no difficulty in locating the claimed line. He turned to Mix and said that he wanted the land, "where the treaty put it [the boundary]."

This maneuver provided the exact opening that Mix had waited for so patiently, and he asked Little Crow the crucial question: "Do you recollect the provisions of the 1851 treaty?" While Little Crow answered in the affirmative and his reply was being interpreted, Mix brought forward a copy of the original treaty that he had Campbell read in Dakota. It described a boundary, which the Senate had struck out, that began at Little Rock River, well above the mouth of the Big Cottonwood. Mix, then, intended to ignore Little Crow's claim that Rice in 1852 and Office of Indian Affairs officials in 1854 had promised a boundary farther south. To this document, Little Crow had no answer, other than to say sadly, "I do not know how to read or write [in English], and supposing the men sent by our Great Father to treat with us were honest, I signed the treaty." Apparently at the end of the day's debate, an employee of the Office of Indian Affairs wrote on the front page of the journal, "Little Crow is bluffed." Indeed, this was a day when all Little Crow's skills as an orator and a politician failed to be of any benefit.

With the chief relatively subdued, Mix then turned in earnest to a discussion of the issue of land. "I do not wish to frighten or unnecessarily alarm him," Mix began through an interpreter, "but he [Little Crow] and his people are now living on the land they occupy by the courtesy of their Great Father." Even so, Mix continued, the Great Father had taken care of the eastern Sioux in legislation passed by Congress authorizing the president to grant them a reservation. Sensing victory, the acting commissioner became charitable, saying, "It is but justice to say the Sioux are primarily indebted to Little Crow" for this guarantee, a reference to Little Crow's 1854 visit. Mix indicated that he wanted to make Sioux title to the reservations permanent, and he wished to divide what lands the Indians occupied into individual farms. The treaty he asked them to consider, however, called upon the eastern Sioux to give up half of their claimed reserve—the land lying northeast of the Minnesota River.

When the Indians returned to the council chamber on May 28, Little Crow was in a foul mood. He seemed to sense by then that the Great

Father had little intention of righting past wrongs. As Mix discussed the terms of the treaty proposal he had previously given them, pointing to the advantages of having eighty-acre farms, Little Crow grew angry and finally, when given the chance to respond, erupted: "You talk well and use fine language and that's all." "This is the way you all do . . . but we never receive half what is promised, or which we ought to get." Halfway through his speech, Little Crow became impassioned and animated. "I recollect you very distinctly," Little Crow noted, referring to his 1854 visit, "you then promised us that we should have this same land forever; and yet now . . . [you] want to take half of it away. We ought when we meet . . . [to] talk like men and not like children." As his anger slowly evaporated, the exasperated chief seemed to sense that he could do nothing about the predicament. "It appears you are getting papers all around me, so that, after a while I will have nothing left," he said in obvious disillusionment. The delegates finally decided to look at the proposal more carefully, Mix warning them that if they refused to sign the treaty, they might have all their lands taken by authorities of the newly formed state of Minnesota.

On June 4, the delegation returned, now keenly aware that rather than having grievances redressed, the Great Father wanted them once again to sacrifice their claim to land. Little Crow was clearly depressed, yet philosophical, and after a long silence in which the Indian delegates smoked profusely, the chief finally rose to speak. "You [Mix] gave us a paper . . . and we had it explained, and from that it would seem that the Sioux Indians own nothing!" No longer astonished at this, Little Crow continued, "When I saw that paper it made me ashamed. We had, we supposed, made a complete treaty, and we were promised a great many things, horses, cattle, flour, plows, and farming utensils, but it now appears that the wind blows it all off." Nevertheless the chief realized that the proposed, new treaty would produce some benefits, such as money with which to pay trade debts. Finally, Little Crow asked that a sum, approaching fifty thousand dollars, be set aside to pay traders. "I want to do what is right," Little Crow noted, indicating that since game had appreciably declined, the Sioux needed their traders more than ever before. Nathan Myrick, Antoine J. Campbell, agent Joseph Brown, William H. Forbes, Louis Robert, and Madison Sweetzer were named individually, after which Little Crow assigned specific figures to each name. Mix tried to humor the chief by complimenting him on his financial ability, but Little Crow remained sullen, refusing through most of this debate to get up from his chair.

Taoyateduta wanted something for his people, too, and a final sum of twenty-five thousand dollars was set aside for them. Unbelievable as it may seem, Mix then left the total compensation for the lands purchased up to Congress, since there was some question whether the government would pay the Sioux anything. A sale price for proposed reservation land at ten cents an acre had been included in the 1851 accord after the Senate struck the article allowing for reservations. When the Indians finally signed the treaty on June 19, it gave them permanent title to the ten-mile strip of land on the southwest bank of the Minnesota River and allowed for eighty-acre allotments, or farms, to be assigned. On the other hand, it promised no new annuities, it did not rectify failures of the government to fulfill promises made in 1837 and 1851, and it took from the Sioux their lands north of the Minnesota River that they had always considered their own.

While the Mdewakanton delegation remained unhappy with this state of affairs, they had few alternatives. Mix told them plainly that the federal government would not prevent the newly organized state of Minnesota from taking by force "what your Great Father proposes to buy and pay for." In other words, if they did not sign, the eastern Sioux would forfeit their entire reservation. When Little Crow made one, last, feeble attempt to obtain justice, even threatening not to sign the treaty, Mix berated him in the Indian fashion: "In this matter [the treaty negotiation], he acts like a child." It was a heavy insult about which the chief also could do nothing.

The Sissetons and Wahpetons received similar treatment at the hands of Mix, signing a treaty that relinquished their claims to the northeast side of the Minnesota River and legalized allotment. Yet they remained less disturbed over the result of the negotiation because their delegation consisted mostly of native farmers who supported allotment. Their tribal leaders who might have opposed the treaty were out on the prairie hunting buffalo.

To mitigate the unsatisfactory results for the Indians of the treaty councils, the government did its best to provide ample presents for each delegate. Most chiefs, including Little Crow, received new suits of clothing, and while in New York City, the delegates were given a host of other items, such as swords and flags. For his part in the negotiation, Little Crow was handed two thousand dollars in cash, part of which he supposedly placed in a St. Paul bank upon his return. Mix promised the Mdewakanton chiefs yet another two thousand dollars worth of presents to distribute to tribal members when the delegates returned to Minnesota.[19]

The long period spent in Washington—over three months—gave the delegation time for sightseeing and observing American society. The Dakota leaders spent at least one evening at the theater, "where they were evidently somewhat astonished, although they endeavored to affect nonchalance."[20] They met many dignitaries, starting with the secretary of the interior, who also warned them against using "fire water." In addition, the Sioux delegation happened to be in Washington at the same time as a Turkish military entourage. The Turks, headed by Vice-Admiral Mohammed Pacha, met the Sioux at the Washington arsenal, where both groups watched a demonstration of the newest weaponry. A newspaper editor could not help but contrast the two delegations, the Sioux in their finery, colorful beyond imagination, with attending war clubs, pipes, tomahawks, and painted faces, and the Turks "in their magnificent uniforms, the collars, cuffs, and seams of which are covered with heavy gold embroidery and various decorations." After the ordnance demonstration, Little Crow gave a speech, and the members of the Sioux delegation danced. While Little Crow's harangue was delivered with "expressive gesticulation," much of it a description of his efforts to capture Inkpaduta, the translation was poor, and the reporter lamented the fact that he could not understand the entire story.[21]

Finally, some delegates took in the night life of Washington, despite warnings from Mix and the secretary of the interior. During these outings, which generated a few charges of rowdiness in the Washington papers, a Wahpeton full-blood named John Otherday became so enamored of a saloon waitress that he took her back to Minnesota and later married her. Little Crow, on the other hand, chose more demure company, being invited to a gala dinner attended by the cream of Washington society. According to one account, he performed admirably as "toastmaster."[22]

Yet circulating in Washington's high society did not disguise the bitterness that remained from Little Crow's discussions with Mix. Near the end of the negotiations, Taoyateduta met his old friend Lawrence Taliaferro, who was then in Washington lobbying for a job as army storekeeper. Taliaferro recorded the meeting, a rather sorrowful affair. Little Crow spoke nostalgically of the past, of Taliaferro's good counsel, and of the former agent's dealings with his grandfather and father. Little Crow was not as kind when reminiscing about the agents who had followed Taliaferro; most had sided with the traders rather than protecting the

Indians' rights. Finally Little Crow spoke of the present. "We have lost confidence in the promises of our Great Father," he said matter-of-factly, "bad men have nearly destroyed us." He was referring to Mix, who Little Crow felt had lied to him and now wanted to "divide our lands and [make us] live like white people."[23]

After the delegation returned to Redwood Agency, Little Crow did his best to sell the treaty to his people, fully aware that he had played a central role in negotiating it and that alternatives did not exist. Taoyateduta, as well as the other chiefs in the delegation, tried to emphasize the good points, of which there were very few. They talked of the presents mostly, telling skeptical young men that the Great Father would reward them generously for the lands northeast of the reserve. Unfortunately, when amounts were discussed, the numbers used escalated far beyond the puny sums set aside for the Indians; one rumor set the figure at two hundred thousand dollars, substantially more than any sum discussed in Washington. Because the tribe's expectations were high, the situation became extremely embarrassing for chiefs like Little Crow when sums of that magnitude failed to arrive by fall. The Senate had not yet acted on the treaties, and not even the two thousand dollars worth of presents promised Little Crow had been delivered.[24]

Frustration over the nonpayment of treaty moneys bred trouble. "The chiefs are being accused of having spoken falsely to their young men" regarding the treaty, agent Brown reported in September. Some young warriors considered assassinating the chiefs responsible, especially Little Crow.[25] While Taoyateduta had never feared death in the past, he quickly discarded the broadcloth coat and kid gloves that he had worn on his return to the agency. This "civilized apparel," provoked "scorn and sorrow" among the older members of his band.[26] Nonetheless, serious damage had been done to his standing within the Mdewakanton power structure. As one of the tribe's soldiers later wrote: "The selling of that strip north of the Minnesota caused great dissatisfaction among the Sioux, and Little Crow was always blamed for the part he took in the sale."[27] Although other chiefs had also agreed to the treaty, sometime that fall or the next spring, Little Crow's role as Mdewakanton speaker was successfully challenged. Red Owl, an accomplished speaker from Wabasha's band who often represented the soldiers' lodge, slowly emerged as the man whom the tribe now increasingly turned to in council. By 1859, Little Crow virtually disappears from the sources, failing to show up at an important council held at Fort Ridgely over Christmas.[28]

While the Mdewakantons mulled over the treaty negotiations, massive change finally began on their reservation. The transformation was engineered by Joseph R. Brown, who had assumed control of the reservation in the fall of 1857. Brown was an unusual and energetic man, a land speculator and entrepreneur, but he clearly sympathized with the Sioux and their ways. He had lived with them for thirty-odd years, eventually marrying a mixed-blood Sisseton woman who bore him a large family. While the missionaries were appalled at the selection of Brown, whom they considered to be completely immoral, within weeks of assuming command at Redwood, he began planning an agricultural revolution.[29] The first fruits of his work were apparent by the following spring.

Brown wanted to end the Indians' dependency upon annuities and upon white laborers, who did most of the farming. He removed some whites from the Redwood payroll, thereby freeing money for other uses. Next he convinced Mix to release large sums of money that the Indian office had withheld from the eastern Sioux for years, providing funds for massive development.[30] But the key to Brown's new program was his willingness to pay and reward Indians who would do farm labor, such as building fences and houses and plowing fields. He understood that reward in the form of money or goods was, to the Sioux, a means of reinforcing kinship obligation. He intended to make Dakota men, who received material benefit from the government, see this assistance as an individual gift, rather than something that the government owed them. Brown realized that this would place an obligation on Dakota men to listen to his advice and become farmers.[31]

Brown knew that the Indians lacked some skills and that whites had to be kept on to break the tough prairie sod, care for stock, and operate the sawmills that provided the lumber necessary for the construction of houses and government buildings. In time, these men could be replaced as Indians learned these jobs. Finally, Brown hired teachers who opened the first government schools at both reservations. While the teachers, who worked in the English language, made little progress in comparison to the missionaries, who taught in Dakota, establishing the schools fulfilled one of the major promises of the 1851 treaties.[32]

The material changes brought about by Brown's energetic efforts immediately became evident. Houses literally sprang up all over the lower reservation, forty-five being constructed during the summer of 1858 alone. Although the frame structures were poorly built and most were replaced by more permanent brick houses over the next two years, Sioux Indians cut the logs for milling and did much of the building. Virtually every Indian who wanted a house found one ready for occupation by fall. Brown also had a large crew working along the Minnesota River, staking off five-acre plots for each individual house and breaking the land for seeding. Similar changes, although on a somewhat smaller scale, occurred at Yellow Medicine where the year before there had nearly been a war. By September 1858, Cullen reported that Brown had nearly doubled the acreage under cultivation; the crops of corn and potatoes proved bountiful.[33]

Changes of a cultural nature occurred more slowly, but the progress at Redwood prompted a number of men to agree to break their tribal ties. In the fall, twelve farmers, almost all Mdewakantons, joined the "pantaloon band" that had been established two years before, discarding their Indian dress, cutting their hair, and pledging never to use liquor. "They are the foundation stones," Brown proclaimed in September. The agent remained convinced that many others would soon join them when the annuities were handed out two months later.[34] Brown and Cullen intended to give two pairs of pants, two coats, two shirts, a yoke of oxen, and a cow to every Indian male who would cut his hair and join the "Improvement Sioux." The entire outfit cost ten times the annual annuity delivered to individual Indians and was paid for out of the funds released by Mix. Presents of this magnitude made Brown a popular man and brought many recruits. By November, when the annuities were distributed, nearly two dozen more Mdewakanton men had joined the improvement band, and over the next year, an astonishing two hundred more followed.[35]

The numbers attracted to the improvement group grew so rapidly that Brown and Cullen ran short of cows, oxen, and clothing to give the eager participants. More importantly, several prominent men joined the movement, among them Wabasha, Wakute, and Mankato. Cullen personally cut their scalp locks on July 26, 1859.[36] Thus within two years of the 1858 treaty the landscape at Redwood Agency changed, with many Indians living on small farms that had brick houses and fenced fields of from two to five acres. The old villages that existed north and south of the agency were slowly but surely disappearing.[37]

Despite having grown accustomed to working closely with whites, Little Crow viewed these changes with deep concern. Through his years of contact with them, his trips to Washington, and his missionary education, he had even learned a smattering of English, although he never used it in public and claimed during the treaty negotiation that he could not read English. After returning to the agency in 1858, he had moved into a two-story log house, described as "well roofed and floored," and had government farmers break twelve acres for his four wives to cultivate.[38]

But this minimal acceptance of white culture hardly compromised his strong spiritual commitment to traditional Dakota values. Little Crow believed that it was wrong to abandon the centuries-old Sioux teachings. Living in houses and eating government-issued pork and bread did not affect his religious beliefs, but cutting one's hair, permanently donning white clothing, and becoming a farmer surely did.

What made matters even worse for him was the fact that many men from his village converted to the improvement band. They now sold corn to the government agent, rather than sharing it with relatives, and they no longer showed as much respect for sacred feasts, dances, and ceremonies that had preserved the Dakota people from evil and destruction for centuries.[39] As physician Asa Daniels noted, Little Crow viewed this change among his people with "sullen contempt." While he could tolerate the conversion of a few men, such as White Dog, Joseph Napeśniduta, and Medicine Bottle to the farm program, as others joined them, the sense of community began to crumble. Indeed, the total number of warriors in his band fell from seventy-seven to forty-three between 1857 and 1860, and overall population declined by more than a hundred people. Those leaving by and large were attached to White Dog's "pantaloon band," as Brown called it, and the numbers of improvement Indians at Redwood increased each year.[40]

Superintendent Cullen and agent Brown tried vigorously to persuade Little Crow to join the farmers near his village and to accept the new school program. Cullen had a long discussion with him regarding his failure to do so in November 1859. Upon being asked why he would not become a farmer, Taoyateduta simply answered that making such a change necessitated adopting the white man's religion, something that he totally rejected. Cullen found the chief's linking of religion and occupation interesting, and he suggested to Little Crow that he could easily "have his hair cut and put on pantaloons" without abandoning his Indian faith.[41] Taoyateduta thought such a notion funny and laughed at Cullen's ignorance. Sacred feasts, dances, hunting, warfare, life itself—virtually everything important to a Sioux man—was intertwined with religion and one's relationship with the spirit world. Little Crow believed that if he gave up what he was, he must also relinquish his religion. If he did so, he would never be allowed to journey to that land beyond, where his father and his grandfather now lived. "A man could not dress and work like a white man," he often told the missionaries, "and at the same time adhere to the religion of the Dakotas."[42] Little Crow's religious convictions brought him to oppose schools by the latter 1850s, since religion was often part of the curriculum. Whereas he had never found the missionary teaching threatening in the past, he now talked against it and convinced several of his farming-oriented relatives, including his brother-in-law Peter Tapetatanka, to stop teaching for the missionaries.[43]

This strong attachment to Dakota religion came from Taoyateduta's upbringing. Like his father and his grandfather, he considered himself to be a wicaśta wakan, or a shaman. He guarded his medicine sack, sacred gourd, and armor and refused to surrender them. Shamans possessed considerable power in Sioux villages, organizing and leading war parties, acting as spiritual leaders for young men, and curing the sick.[44] While Taoyateduta had frequently turned to the white doctor at the agency for help, he never believed strongly in white medicine. Indeed, when he had been so seriously wounded in 1846, he scorned the advice of the surgeon at Fort Snelling and turned to a wicaśta wakan. The shamans were mystics who were revered for their knowledge and their power—a power that agent Brown realized the government could never subvert with presents. The real threat to the influence of wicaśta wakans, such as Little Crow, came from the farming program and its attendant inroads upon Dakota communalism. Brown and the missionaries knew that shamans could do little to halt the massive changes underway as the process of decentralization on the reservation moved inexorably onward.[45]

The advocates of acculturation found a new source of support in their struggle with the shamans as white settlers poured onto the lands just north of the reservation and opened farms. Within one year's time, their numbers reached several thousand. Although young Dakota hunters still skirted these communities and reached old woodland hunting grounds in the Big Woods to the east, the white settlers' move up the north side of the Minnesota River onto lands directly opposite the reservations foreordained the end of the Dakotas' hunting and gathering existence and brought considerable disillusionment to reservation inhabitants. This quick occupation of what had always been considered Sioux land came before Congress had even acted on the 1858 treaty.[46]

The whites who settled north and south of Beaver Creek, just across the river from Redwood Agency, were squatters in one sense and legal settlers in another. The land office had mistakenly opened the region to settlement before Indian title had been extinguished. Once the government realized the error, it became almost impossible to remove the settlers, since local politicians came to their support. Agent Brown wanted them off the land, some observers felt, so that he could establish claims from the "half-breed" scrip assigned to his children, but he lacked any authority over the lands in question. Lieutenant Colonel John Abercrombie at Fort Ridgely refused to order them out and asked Washington for instructions. After issuing orders to expel them, Washington officials quickly changed their minds when Minnesota politicians protested.[47] All the Mdewakantons could do was watch as valuable timber was cut and farms opened. Rumors of discontent mounted, and attacks on the stock of white farmers increased.[48]

Reports of depredations started reaching the Indian agent by the summer of 1859. Although the claims often seemed trivial, the government paid compensation for losses, the Indians forfeiting funds whenever evidence showed the destruction of pigs, cattle, or horses.[49] On several occasions, the killing of stock occurred during the return of Dakota war parties from raids on the Ojibway, convincing Brown to deduct money directly from the annuity of individual Indians rather than from the tribe as a whole.[50] Obviously the men being punished were young warrior-hunters, who soon began to hide or deny their pillaging. When they were caught, however, the agent wrote in big letters the word "war" alongside their names on the annuity rolls. Although most chiefs spoke out strongly against men who killed the stock of white settlers, at least one, Red Owl, the Mdewakanton speaker, defended it. Until his death in 1861, he remained a strong opponent of the farm program and a defender of the young, impetuous men who preferred a traditional life.[51]

Depredations became a mechanism by which discontented hunters vented their anger. Traditionally Sioux Indians took revenge for insults by destroying property and whenever possible openly killed a horse belonging to the offending party or slashed his tepee. Since by the late 1850s these acts resulted in punishment, the alternative was to kill animals belonging to an inoffensive outsider, such as a white settler. As Brown distributed more goods to the farmers and ignored the hunters, young Dakota warriors turned to material violence as a form of protest for this obvious social insult. Although a few men killed the oxen issued to farmer Indians, the increase in attacks on animals occurred in and about the new towns of Forest City, Hutchinson, and Long Prairie, and in the region near Beaver Creek.[52]

This disenchantment increased markedly after the Senate finally ratified the 1858 treaty, and the money derived from it went into the hands of traders. The treaty business had taken a long time to settle in the Senate, a considerable debate ensuing over the issue of just compensation for the lands taken from the Dakotas. Whereas Brown thought a fair price was five dollars an acre, the Senate finally settled upon thirty cents, or what amounted to about ninety-six thousand dollars for the Mdewakantons and Wahpekutes. The Sissetons and Wahpetons were to receive nearly double that figure since they had relinquished claims to more land. While Mix had promised Little Crow that twenty-five thousand dollars of the sale price would be turned over to the tribe in the form of annuities, when the traders finally met with the Indians they laid claim to an additional $34,150.47, equaling a total sum in excess of the ninety-six thousand dollars allowed the Mdewakantons. Traders claimed that credits had been given in the interim, or between June 1858 and December 1860.[53]

The Senate had ordered that the Indians be allowed to examine claims in open council. Thus when the time came to deal with the debts, superintendent Cullen and the traders convinced five chiefs, including Little Crow and Wabasha, and seventeen men to meet with them in December and work out a settlement. Discussions lasted for two days, with the Indians initially demanding that the money from the sale be handed over to them. "The Indians . . . remarked that they wanted the money, and wanted to use it for what they had a mind to," trader Nathan Myrick later stated. Myrick ordered his store to be closed, and yet another crisis arose over the 1858 treaty. Cullen contemplated returning to Washington with the treaty funds.[54]

Just as the impasse seemed impossible to break, Little Crow rose to speak. "We know we set apart money to pay our debts, while in Washington," he noted. He expressed concern that the payments to be made would not cover all Indian indebtedness. "We do not want to have the traders running after us hereafter whenever we kill a muskrat," he continued. His wish was to have the trader books examined by Cullen, whom he trusted, and all debts canceled by the payment, regardless of whether the treaty provided funds sufficient to do so. While Wabasha and others protested, the threats of traders to close stores and the belief that the Mdewakantons would be deprived of all benefits from the treaty soon brought general agreement. Unfortunately, as the councils ended the Episcopal bishop, Henry Benjamin Whipple, mentioned that Little Crow received a "new wagon"—a suggestion of bribery.[55]

Superintendent Cullen presided at the final council where the debate resulted in a consensus agreement. Many Indians reluctantly decided to support the debt payments because that fall they had taken a goodly number of muskrats that they hoped to market. Moreover, the traders had agreed that if the Indians turned over the government money, all debts would be wiped off the account books. Nevertheless, the incident further damaged Little Crow's prestige. As an Indian observer noted many years later: "Little Crow was discredited among the Sioux for his consent to allowing traders . . . to absorb the money paid by the government for the east half of the lower reservation."[56]

At least some Dakota warriors and farmers understood the necessity of paying their debts to traders, in part because the kinship and economic ties between the traders and the Mdewakantons remained extensive. Little Crow's brother, White Spider, for example, worked as a clerk in William H. Forbes's store. There is some evidence, however, that a large number of Mdewakantons concluded that the traders had been overly greedy, coveting much more than what had been negotiated at Washington two years before. A few Mdewakantons forcefully told Cullen during the council that their willingness to pay the extra money from the treaty proceeds was based solely upon one condition: *"That this should include all debts owing by them up to the date of that council."*[57]

In the aftermath of the December 1860 agreement the relations between Indian hunters and traders deteriorated. This estrangement occurred to some extent because Mdewakanton hunters were increasingly forced to go heavily into debt to the traders in order to obtain food and blankets. Hunters came to see this constant pressure of debt as insulting. As Big Eagle noted much later: "The Indians seemed to think the traders ought not to be too hard on them . . . but do as the Indians did among one another, and put off the payment until they were better able to make it."[58]

With discontent building on several levels at Redwood Agency by 1860—between native hunters and farmers, government officials and traditional Indians, and traders and Mdewakanton Indians of both the major factions—it was not the right time to change administrative personnel on the reservation. Nonetheless, upon the election of Abraham Lincoln, the patronage system brought a whole new set of white administrators into power in spring 1861, led by superintendent Clark W. Thompson and agent Thomas J. Galbraith. Neither understood the Sioux people very well, and both lacked the dedication exhibited by the likes of Brown and Cullen. In addition, the two officials hoped to push the advancements made by their predecessors one step farther; Galbraith concluded that the annuity system should be changed so that Dakota men would be rewarded only for work. Annuities, he believed, were not a right of each Dakota man to claim. Galbraith tended to hand out goods to farmers haphazardly every month whenever they needed them, and to hunters, only at the annual distribution. This policy only pushed a wedge deeper between the hunters and the farmers in the Mdewakanton reservation community.[59]

Agent Galbraith and superintendent Thompson faced their first trials as administrators in early June 1861 when they proceeded to Redwood to pay annuities and hold a council with the Mdewakantons. The newly elected Republican governor of Minnesota, Alexander Ramsey, joined the party and, as the *Weekly Pioneer and Democrat* reported, opened the council with a short address. He was followed by Red Owl, spokesman for the tribe. Red Owl's oratory was "energetic" and "forcible," and the Indians nearby followed each interpreted remark with a "hearty 'ugh' of approval." Red Owl complained vociferously of the administrative handling of the reservation and offered a long list of problems.[60]

Red Owl was even less congenial a month later when Galbraith spoke with him about some white squatters who had moved across the southern boundary of the reservation and opened farms. While they were clearly on Indian lands, Congress had passed a resolution recommending that the Sioux allow them to stay and file one-hundred-sixty-acre preemption claims. Galbraith was instructed to sound out the Mdewakantons. Red Owl's reply was "pointed." "The Great Father has plenty of land elsewhere which he can give to these whites," he said and insisted that they move. Even the farmer Indians concurred in this decision. They noted that the white settlers in question gave liquor to the "blanket," or hunter, Indians, and the latter, while intoxicated, killed cattle and otherwise abused the Indian farmers.[61]

The growing resentment that Galbraith sensed on the Redwood reservation, however, seemed minor in comparison to the discontent at Yellow Medicine. While the government had tried to convince large numbers of Sissetons and Wahpetons to join farmer bands, the majority not only refused but inaugurated a violent campaign to destroy the Indians who left their villages for farming. The agent described most of the upper Indians as "restive, turbulent, [and] saucy." The intimidation policy forced many farmers to backslide over the winter of 1861–62, putting on white man's clothes one day in order to get assistance from the agent and changing to a blanket the next to avoid assault from fellow tribesmen. Both Brown and Galbraith asked the army to station troops at Yellow Medicine to protect the farmers, and several companies were there during the summer months. As long as the troops remained, the discontented elements fled en masse to Lake Traverse or beyond. On the plains, they commiserated with the Yanktons and Yanktonais, who also had grown to distrust and dislike the whites.[62]

As the unrest mounted, the traditionalists among the Mdewakantons lost their leader. Red Owl died at Redwood in August 1861. He, and to a lesser extent Shakopee, had been the spokesman for the young men of the tribe who wished to continue hunting and avoid farming. Unfortunately, Shakopee had died the year before. The only possible successor to Red Owl was the somewhat discredited Little Crow, who still had not openly embraced farming.[63] Despite his importance, however, there was no need to fill the vacant speakership that fall since most annuities had already been handed out. Indeed, the Mdewakantons were beginning to think about leaving the reservation to winter in the Big Woods, for a major calamity had occurred that fall the effects of which were just being realized. Cutworms had invaded the corn crops, and many Mdewakantons realized that there would be little food for them at Redwood.[64] One of the men who decided to leave was Little Crow. He had determined to winter with his band in the vicinity of Lake Judson, a couple of miles north of Hutchinson.[65]

Dr. John Benjamin lived in the vicinity of the lake and by fall had developed friendly relations with the famous chief. He found Little Crow to have a positive attitude about the future. The doctor fed him along with a few of his warriors during the harshest portion of the winter. In return, Taoyateduta gave Benjamin a picture of himself taken in St. Paul at a photographer's studio. The photograph showed an Indian, in a "full dress suit," with a "necktie and flowing collar," the clothing donned at Ramsey's request. Yet it also showed an Indian who had yet to cut his hair.[66]

While Little Crow was perceived by some as a chief who occasionally did the white man's bidding, he still preferred the chase to farming and sympathized with the majority of his people who refused to join the improvement groups. He defiantly defended his religion and his culture, unlike the remainder of the band chiefs at the agency. Wabasha, Wakute, Traveling Hail, Mankato, and Big Eagle had all succumbed to farming and were listening to the missionaries. Considering the actions of these men, Little Crow must have viewed himself as something of an anachronism, but he remained the most traditional of the major Mdewakanton leaders in a society that was still very traditional. Many young Dakota men continued to go to war against the Ojibway and formed part of a new generation that had come of age on the reservation and needed direction. Such young men had few reasons to turn for advice to leaders who had become farmers, to men who had seemingly forsaken their culture. Surely Little Crow's optimistic mood over the winter came from his confidence that the Mdewakantons would once again rely on him for leadership and guidance the following spring.

7

The Failure of Accommodation

THE WEATHER in Minnesota over the winter 1861–62 was unusually cold. The fierce snowstorms hardened the hearts of many Dakota men who watched family members suffer, their faces revealing the gaunt look that attended starvation. Little Crow himself faced privation. The chief, who had played a pivotal role in helping whites purchase much of the state, was reduced to trading his firearms for food and relying on friends for occasional meals. Understandably, many Dakota Indians were in an ugly mood when they returned that spring to the prairie agencies at Yellow Medicine and Redwood. And the spring did not bring the kind of rejuvenation that the season implied; there was little if any food at the agencies—annuities were not even expected for several months—and most of what was in the warehouses had been set aside for the white workers or the farmer Indians.[1]

The lack of food that spring prompted vehement protests at both agencies. Indians complained bitterly of the policy of agent Galbraith to do "everything for the 'dutchmen'," the contemptuous name used to identify farmer Indians, and nothing for the men of the various tribes who continued to hunt. Galbraith allowed farmer Indians to get "groceries" from the warehouses upon request, denying those Indians who hunted such access. Moreover, young Dakota hunters and warriors showed concern about their annuities. The American Civil War was entering its second year, and rumors floated about the agencies suggesting that the Lincoln administration would be unable to fulfill its obligations to feed and clothe the eastern Sioux. The uneasiness regarding annuities provoked angry discussions among agency Indians, the most heated debates occurring in the soldiers' lodge as the warriors reassembled at Redwood Agency. The lodge had increasingly become a center of political activism in the years just prior to the Civil War.[2]

Although a large number of Mdewakanton men adopted farming in the

116

late 1850s, the soldiers' lodge as an institution continued to function at both Redwood and Yellow Medicine agencies. The organization at Redwood was still occasionally employed in a traditional fashion during deer hunts east of the Minnesota River. But the soldiers, or young men, also used the society as a vehicle for protest, especially after it became apparent that solving problems in council with agency administrators was growing increasingly difficult. An example of how the lodge was used occurred in October 1857 when Red Owl appealed to authorities at Fort Ridgely about a certain Frenchman's attempt to occupy agency lands. "Red Owl, who I understand has been appointed captain of police [head of the soldiers' lodge], & some twenty five of his policemen from different bands, called on me today to complain of a Mr. Jonis La Croix who they state without any authority is building, [and] cutting down timber on their reserve, and [they] requested me to put him off," the commanding officer, Captain Alfred Sully, reported.[3] Most of the Mdewakanton bands seemed to be represented in the lodge, and young men who were still involved in the hunt dominated it.

Lodge activities surfaced only infrequently at Redwood after 1857, due mostly to the growing militancy of the organization and the attending need of members to keep their deliberations secret. This condition pertained especially after the lodge became the center of opposition to the government farming movement and was joined by a group of other societies that underwent a revival in the late 1850s. A mixed-blood observer, Thomas A. Robertson, in his memoirs listed the major societies that suddenly emerged during the period; among the most important were the Bear Dance society, the Elk Lodge, the Raw Fish Eaters Lodge, the Dog Liver Eaters Lodge, and the Sacred Dance.[4] These organizations became bastions of traditional culture as they encouraged feasting and dancing and opposed Christianity, the destruction and loss of hunting territory, and the forced adoption of farming. The secret societies and their increasing opposition to the government programs was by no means limited to Redwood Agency. Indeed, the soldiers' lodge at Yellow Medicine grew to such importance during this period that agent Galbraith noted that it controlled the actions of the chiefs and virtually threatened the peace at the agency during the 1861 distribution. When he called for troops to provide security, many Sissetons and Wahpetons sparred with them, even mounting a false charge at one point that was turned back by the firing of a cannon.[5]

Galbraith concluded that the Yellow Medicine lodge consisted of "bad persons" from various bands. Obviously, it had become a rallying organization for blanket Indians, particularly young warriors who disliked the agent's policy of refusing annuities to those men who participated in intertribal war or killed agency stock. Many friendly farmer Indians at Yellow Medicine told Galbraith privately that the lodge had the power to take lives, that lodge members threatened to shoot any chief who refused to follow its lead, and that there was little that tribal leaders could do to stand up to it. The agent believed Inkpaduta had to be at the heart of this new "reign of terror."[6] While evidence tying Inkpaduta to either soldiers' lodge had no basis in fact, the lodges at both agencies had clearly assumed a political role uncharacteristic of their history.

Several months before the annuity distribution, the young hunters realized that the traders were still demanding payment for past credits. Most Indians had thought that the December 1860 agreement as well as the annuity payment of 1861 had been sufficient to cover those old debts. Andrew J. Myrick concluded that whites had encouraged such thinking, writing his brother on May 18: "Some say they [the young Dakota hunters] were told so by Prescott [a government farmer], others by Forbes [a trader]."[7] Whoever the source, the concern regarding the annuities provoked a serious discussion in the Mdewakanton soldiers' lodge. Young men at Redwood were debating their relationship with government officials and traders outside the framework of the traditional, formal council.

Particularly galling to Mdewakanton soldiers was the manner in which the agent traditionally handled annuity distributions. The agents never actually counted out the money sent by the government, and the sum often fell short of what the government owed. When the agent handed out funds to individual Indians, traders or their mixed-blood representatives stepped forward and demanded the cash, showing the agent a credit book that listed the Indian men who had received advances. Several of these credit books, which have survived, show that traders gave individual Indians credit based primarily upon how many dependents they had in their families. Sarah Wakefield, who witnessed the 1861 annuity distribution at Yellow Medicine, noted that the Indians had no way of knowing what they owed, and the traders generally asked for all the money that each Indian had coming. To make matters more difficult for Dakota hunters, most of the food annuities were given to farmer Indians as rewards instead of being evenly distributed to each adult male.[8]

Discussions in the Mdewakanton soldiers' lodge regarding the annuities should have attracted the Sioux chiefs, yet most, including Little Crow, did not join in the debate. Perhaps their absence is explained by the fact that the soldiers' lodge was traditionally governed by "soldiers," or warriors, rather than chiefs. More than likely, however, the young men now believed that most chiefs lacked sympathy for their problems and cooperated fully with the whites. In early spring 1862, even Little Crow still seemed intent on working with reservation administrators. At one point, he wrote a letter to an Ojibway village in northern Minnesota warning the inhabitants that a war party of young Dakota men was stalking the Ojibway domain.[9] While he probably sympathized with their problems, Little Crow showed no outward signs of joining the soldiers.

At least part of the war party that Little Crow tried to stop came from the two camps that had been under the leadership of Shakopee, who had located his village just above the Redwood River when moving to the agency in 1854. A splinter faction under his brother, Red Middle Voice, had continued farther up the Minnesota River, settling at Rice Creek. After Shakopee's death during the summer of 1860, his young, rather impetuous son, called Little Six or Young Shakopee by the whites, had taken charge of the main village. Many band members, believing that Red Middle Voice was a more experienced leader, moved to his village, which became a center of militant activity. Both Red Middle Voice and Little Six sympathized with the soldiers' lodge.[10]

As the selection of a new speaker for the tribe drew near in the spring of 1862, Dakota Indians who wished to continue as hunters lacked a chief of distinction who could represent them. Red Owl, once their leader, had died the previous year, while Red Middle Voice had never spoken in council and was generally distrusted by whites. The only choice likely to be acceptable to the young men was Little Crow. He at least had remained a traditionalist, although he lived in a frame house. Taoyateduta though had many liabilities. As David Weston, a farmer Indian, later testified, Little Crow "was not followed at all" by the improvement Indians. Most Mdewakanton farmer Indians supported Traveling Hail, a farmer who at one time had been a member of Cloud Man's band, or Big Eagle, a relatively new leader of a moderate political mold who grew up in Black Dog's village.[11] The selection of a speaker, coming at a time of growing unrest, served as a weather vane; it was a test of will between traditional and improvement Indians.

Taoyateduta no doubt hoped that he could convince a sufficient number of elders that he had more experience than either Traveling Hail or Big Eagle. But Little Crow still refused to endorse the farming program, and as the counselors who made the decision finally arrived at a consensus in early June, they selected Traveling Hail. The choice made perfect sense.

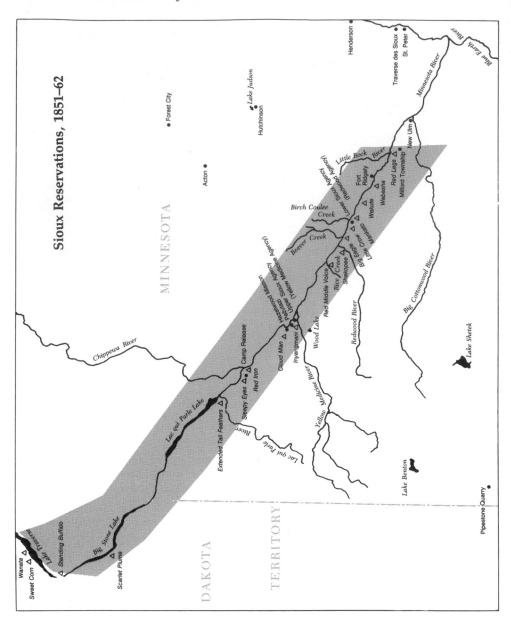

Sioux Reservations, 1851–62

Little Crow had been "distrusted" by many Indians after the 1858 treaty, and he had acted as speaker only once since the negotiation, helping to form consensus during the December 1860 councils with Cullen. His role even in this decision had attracted criticism. More importantly, agent Galbraith had lobbied extensively for Traveling Hail, whose band always had been closely allied with whites. Most of the important Mdewakanton chiefs were now farmers and followed his lead because they wanted a speaker who would have influence with government officials.[12] On the other hand, the election demonstrated that Indians who opposed the farm programs no longer had a say in political affairs.

That Little Crow learned from the election is evident from a discussion he had with Galbraith a short time after the elders had reached their decision. Galbraith indicated that Little Crow was increasingly receptive to becoming a "white man." He had decided to give up his support of the "blanket Indians" and turn his attention to adopting white civilization. By late June, he was attending services at the Episcopal mission, and he began to work with his hands, digging the cellar for his new brick house himself. In his existing frame house, he had installed a cookstove and furniture.[13] It was a modest beginning, but Taoyateduta seemed to have crossed the barrier that he had so vigorously erected only a few years before, deciding to change both his religion and the way in which he lived by becoming a "white man."

Certainly Little Crow had thought hard about the implications of such a change. He had showed a strong determination to remain traditional in the past, but he was an open-minded man who adapted well to most situations. If becoming a farmer was the only way in which he could retain a political role within his tribe, then he seemed compelled to try this new life. So many others, a large number of whom were his relatives, had already done so, and they could serve as a political power base. Even so, some bitterness remained after his political defeat. Big Eagle noted many years later that Taoyateduta "felt sore" at being spurned by his people.[14] His one hope seemed to be that sooner or later his services would once again be required by government officials. Such an opportunity appeared much sooner than he expected, as the long June days unfolded one after another without any visible sign of relief from the hunger that stalked the agencies.

The trouble began at Redwood Agency in late June after many Dakota men were denied credit at the traders' stores. This change of policy occurred for two reasons: traders feared that the government would not be able to send all of the annuity money due the Sioux, thus cutting deeply into the cash being made available, and they learned of a plot organized by the soldiers' lodge supposedly to defraud them. Andrew Myrick was informed of the conspiracy in July, learning from three Indians that the soldiers intended to obtain as much credit as possible and then refuse to pay the traders at the distribution that summer. While Myrick probably discounted the information at first, he knew that since May many soldiers had been intimating that they would not defray their "debts" at the upcoming payment. In addition, Myrick learned in early July that lodge members had gone on a secret mission to see Captain John S. Marsh at Fort Ridgely and asked him not to use troops to force a payment. Marsh's answer, although not recorded, satisfied the Indians that he would remain neutral. Whereas the traders had begun restricting credit as early as May, this revelation prompted them to stop all loans. Since Indians who hunted had no money and could buy nothing from government stores, they were virtually cut off from food.[15]

When the Dakota soldiers learned that their plans had been exposed by three fellow Indians, they were enraged, and finding a horse belonging to one of the men, they cut it to pieces, along with all of the man's belongings. Upon discovering who the two others were, they carried them out into the middle of the agency grounds and stripped them naked in public. After the formal chastisement, the soldiers marched over to Myrick's store and had a shouting match with him. "You have said you had closed your stores . . . and that we should eat grass," a Dakota soldier defiantly began. "We warn you not to cut another stick of wood nor to cut our grass." Throughout early July, various other encounters followed at the Lower Agency as young Indians warned traders or their mixed-blood employees not to cut wood or take hay, and the commercial cadre at the stores responded by telling the Dakota men to "eat grass" or "wild potatoes."[16]

Meanwhile, similar confrontations occurred at Yellow Medicine, where between three and four thousand Sisseton and Wahpeton people—fully three-fourths of those assigned to the agency—awaited their annuities. Their chiefs approached Galbraith on June 20 and demanded their annuity goods and money. Galbraith promised to make the payment on July 20 and then departed for the Lower Agency after telling the Indians to disperse and hunt until the money arrived. On returning to Yellow Medicine on July 14, Galbraith found that the number of destitute Indians had increased appreciably. "They feared they would not get their money because white men had been telling them so," Galbraith reported.[17] Partly because of his refusal to issue provisions—he was saving what he had for

122

the white agency staff—the agent asked for soldiers for protection. More than a hundred men under Lieutenant Timothy J. Sheehan marched from Fort Ridgely to the agency in late June and arrived just in time to face nearly a thousand hostile men who demanded food for their families. Included in the throng were a few Mdewakanton warriors as well as a handful of Yanktons and Yanktonais.[18]

The Indians at Yellow Medicine were even more desperate than those at Redwood—many had been surviving for weeks on roots or a few dry ears of corn issued by the agent—they also remained angry because of a growing feud they, too, were having with their traders. The year before a small trading firm named Carothers and Blake had claimed that Sissetons took roughly five thousand dollars worth of goods from the firm's Lake Traverse store. The claimants bypassed the normal channels and went directly to Washington where the commissioner of Indian affairs sanctioned the claim and deducted the money before the annuity cash was shipped west. Sisseton and Wahpeton leaders were understandably outraged, since no more than a few blankets had been taken, and they had agreed to pay traders a huge sum of money just the year before to cover their debts under the 1858 treaty. By July 1862, the soldiers' lodge at the Upper Agency had decided to prevent the agent from giving traders any of the annuity money, telling Sheehan, who agreed to listen to their complaints, "we do not want to let the traders come to the paytable. . . . They take all our money out of our hands."[19]

Although the standoff between traders and Indians foreordained trouble, it was clearly overshadowed by the growing specter of starvation that stalked the Yellow Medicine Agency by early August 1862. All Galbraith seemed intent on doing was preserving the rather meager supply of food that he had in the storehouse. His failure to feed the Indians resulted in violence on August 4, when a crowd of angry Indians surprised Sheehan and broke into the warehouse. They carried off more than a hundred sacks of flour before the troops stopped them. During the mad scuffle, several soldiers were injured, and Sheehan threatened to blow up the building with a cannon shot in order to prevent further pillaging. That afternoon, Sheehan finally convinced the Indians to talk over their problems. In the council that followed, it became clear that the soldiers' lodge was behind the attack on the warehouse. Sheehan soon realized that peace could not be restored until there was a distribution of food. After repeated attempts to convince Galbraith, who cowered in his brick house, to hold a general distribution failed, Sheehan very wisely sent off an urgent request for reinforcements to his superior, Captain Marsh, back at Fort Ridgely.[20]

The Hazelwood mission of Reverend Stephen R. Riggs in about 1860

On Sunday, August 17, 1862, a group of Indians gathered at Dr. Thomas Williamson's house at Yellow Medicine; the doctor is wearing a light-colored hat, and his wife is in a sunbonnet (left, center). Adrian J. Ebell, the photographer, safe-guarded his camera and glass-plate negatives as he fled with the refugees two days later.

124

*Sioux women
winnowing wheat,
photographed by Ebell*

*Women and children guarding a cornfield from blackbirds in mid-August
1862, photographed by Ebell*

An unidentified farmer Indian and his family stood in front of a new brick house at the Upper Agency. Some people in this picture appeared in others of Ebell's photographs.

When word filtered down to Redwood Agency of the conflict, Little Crow hurriedly rode to Yellow Medicine. His sense for trouble had enabled him in the past to use confrontations of this sort as a vehicle to enhance his reputation as a leader. He arrived at the Sisseton-Wahpeton agency in time to attend a series of councils begun by Galbraith on August 5 and joined by the missionary Stephen Return Riggs. The Indians made it clear that they were in desperate need of assistance and wanted to know when money and food would arrive with which to care for their families. Galbraith had only vague promises to offer them.[21]

Little Crow rose to speak the next morning, with Galbraith, several clerks from the agency stores, Andrew J. Myrick, and the young missionary John P. Williamson in attendance. Little Crow was certainly the most important Indian taking part in the discussions; in fact, the two surviving accounts of the negotiation identify no Indian participant other than Little Crow. He began his address slowly, working toward a solution through dialogue. He first noted that the government payment was overdue and that something had to be done. While he and other leaders present realized that Galbraith had little in his warehouse, Little Crow astutely pointed to the four traders' stores at Yellow Medicine and suggested that Galbraith "make some arrangement" with the traders whereby they might assist the Indians until annuities arrived. It had been done before, but no one had thought of it until then, and the traders' stores were full of goods and food.

Little Crow's solution to the problem seemed more than reasonable, and he doubtless expected the most important trader present, Myrick, to be supportive. Little Crow had transferred his own trading account to Myrick's Redwood store in 1860, and he had argued in favor of the traders' claims during the debate over the distribution of treaty money in December of the same year. No Mdewakanton chief had been more consistently committed to reimbursing the traders for their assistance. After stating his case, however, Taoyateduta concluded with an offhand remark: "When men are hungry they help themselves." Whether meant as a justification for the raid on the warehouse or as a threat to the traders, Little Crow did not indicate.

The interpreter, obviously sensing the latter to be the case, refused to render Little Crow's statement into English. This difficulty forced Galbraith to turn instead to John P. Williamson, the young missionary son of Thomas S. Williamson, who knew the Dakota language well. When asked, he gave an accurate translation, whereupon Galbraith turned to the traders, saying: "Well, it's up to you now. What will you do?" Since most of the stores at Yellow Medicine were operated by clerks rather than owners, the storekeepers turned to Myrick. After being prodded by Galbraith, Myrick deliberately rose and slowly walked from the council, obviously showing his increasing disgust with the entire situation, at which point the agent rather angrily demanded an answer. Myrick turned and scornfully said: "So far as I am concerned, if they are hungry, let them eat grass." The Indians sat silent, being unaware of the text of Myrick's statement. But when Williamson finished the translation, they jumped up from their positions and began a series of "weird and savage war-whoops." The insult that had been commonly employed by traders and clerks at Redwood now had been hurled at Little Crow and the many Sissetons and Wahpetons present.[22]

Fortunately Captain Marsh arrived that afternoon and called for an immediate council in an attempt to repair the damage that Myrick had caused. Marsh ordered Galbraith to open his warehouse and issue whatever he had to the Indians, further declaring that he would "arrest the traders" if they so much as "appeared to cause [any more] dissatisfaction amongst the Indians." Marsh had obviously been informed by Galbraith and Sheehan of the traders' role in causing the unrest. Later evidence showed that Galbraith was convinced that the traders had been telling the Indians that their annuities would never come, using the threat as a weapon against the soldiers' lodges. Marsh, Galbraith, Little Crow, and representatives of the upper Sioux continued their talks for two more days, during which time Little Crow asked the agent to distribute food at Redwood as well. Galbraith solemnly promised to do so under the realization that Marsh would most likely order him to comply with the request if he refused. The discussion and the food—130 barrels of flour and 30 barrels of pork—placated the upper Indians, and on August 9 the majority of them left the agency for buffalo hunting west of Big Stone Lake.[23]

The crisis had passed by August 12, and Galbraith turned to recruiting mixed-bloods for the war effort in the East. Sheehan, meanwhile, marched his troops back to Fort Ridgely and prepared to leave for a new assignment at Fort Ripley in central Minnesota. Three days later, Galbraith and his recruits came down to Redwood, where the agent had an interview with Little Crow. Galbraith reported the chief to be "well pleased and satisfied," since corn from government fields was being harvested, and Galbraith had at least begun the annuity distribution. That same day, Little Crow and Andrew Robertson negotiated the purchase of two cows from a nearby farmer, one Jonathan W. Earle. The chief gave as security his favorite double-barreled shotgun. Thus the specter of starvation, ominous in late July, had passed at the agency, as trades of this sort coupled with the harvest of an abundant corn crop provided sufficient food to hold the Indians over until the cash annuity arrived. Such conditions prompted Galbraith to decide against giving out the provisions he had promised the Mdewakantons. Indeed, Galbraith was so convinced that the problems of July and early August had passed that he left the agency for St. Paul to deliver his new recruits, whom he had named the "Renville Rangers," to the local recruiting office.[24]

The quiet facade witnessed by Galbraith at Redwood concealed the fact that secret meetings of the Mdewakanton soldiers' lodge continued at the Rice Creek village. As Big Eagle later confessed, these councils—influenced heavily by the confrontation with the traders, the events at Yellow Medicine, and the failure of the government to issue cash, which would have benefited Mdewakanton hunters—frequently turned to the "talk of war."[25] Nevertheless, there were many Indians opposed to violent action, since the promise of a bountiful harvest was obvious to everyone. Big Eagle later said that the more reluctant Indians had used the promise of plenty as an argument against starting a war on several occasions during July and early August.[26] But the agent's failure to deliver the food promised and the troubles at Yellow Medicine added fuel to the debates that went on in the soldiers' lodge. While most of the angry young men lived at Rice Creek, others could be found in every village in and about Redwood. Even a few farmers who had good credit ratings had been denied assistance from traders; they found such a situation very difficult to understand.[27]

Myrick's stinging insult and those that followed from other mixed-blood assistants were still fresh in the minds of many Indians, and the indignities had been repeated many times during late July and early August. While it had been hunters and warriors who most frequently bore the onus of these insults, the actions of the traders went against one of the basic tenets of Dakota culture—the belief in sharing with relatives and friends one's material possessions. The exchanges that occurred at both agencies became a clear example of how traders now ignored their kinship responsibilities. The trade had become almost completely a business where creditors were "trusted" in relation to their ability to pay, rather than an exchange that was based to any degree upon kinship obligation.[28] As Big Eagle indicated, most Indians believed that the traders should accept the fact that they were poor and in need of help.[29] In other words, the traders, all of whom either lived with or married Indian women, had a responsibility to assist their Dakota relatives that went beyond the profit motive. Their denial of that duty was socially unacceptable, and to the Sioux such action warranted severe punishment.

Relations with white settlers just outside the borders of the reservations deteriorated even further during the early 1860s. The tremendous increase in white population caused many of the problems, although ethnic conflict also existed. Most newcomers were from Germany or Scandinavia and carried a cultural baggage into Minnesota that was of necessity thrifty, so they saw no reason to share resources with Indians. On one occasion, a white settler refused to parcel out his catch of fish taken from the Minnesota River within sight of the Indians' camps. Moreover, the new horde of settlers harvested what little game still remained in the Big Woods and along the Big Cottonwood River, destroying the last vestiges of a hunting economy, and then sold those furs to the traders at the agencies. Nathan Myrick later claimed that fully 25 percent of his business in skins by 1860 came from nonreservation whites.[30]

Understandably, Dakota hunters slowly came to see these interlopers as selfish people who hoarded food rather than share it. One young white girl, who distinctly remembered the increased hostility of the Indians, later noted that while the Indians had been friendly to begin with, their attitude changed markedly in 1862. "They became disagreeable and ill-natured," she noted in retrospect. "They seldom visited us and when they met us, passed by coldly."[31] Clearly, blanket Indians had come to hate whites in general and placed them in the same category as the farmer Indians. Both groups—but especially the whites—had little regard for the sacred Dakota obligation to work for the betterment of the group rather than the individual. It was simply a matter of time before the deep-seated animosities that were building between these two groups—farmer and hunter—erupted into violence.

Just such a clash occurred on August 17 near the small community of Acton when a party of either four or six Dakota hunters, predominantly from the Rice Creek village, quarreled with a settler and killed five white people. The settler, Robinson Jones, had apparently sold whiskey to the Indians sometime previous to their visit, and he had offended them when they returned, perhaps for more spirits. The young Dakota men involved quickly rode back to their village and late that evening reported their activities to members of the soldiers' lodge. Other Indians were aroused from sleep, and a debate began in the lodge, the soldiers trying to arrive at a consensus. The body discussed the nature of their dependency on whites and the fact that, once the killings were known, the agent would demand monetary compensation and corporal punishment for those responsible. The thought of such an alternative produced much stronger talk and led to the conviction that it was better to launch a full-scale war. The whites could be driven from the Minnesota valley, hunting ground recaptured, and the hated farm program destroyed. As Big Eagle later said, many members of the soldiers' lodge believed that war would once again unite the Mdewakantons and drive from among them those who had sought to ruin their way of life. The thought of defeat in such a war never received serious consideration. The young men of the soldiers' lodge had not been to Washington, D.C., and they knew only of the whites who lived around them; the Americans now had few soldiers with whom to defend the frontier, and the warriors who had been at Acton had found the whites easy to kill.[32]

As the consensus for war evolved at Rice Creek, however, it soon became obvious that the soldiers' lodge was but one hundred men at most. The leaders immediately recognized the necessity of bringing into the conspiracy men from other Mdewakanton villages who sympathized with their cause. But they also saw the need to proceed cautiously, since revealing their plans in each village would have resulted in the calling of village councils that were controlled by farmer Indians. In order to expand the uprising into a general war, the soldiers had to enlist the assistance of an important man, who through force of personality and oratory could attract Mdewakanton men to a national cause but who had not necessarily been connected with the soldiers' lodge. As the sky in the east turned gray, telling of the impending dawn, the soldiers adjourned to wake Little Crow. On horseback and on foot, they marched toward his house and along the way recounted the many wrongs for which whites were responsible; they could no longer live as hunters and warriors in a land such as the Great Father had made. Once in front of Little Crow's house, the emotionally charged atmosphere made the prevention of violence almost impossible. The soldiers woke the chief and demanded that he lead them in a crusade to free their lands from the hated "Dutchmen" as well as the cruel men who worked for the Great Father.[33]

Little Crow, awakened from sleep, immediately sensed the urgency of the young men who peered through the doorway of his small frame house. The warriors insisted that he join them, restating all the arguments that had been made in the soldiers' lodge—the failure of the government to send promised annuities, the thievery of agents and traders, and the debauchery of Indian women by the traders and government workers. Once aware of what they intended to do, however, Taoyeduta sought ways to dissuade them. He initially refused to lead them in war and suggested that they call on Traveling Hail, who was now the spokesman for the Mdewakanton tribe. Taoyateduta recognized that Traveling Hail was not about to start a war and that once the more moderate chiefs were brought into the discussion the soldiers could be talked out of their mission. But the ruse failed because the soldiers knew that the farmers would not fight. They pressed Little Crow once again for an answer.

Taoyateduta, noticing that many of the men involved were young, spirited, and relatively unfamiliar with the American nation, tried another tack. "You are full of the white man's devil-water [liquor]," he stated, now standing impressively in front of the throng. "You are like dogs in the Hot Moon when they run mad and snap at their own shadows." In Dakota society, young men were expected to be rash and aggressive and unconcerned with making rational judgments. Hitting on what was clearly a good argument, Little Crow then tried to reason with the young men. "We are only little herds of buffaloes left scattered . . . [but] the white men are like the locusts when they fly so thick that the whole sky is a snow-storm. You may kill one—two—ten; yes, as many as the leaves in the forest yonder, and their brothers will not miss them." Many Mdewakanton soldiers believed that the Civil War would make it impossible for the Americans to respond, but Little Crow also repudiated this argument: "Do you hear the thunder of their big guns?" he asked. "No; it would take you two moons to run down to where they are fighting, and all the way your path would be among white soldiers."

Unfortunately, the young men at Little Crow's door were beyond the point of meekly accepting such calculated logic. They were primed for war, and when Little Crow vainly tried to prevent it, they finally resorted to questioning his valor. "Ta-o-ya-te-du-ta is a coward," several men in the crowd were overheard as saying. One soldier even threatened Little Crow with a gun. Finally, angry and tiring of the argument, Taoyateduta relented, declaring in what must have been a saddened and rather indignant voice, "You will die like the rabbits when the hungry wolves hunt them in the Hard Moon (January). Ta-o-ya-te-du-ta is not a coward: he will die with you."[34]

Few men were dragged more reluctantly into war. Little Crow knew that fighting the whites would bring disaster to his people. The only rational alternative was to adopt farming. The game could not be brought back; it was impossible to return to the old life. Little Crow himself had finally made his peace with the government acculturation program. He had promised Galbraith to become a "white man," and his sister-in-law, Mrs. Harry Lawrence, later described him as "having put away his Indian dress" and had his hair cut. Even more ironic, the very morning of the Acton killings, Little Crow had awakened early, gone hunting, and walked to the Episcopal mission to attend Sunday services. The Reverend Samuel D. Hinman later noted that the chief was "attentive" and "interested" in the sermon and, as usual, demonstrated the politeness in manners that had made him a favorite with many white reservation people.[35]

The rapid change in Little Crow's plans is explained to some extent by the pressure placed upon him by the young men who began the war. They had abandoned traditional patterns of consensus politics designed to prevent hasty decisions. They refused even to consult with the major civil chiefs. A decision so crucial, so important to the welfare of the tribe, should have been reached by consensus in a formal tribal council. Only about a hundred men came to Little Crow's house to argue for war, and they came predominantly from young Shakopee's and Red Middle Voice's villages, where the soldiers' lodge had been the strongest. Farmer Indians had no knowledge of the events at Little Crow's house that morning; indeed, evidence suggests that members of Taoyateduta's own band, including his head soldier Wakinyantawa, were unaware of the decision. The soldiers failed to consult them because large numbers had moved to farms, abandoning a communal life, or at least sympathized with the farm program. Even the chief now lived in a house, encircled by a handful of tepees. One can only speculate as to the outcome of the early morning council had Taoyateduta been surrounded by the headmen of his own band. Certainly a large number did not want war. Unlike a traditional Dakota warrior who sought assistance from close relatives in time of war, Little Crow was asked to lead a rebellion that had been started by people from Mdewakanton bands other than his own.

Considering these circumstances, one might wonder why Little Crow agreed to join the war effort. He had always been an accommodationist, and he had consistently used his persuasive abilities to prevent violence. The explanation stems partially from the fact that he was a political opportunist who undoubtedly felt flattered at the obvious suggestion of the young men of his tribe that they could not start a war without him. Furthermore, Little Crow had personal reasons for getting involved in such a crusade. Government officials had wronged him on several occasions, and he had felt betrayed. As a mixed-blood, who knew Little Crow well, later said: "He [Little Crow] had been a big gun among them [the eastern Sioux] at one time, but . . . through having more or less sided with the whites had lost much of his influence . . . and thought that he had not gained . . . as much favor from the whites as his attitude had entitled him to."[36] Little Crow undoubtedly concluded that by joining the soldiers, he would be reinstated in his position as speaker for the Mdewakanton tribe.

On the other hand, Little Crow had always been pragmatic. He had consistently worked for solutions that were within the realm of possibility. His decision to join a doomed war effort certainly contradicted his past behavior, but it did not run counter to the traditional obligation of a Sioux warrior to his community and people—that of giving his life when such a sacrifice became necessary for the benefit of the whole. Although he believed that it was the wrong decision, he felt obligated to join the young men and "die" with them. The honor that attended such sacrifice was more important than the dire consequences of the war.

As the morning light broke out over Redwood Agency on August 18, Little Crow, visibly changed from the day before, took the lead of a column of soldiers who prepared to assault the agency. The tragedy often called the "Great Sioux War" had begun.

8

War

MONDAY MORNING came with promise to Redwood Agency. The rising sun warmed the combination of log, frame, and brick buildings that surrounded the large council square. The daylight prompted activity inside the structures among the many different men and women — farmers, carpenters, clerks, teachers, cooks, and missionaries—who worked there. Government laborers, rising early in the large boarding-house and taking advantage of the long summer day, readied themselves for fieldwork by six o'clock. The traders, who had stores about one-quarter of a mile northwest of the agency compound, prepared to open for the week's business. They had sold little merchandise, due to the struggle with the Mdewakanton soldiers' lodge, and optimistically looked to the days ahead for profit. The annuity money, long overdue, was expected daily. Indeed, the cash, more than eighty thousand dollars in gold coin, would arrive at Fort Ridgely later that very day, August 18, 1862.[1] Unfortunately it would never reach the Indians for whom it was intended, for two violent storms suddenly followed the sun's bright entrance. One brought deafening thunder and heavy rain; the other, unbelievable human tragedy.

Just as the traders settled down to breakfast, a long file of painted Dakota warriors, attired in breechcloths, entered the compound from the north. Small parties broke off from the main body and stationed themselves near the stores. It was now seven o'clock. At a signal, the warriors raised their motley array of rifles and shotguns and opened an indiscriminate fire, many weapons being discharged into each trade house. James W. Lynd, a clerk, fell first, being shot as he stood in the doorway of Myrick's newly built store. Moments before, the warrior who killed him was heard muttering in an excited fashion: "Now I will kill the dog who wouldn't give me credit."[2]

An orgy of wild killing followed, Indian warriors becoming more impassioned with each passing shot. Myrick's cook, a German affectionately called "old Fritz," fell seconds after Lynd, and Andrew Myrick himself was slain as he tried to escape from a second-story window in his store. Myrick was supposedly shot first by an Indian who wished to avenge his sister. Myrick had fathered three children with the man's sister and then abandoned her for a younger, more attractive woman. Maddened warriors shot several arrows into Myrick and thrust an old scythe into his ribs.[3] As Dakota men broke into the other three commercial establishments, trader François La Bathe and half a dozen other clerks met a similar fate. Only two men, who were wounded in the attack, survived the rage of the Indian warriors. The looting of the stores, however, brought an end to the organization apparent at the beginning of the bloodbath.[4] Most warriors commenced loading carts and wagons with spoils, leaving only a few Indians to confront other whites at the agency below.

For the most part, white men who had been part of either the trading enterprise or the agency staff received no quarter. A Dakota warrior shot George Gleason, Galbraith's clerk, as he approached Redwood on the Yellow Medicine road. At the agency itself, several more whites were killed, mostly laborers who tended stock or worked in the fields. The hatred that many Dakotas had for the agency physician, Philander Humphrey (even his son admitted that Humphrey had a "hasty temper"), resulted in his death. Humphrey, his wife, and children had managed to escape to a house a few miles below the agency. Dakota men found them and killed everyone inside the building, burning it to the ground thereafter. Even Philander Prescott, the old interpreter who had lived with the Sioux for forty-odd years, was not spared. Prescott had been warned by the soldiers to stay inside but decided instead to run for his life. He was killed while trying to flee to the Minnesota River ferry. While large numbers of people escaped the agency via the ferry, the Indians soon killed the ferryman, Hubert Millier, ending that avenue of flight. In all, of more than eighty people at the trade houses and agency, twenty were killed outright, ten taken captive, and the remainder sent fleeing toward Fort Ridgely.[5]

The turmoil that enveloped the agency, however, did not prevent several Dakota men from saving friends and kinsmen. Indeed, many survivors were warned by Indians in the attacking party. As the shooting started, for example, Little Crow left the scene by the stores and headed for the Episcopal mission. When the Reverend Samuel Hinman asked him what was happening, Taoyateduta only "looked a look of terrible fierceness" and proceeded on. Little Crow would urge young warriors to kill white men on several occasions during the war, but he did not wish to see Hinman die, and both the missionary and his assistant, Emily West,

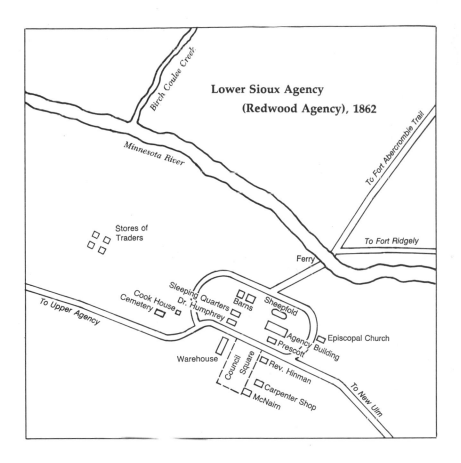

Birch Coulee Creek

Lower Sioux Agency

(Redwood Agency), 1862

To Fort Abercrombie Trail

Minnesota River

Stores of
Traders

To Fort Ridgely

Ferry

Sleeping Quarters

Cook House

Dr. Humphrey

Cemetery

Barns

Sheepfold

Agency Building

Episcopal Church

Prescott

To Upper Agency

Warehouse

Council Square

Rev. Hinman

Carpenter Shop

McNairn

To New Ulm

escaped to Fort Ridgely.[6] Little Crow's head soldier, Wakinyantawa, saved the life of George Spencer, a clerk in William Forbes's store. Although Little Crow no longer traded there, many of his band members did, and Wakinyantawa had developed especially strong kinship attachments with Spencer.[7] As farmer Indians learned of the outbreak, many proceeded to the agency with the intention of saving friends. At Yellow Medicine, especially, virtually all the Americans received ample warning and escaped. Big Eagle, who later fought actively in the war, noted that many of his friends went to the agency to save favorites. Even the violent Shakopee directed several people to stay off the main roads and to work their way to the fort.[8]

Nevertheless, this magnanimity was certainly the exception, especially after Little Crow and his soldiers defeated a company of troops sent from Fort Ridgely. Captain John S. Marsh learned of trouble at the agency at 10:00 in the morning and quickly assembled a forty-three-man column. Marsh underestimated the difficulties and was ambushed, losing half of his command as he and his men prepared to board the ferry and cross the Minnesota River to the agency. The destruction of Marsh's command gave many warriors the added confidence to carry the war effort beyond the confines of the agency. The tendency to split up into raiding parties, however, and open an onslaught against the surrounding white settlements ruined any chance of overrunning Fort Ridgely, the key to the Minnesota River valley. Indeed, Little Crow could only muster a hundred-odd men on the morning of August 19 with which to assault the fort, and an attack was postponed.[9]

The fighting in the settlements opened a new phase of the war. Unlike the Americans at the agency, the settlers had had only sporadic contact with the Indians, many having lived in the area less than a year. The white farmers seldom had the opportunity to develop any substantial bonds with the Sioux, even though many later claimed that a friendly exchange of game and furs for food and liquor had occurred regularly. Actually, the Sioux had little to barter and were perceived most of the time as beggars.[10] On the other hand, the warriors blamed the white farmers for killing game and turning hunting grounds into farms. The members of the Mdewakanton soldiers' lodge particularly disliked the German and Scandinavian settlers, who shared very little with them. Their attitude was best exemplified during the early hours of fighting by the angry cry of Shakopee: "The gutteral speakers [Germans] have made me so angry that I will cut off their heads while they are still breathing."[11]

The killing of white settlers in the countryside began in earnest shortly after noon.

Most of the Dakota warriors who sought revenge among the white farmers turned either to the Beaver Creek settlements just across the Minnesota River from Redwood or to Milford Township, northwest of New Ulm in Brown County. Many Dakota men, including Little Crow, believed that the whites in these settlements had stolen land from them. Within the Milford settlements, fifty-odd settlers—mostly German speakers—were killed in a few hours. In most cases, women and children fell to the same hatchets and shotguns that killed the men of the community. Dakota warriors had never discriminated in war; the killing of an enemy of any age or either sex led to the right to wear an eagle feather. Similar carnage—probably precipitated by Shakopee's soldiers—occurred north and south of the Beaver Creek region, where some estimates placed the white population in the thousands. While many settlers managed to reach safety at places like New Ulm or the fort, several hundred people suffered horrible deaths. The acts of brutality included the mutilation of bodies, heads and limbs occasionally being severed. Such acts were in keeping with traditional Sioux warfare. Dakota warriors did not believe that enemies should be left physically intact, since they would have to fight the same adversaries again in the world beyond their own.[12]

The killing continued in the settlements from the early afternoon of August 18 into August 21. During this time, Dakota raiding parties reached well beyond the confines of the upper Minnesota valley. Their warriors ranged as far south as the Iowa border, eastward into the counties adjacent to the Mississippi, and into the southwestern regions of the state, nearly wiping out a small settlement at Lake Shetek. In all, more than four hundred civilians lost their lives, and about a hundred women and children were taken captive in those four days.[13] Little Crow had joined a race war that augured the extermination of one side or the other.

Taoyateduta soon learned, however, that the soldiers' lodge would take his advice only when the members agreed with it. Neither the leaders of the lodge nor its members intended to allow him to run the war effort. Taoyateduta should not have been surprised at this turn of events, since in more traditional times, band chiefs often had little influence upon the decisions of a soldiers' lodge. While much had changed during the reservation years, especially in regard to the growing political role of the lodge, Dakota war leaders, or "head soldiers," still had more influence in the lodges than band, or civil, chiefs. Chiefs like Little Crow, even those who had been tribal speakers, had no legitimate political power in a lodge, other than the ability to influence events through speaking. Taoyateduta had assumed a leadership role in a war that he could not control.[14]

The burgeoning war went beyond traditional leadership patterns in other ways. The Mdewakantons had never fought an all-out war, and institutions designed to fight guerrilla campaigns against other tribal enemies were obsolete. Furthermore, tribal factionalism complicated matters for the leaders of the war effort. In the case of Little Crow, most of his relatives and many of the members of his band belonged to the farmer element on the reservation. This included one of his closest associates, his "head soldier" Wakinyantawa, who refused to take part in the fighting. Wakinyantawa was joined by yet another of Little Crow's head soldiers, Tunkanwicaste, or Stone Man, who spent most of his time trying to protect captive whites. Yet these very circumstances made Little Crow's support of the war all the more crucial, since the soldiers desperately needed support from Indian farmers. While leaders of the soldiers' lodge must have questioned the leadership abilities of a man who came from a band dominated by the farmer element, they realized that he possessed organizational and oratorical skills unmatched in the Sioux community and that he alone might bring unity to the Mdewakanton cause. Thus when the Dakota marauders returned to the vicinity of the Lower Agency on August 19, they congregated at Taoyateduta's village. It quickly became the headquarters for the war effort, and Little Crow was thereafter perceived by whites as the leader of the outbreak.[15]

The celebrating in Little Crow's camp soon attracted farmer Indians and mixed-bloods, who either joined the war effort willingly or were prodded into supporting it. Little Crow's village, which had been a small enclave consisting of his house and a few tepees, grew by the evening of August 19 to two hundred lodges. It was an encampment thrown together haphazardly with virtually no concern for defense or any consensus among its members as to what action to undertake next. Most young men bragged of their success, tormented white captives, feasted on food taken from the tables of settlers, and remained convinced that they had defeated the Americans in one swift and disconnected blow.[16]

Little Crow knew better. Now determined to see the war through to its conclusion, he tried to create order out of the chaos. He had apparently spent much of the afternoon of August 18 thinking about the issues that needed to be addressed. One white captive who saw him on that evening noted that he was constantly "walking the floor" of his house, seeming to consider his options.[17] The most immediate problem that Little Crow faced was the disposition of the large number of captives, both white and mixed-blood. While Big Eagle wanted them to be turned over to the Americans at the fort, Little Crow quickly disagreed. He planned to use them for protection, saying in substance that "they should suffer with us," and the soldiers supported his position. He openly reveled in the plight of some whites, at one point toying with a scared, teen-age German girl as she sat outside a tent crying. Little Crow raised his hatchet and brandished it above her head as if to kill her and then walked away, laughing.[18]

Little Crow never harmed any captives taken during the fighting and even opened his house to several white women who needed a place of refuge, but his actions in regard to this unfortunate girl suggest that he enjoyed the excitement created by the war and the new-found power that the Sioux had over the lives of the whites in the camp. Indeed, although he had initially opposed the war, the fighting invigorated him. Perhaps this reaction is explained by the fact that he had always thrived on a crisis. Above all, he looked forward to the political challenge involved in trying to control the seemingly disorganized revolution that he had agreed to endorse. He attempted to assume leadership as soon as the warriors started considering their strategy.

As the soldiers began to return to Little Crow's village on Tuesday, August 19, Little Crow had several opportunities to influence the direction of the war. At one point, he spoke out strongly against the actions of the young men, pointing out that they had been "too hasty" in going into the countryside and attacking the settlements. Little Crow hoped to stop the killing of civilians and confine the attention of the Dakota warriors to those who had been "robbing us for so long." Although most warriors probably disagreed with him, Little Crow told the Dakota soldiers that making war on women and children only sapped the strength of the young men and ruined any chance of winning the war. Taoyateduta realized that pushing the whites out of the Minnesota valley would not bring victory; the whites had massive populations from which to draw soldiers. Victory could come only through a negotiated settlement, something that Little Crow apparently still considered as possible on August 19. Worried about how the whites would view the atrocities that had occurred, he harangued the young men over the need to "make war after the manner of white men."[19]

Taoyateduta, recognizing that a war of this sort necessitated the development of strong allies, was encouraged when some Mdewakanton farmers joined the movement on August 18. Most farmers had not participated in the killing of settlers, but some seemed to be swept up in the currents rushing through Little Crow's camp. As Big Eagle later noted, once the die was cast, some farmer Indians like himself decided to take off their white man's clothing and become warriors once again. Kinship ties had much to do with their decisions; while they had broken with many traditions, farmer Indians still had obligations to assist many of their relatives who were actively supporting the war. This dichotomy of supposedly rejecting past kinship responsibilities during the late 1850s and then rallying briefly to them seems to defy explanation, but it must be remembered that the farmers had been supported by the government, which in turn had not met its obligations. Many farmer Indians put on white man's clothing in order to benefit from annuities and willingly took it off when those supplies failed to arrive. On the other hand, large numbers of farmer Indians merely appeared to be converted to the cause of the rebellion; and, as later evidence would show, some converted warriors frequently loaded their weapons with powder only in order not to harm anyone. At most, no more than one hundred farmers actively participated in the fighting.[20]

The mixed-bloods remained even less cooperative; indeed, a considerable amount of animosity existed between the Sioux mixed-bloods and their full-blood relatives. Oftentimes this distrust resulted from the tendency of mixed-bloods to deny their social responsibility. On one occasion, full-bloods attempted to kill a mixed-blood Dakota woman and her French-Canadian husband, Louis Brisbois. "One of the Indians hit the woman [Mrs. Brisbois] in the face and said something about having treated them [the full-bloods] bad at some time when they went to her home."[21] While the Dakota blood that filled their veins prevented the mass killing of mixed-bloods — only one was actually shot — they became prisoners in Little Crow's camp much like the white women and children. Whereas relatedness frequently affected the way mixed-bloods were treated by individual hostiles, at various times over the weeks to follow full-bloods threatened to kill all mixed-bloods. Little Crow even warned the mixed-bloods that they would be slaughtered if they attempted to escape from his camp.[22]

Little Crow, although taking a hard line toward white captives and mixed-bloods in general, dealt more liberally with those who could help the war effort. This was especially true of Joseph R. Brown's mixed-blood family, who were captured along with several whites by Shakopee, Cut Nose, and several other warriors on August 19. Little Crow ordered that they be confined in his house, and during the late evening hours he spoke often with Susan Brown, who was a half-sister of Gabriel Renville, one of Little Crow's relatives. "He appeared very sad," reported Mrs. Brown, and explained that the war was forced upon him only after it became obvious that the government would punish the Acton murderers. Yet after it began, Little Crow strongly asserted that he intended to push for a favorable ending with all his "energies." He told Mrs. Brown that the Winnebagoes in the southern part of the state and the Ojibway from the north would soon join the effort and that her relatives, the Sissetons and Wahpetons, were certainly welcome. Little Crow optimistically believed that other Dakota tribes would fight on the side of the Mdewakantons, and he accordingly treated Brown family members, who were closely related to the Sisseton leaders Wanata and Burning Earth, with great kindness. They, and two white men who were captured with them, were allowed to leave with several of their relatives who came down from Yellow Medicine to get them.[23]

While Little Crow worked on strategy—addressing questions regarding captives, fighting techniques, and allies—his warriors implemented a cultural revitalization movement on August 18. The members of the soldiers' lodge ordered Indian farmers, mixed-bloods, and white captives to take off their white man's clothing and don Indian dress. Tepees became the only acceptable housing, and women ran about camp looking for materials with which to make them. This transition, in conjunction with the consumption and adaptation of all sorts of stolen items from farms and stores, produced a rather colorful atmosphere. Indian women cannibalized clocks, using the mechanism for earrings and medallions. Warriors tied bolts of cloth to the tails of their horses and raced through the camp. Indian women dressed their children in silk and lace. And above all, there were constant feasts, harangues, and the overuse of liquor. The terror-stricken Americans who survived to describe the scene looked upon the whole spectacle with utter amazement.[24]

The events at the camp made it difficult for the Dakota to concentrate on the war itself. While Little Crow and others urged an offensive against Fort Ridgely on the morning of August 19, not until a council convened that evening was such a strategy adopted. The Indian leaders present, especially Little Crow, Big Eagle, and Medicine Bottle, fully understood that they had to dislodge the remaining American troops at Fort Ridgely if they were to regain the Minnesota River valley. The soldiers' lodge, under the leadership of Cut Nose, Shakopee, and Gray Bird, Little Crow's hastily selected new head soldier, agreed with this logic and gave the orders to organize the campaign. Large numbers of wagons were collected for the purpose of carrying home plunder. Only Wabasha and Wakute, opposed to the war from the beginning, dared to say anything against the decision, but few Indians listened to them. Late that night, the soldiers planned the assault, hoping to divert the attention of the American defenders with several false charges and carry the garrison with one, last frontal attack. The next morning, four hundred Sioux filed out of the village with Little Crow mounted on a white horse at their head. The campaign to seize the valley had begun.[25]

After the defeat of Marsh at the ferry two days before, the Minnesota troops were woefully unprepared for such an attack. Only forty men remained at Fort Ridgely with an inexperienced officer, nineteen years of age, at their head, and, as one observer noted, the volunteers were "not very reliable." Worse, Fort Ridgely had been built on a plateau, about three-fourths of a mile from the Minnesota River. On three sides, ravines carried runoff to the river. Although the fort had been situated on high ground, the creeks and ravines provided excellent staging areas for an Indian attack.[26]

Luckily, messengers reached Lieutenant Sheehan while on his way to a new posting along the headwaters of the Mississippi River, and he returned to Fort Ridgely on the morning of August 19. A steady officer, Sheehan brought with him approximately forty reinforcements. Word of the killings reached agent Galbraith at St. Peter on the afternoon of the eighteenth, and his Renville Rangers also rushed back to the fort. Along with about two dozen settlers who were under arms, Sheehan had a force of 180 men by Tuesday evening of the nineteenth. Although the garrison had no walls for protection, which was typical of western forts, Sheehan did manage to construct some breastworks to connect the innermost buildings. The low, makeshift "walls" allowed for the effective use of the cannon that had been left behind by regular army artillery.[27]

The battle commenced at about two o'clock, Wednesday, starting on the west side of the fort. Little Crow, Sheehan noted, directed the forces on the west approach, while Gray Bird, Shakopee, and Cut Nose led the soldiers' lodge, and Mankato and his chief soldier, The Thief, quickly demonstrated unusual boldness in taking advantage of the terrain. Using ravines for cover, these leaders and others urged the Indians forward. Most of the outer buildings on the northern perimeter of the fort—mills, an old stable, and log houses—fell under their control after Little Crow feigned an attack on the west side. As the fighting intensified, an all-out assault took place on the northeast breastworks, the Dakota overwhelming several positions and nearly driving the whites out. But Sheehan's men regained their composure, due mostly to the effective use of the artillery, and retook the position, both sides losing several men in the exchange. By evening the fighting subsided, and a heavy rain began to fall, but the American soldiers remained at their posts throughout the night. The first light on Thursday morning revealed that most of the Indians had withdrawn, and only scattered firing occurred over the next day and a half.[28]

In the meantime, Little Crow's call for allies had spread north into the villages of the Sissetons and Wahpetons, most of whom were camped on the plains west of Big Stone Lake. Although they had sparred with whites in years past, their warriors now responded slowly to the news. A few men, acting in a hostile fashion, drove government employees out of buildings at Yellow Medicine during the evening of August 18, but the missionary families at Yellow Medicine did not flee until the early hours of the next morning. The Sissetons and Wahpetons also harassed the Americans at Fort Abercrombie, located along the Red River near present-day Breckenridge, Minnesota. It was not until August 21, however, that approximately four hundred Sissetons and Wahpetons reached Redwood with the intention of joining the war. While their recognized head chiefs failed to participate in the fighting that followed and later testimony suggested that the majority of tribal members remained aloof, these young men added considerably to the forces at Little Crow's camp. Buttressed by such additions, the Mdewakantons decided once again to attack Fort Ridgely in what was called by one participant "a grand affair."[29]

Perhaps as many as eight hundred men departed from Little Crow's village to storm the fort on Friday, August 22. Little Crow rode to the battle in high style in a handsome buggy driven by David Faribault, a mixed-blood. Antoine J. Campbell, another mixed-blood assistant, also remained at Little Crow's side. He had been with Little Crow on the campaign against Inkpaduta in 1857, and both Campbell and Faribault were kinsmen and friends of the chief. Mankato and his head soldier, The Thief, joined Cut Nose and Little Crow in planning the attack. Large numbers of farmer Indians and mixed-bloods marched with the army, some willingly and others through coercion. The fighting began at one o'clock, with a slow, deliberate assault on all sides of the fort. A strong wind blew from the south, and as the cannon and the Indians ignited buildings and prairie grass, it soon looked as though the entire garrison would be enveloped in flames. A series of charges followed, with the Indians trying to mount a final blow to overrun the garrison at four o'clock. The charge, originating near the southwest corner of the fort, was broken up by a cannon shot. American defenders later mentioned that they could hear Little Crow haranguing his men just prior to the onslaught. While casualties in the fort increased to more than sixty and water and bullets ran low, at day's end the stubborn defenders held fast, and the Indians slowly withdrew.[30]

After failing to overrun the fort—a great disappointment—the Dakota army turned toward New Ulm on Saturday, August 23, prompting the most savage fight of the war. Although hundreds of frightened settlers had flocked to the town for protection, few were armed. Fortunately, at least two hundred men had reached this predominantly German community from the river towns below. Outgunned perhaps two to one and without cannon or strong barricades, the people of New Ulm faced a truly uncertain future when Dakota Indians surrounded the small community in the late morning hours. The citizen army tried to form and hold a line on a plain in front of the town, but the Indian forces, opening up in a bold fashion, provoked such fear among the defenders that the whites broke and ran. Quickly, the Sioux seized the outer buildings and pressed forward to the center of town. Soon, New Ulm was ablaze.[31]

Fierce fighting continued for several hours, causing a reported sixty casualties among the American defenders alone. At one point, it seemed certain that the enclave of settlers and citizen soldiers would be overrun by Sioux mounting a brutal assault. Little Crow came close enough to the whites to leave his "totem," a crow's skin, on the body of a dead defender. Nevertheless, the whites at New Ulm held on, and the Indians could not penetrate a four-block-square section of the city—literally the only buildings untouched by fire—at the end of the day's fighting.[32] Consequently any thought of marching down the Minnesota valley and wreaking devastation among the lower river settlements came to an end.

Little Crow had played a major role in all the battles, and upon returning to his village late in the evening of August 25, he undoubtedly knew that the most favorable opportunities for pushing the whites back to the Mississippi had passed. Along with the other leaders, he then agreed to a gradual withdrawal to the north, camping first near the Rice Creek village and moving just above Yellow Medicine on August 28.[33] As the Dakotas marched northward, a few farmer Indians in the group organized resistance to the soldiers' lodge and Little Crow and held secret nighttime meetings in the tents of Wabasha, Wakute, and Taopi, a farmer Indian.[34] The failure to take the fort also apparently prompted some Sissetons and Wahpetons to return to the plains, abandoning the Mdewakanton cause.

The plotting of a handful of Mdewakanton farmers and the desertion by the plains allies, however, hardly deserves a notice in comparison to

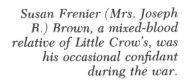

Susan Frenier (Mrs. Joseph R.) Brown, a mixed-blood relative of Little Crow's, was his occasional confidant during the war.

Joseph R. Brown while Indian agent attempted to make the Indians self-sufficient farmers.

Little Six (Shakopee) was a traditionalist and one of the leaders of the war. Later he was a prisoner at Fort Snelling where this photograph was taken.

Cut Nose, a leader of the Mdewakanton soldiers' lodge

Big Eagle was a subchief who became a farmer but ultimately supported the war, for which his reminiscences are a valuable source. He was probably photographed at the time of the 1858 treaty negotiations.

Wabasha, in about 1860

White Spider,
Little Crow's half-brother

150

the opposition that surfaced when Little Crow and his people reached Yellow Medicine. After a few upper Indians had pillaged the stores and buildings, the Upper Agency had been abandoned. About a dozen mission Indians had remained behind, among them Gabriel Renville, Paul Mazakutemani, Joseph Akipa Renville, and several others who had lived at either Hazelwood or Williamson's Yellow Medicine mission. These men were all relatives of Little Crow's, and they all opposed the war. Several were also related to the Brown family and were the ones who had gone to Little Crow's village to fetch Susan Brown and her children. After Little Crow's arrival, he proceeded to the house once occupied by the agency physician, Dr. J. L. Wakefield, and ordered the farmer Indians to abandon it. The Mdewakantons then burned it and all other agency buildings to the ground.[35]

The farmer Indians left the agency without protest, but shortly thereafter they toured the Mdewakanton camps, noticing the many white captives being held and deciding to discuss with the soldiers what was to be done with them. Paul Mazakutemani, Little Crow's cousin, spoke during this council telling the Mdewakantons to "give me these white captives." He asked why the Mdewakantons did not simply make war on the white soldiers and rebuked them for their actions against civilians. "No one who fights against the white people ever becomes rich, or remains two days in one place," he exclaimed. Although Little Crow undoubtedly agreed with this assessment, having said much the same thing a few days earlier, he now remained silent. Strike the Pawnee, son of White Lodge, arose and answered Paul: "If we [the Mdewakantons] are to die, these captives shall die with us."[36] All the other soldiers at the council gave strong verbal support to this commitment.

After moving on to Hazelwood, the Sissetons and Wahpetons, who had been forced from Wakefield's house, were approached by four Mdewakantons who asked them to join the rebellion. But the mission Indians refused and prepared instead to intensify their campaign for the release of the captives. They planned to force the hand of the Mdewakantons by calling them to a feast and appealing to their sense of obligation. Just as a fat calf was being cooked for the occasion, two hundred Mdewakanton warriors suddenly appeared. Intent on mischief, they were clearly deflated when the mission Indians asked them to come and eat. As the two groups sat down to feast and talk, Paul Mazakutemani harangued them regarding the issue of the captives, scoffing at their haughtiness and lamenting the fact that the war had been started. Paul particularly criticized the argument made by some Mdewakantons that the British in Canada would come to their aid in the war, concluding by saying, "The British will dislike everyone who is wicked and disobedient." The Mdewakanton soldiers, refusing to budge, replied, "The braves [soldiers] say they will not give you the captives. . . . The Mdewakantons are *men*, and as long as one of them lives they will not stop pointing their guns at the Americans."[37] As the soldiers departed from the council, they warned that they would come again the next day and force the Indians near Hazelwood to join them. That night the Sissetons and Wahpetons near the mission prepared to defend themselves and formed a soldiers' lodge, with Gabriel Renville acting as chief soldier and Paul as speaker.[38]

Little Crow had avoided the debate over the captives, saying nothing when the issue first came up at his camp and apparently not attending the council held later on the evening of August 28 at Hazelwood. He had an obvious reason; the mission Indians were all his relatives, and he wished to avoid debating them, for he well understood their views on the war. Unfortunately the confrontation widened as the Mdewakantons rode to the Sisseton and Wahpeton camp the next morning and attempted to destroy it. They quickly discovered, however, that the Sissetons and Wahpetons had reinforced their position during the night, and the hostile lower Indians elected not to challenge the authority of the new soldiers' lodge.[39]

As the angry Mdewakantons departed, Gabriel Renville and his fellow soldiers, more than a hundred strong, mounted and followed them back openly singing their war songs as they rode toward the Mdewakanton camp. They intended to demand the return of all property taken from mixed-bloods. A tense situation then unfolded as the armed Sissetons and Wahpetons rode through Little Crow's camp in a brief display of horsemanship, shooting their guns in the air and acting in a threatening fashion. When they finally stopped in front of the Mdewakanton soldiers' lodge, several brief individual confrontations occurred, but no serious fighting. Leaders from both sides called for yet another council, which this time attracted more than a thousand people.[40]

Paul opened the debate with a long, detailed speech. "You have been threatening us and trying to get us to join you in what you have done," he began, speaking directly to Little Crow. Paul then announced that the Sissetons and Wahpetons wanted nothing to do with this war, and in order to preserve their independence, they had formed a soldiers' lodge. While avoiding the issue of the white captives, Paul berated the Mdewakantons for holding the mixed-bloods against their will and for taking their property. He declared that several mixed-bloods intended to recover whatever property could be found, which turned out to be a few horses and a couple of wagons. Fighting broke out as the animals were taken, one Mdewakanton soldier being knocked down during the melee.[41]

Little Crow made no attempt to halt the recovery, but it must have pained him to witness the divisiveness that it represented. When he finally responded to his cousin Paul Mazakutemani during the council, he said that he willingly had agreed to join the war against the Americans and that he had no intention of abandoning the cause at such a late date. Yet he did not ask his Sisseton and Wahpeton relatives to join the rebellion, and he did not defend it or boast of its success. In what must have been a dejected voice, he strongly implied that the Sioux had lost the war and that he never intended to be taken alive. He believed that the whites would make a show of him, and he swore that no white man would touch him until after he had been killed. At that, the debate ended and the Sissetons and Wahpetons departed.[42] From then on, there would be two camps, one hostile and one friendly toward Americans. Little Crow moved his followers to within one-half mile of Hazelwood the next day, August 30.[43] The move was necessary in order to put the Yellow Medicine River between the Indians and the newly reinforced garrison at Fort Ridgely.

A twelve-hundred-man column of Minnesota militia under the command of Colonel Henry Hastings Sibley, the fur trader and politician and old acquaintance of Little Crow, had reached Fort Ridgely on August 28. Three days later, Sibley ordered the former agent, Joseph R. Brown, and 150 men to scout the Redwood Agency grounds, to bury the dead, and to look for any survivors. Brown's patrol reached as far north as Little Crow's original village, interring forty-one bodies in the vicinity of the agency alone, and then crossed over to the east side of the Minnesota River to scout the vicinity of Beaver Creek. As the column marched east, however, Indians saw it and hurried to report the news to the Mdewakanton soldiers' lodge.[44]

The warriors at Little Crow's camp debated what course to follow on the evening of August 31. A white captive witnessed the council and left a description. Little Crow and twenty or thirty soldiers walked out onto the prairie and seated themselves on the ground in a large circle. A kettle filled with dog stew hung over a fire in the center. Ironically, the United States flag was draped from a staff nearby. One by one, the men stoically rose and addressed the party, after which they dipped a ladle into the stew and ate. According to the decision they reached, Gray Bird, Mankato, Big Eagle, and half of the soldiers would march south along the river and seize whatever prizes appeared. Plunder was probably their primary motive, even though large amounts of arms, munitions, and food had been taken from the trade stores and settlers' houses. As a report had circulated in the Indian camp that New Ulm had been abandoned, the Indians probably hoped to loot the town. Little Crow, meanwhile, would head overland with a second party of 110 men toward the Big Woods. He intended to protect the flank of the main party and eventually assault such places as Henderson and Forest City, the most western of the Minnesota frontier towns still occupied.[45]

The next evening, Gray Bird's party reached Little Crow's old village. From a hilltop, their scouts could see white soldiers, the detachment that had been actively burying bodies for two days. Now tired and feeling relatively secure after reconnoitering much of the river valley and seeing no Indians, Brown's inexperienced militia selected a campsite on Birch Coulee, a ravine just south of Beaver Creek. During the night, the Indians silently surrounded the exhausted soldiers and at daybreak opened a murderous fire from concealed positions. Located on an exposed plain, without water or protection, the soldiers tried to form lines but quickly realized that standard tactics would not work. Most fell to the ground and dug holes for protection wherever possible. Within an hour, fully sixty casualties had been suffered. Virtually all the horses, more than eighty in number, were dead; most were being used for breastworks. When relief arrived the next day—Sibley and eight companies moved cautiously to the scene for fear of ambush—the intensity of the struggle became evident. Along with the wounded and dead soldiers, tents, wagons, virtually everything, had been riddled with bullets. The punishment of the eastern Sioux, thought to be a simple matter by some white Minnesotans, took on new meaning after the Birch Coulee debacle. In a letter to his wife, Sibley exclaimed that Dakota warriors fought "like devils."[46]

Due to Little Crow's raid into the Big Woods, Brown and his men did not face the entire Indian force. While the fighting was underway, Little Crow was moving deeper into the Big Woods, traveling more than thirty miles the first day, looking for targets of opportunity. But on September 2 a squabble broke out, and the party divided into two factions, both camping near Acton. At least one source suggests that the argument centered on the issue of attacking the towns of Hutchinson and Forest City. Little Crow wanted to avoid assaulting the towns, since each community had constructed a stout stockade and civilians were involved.[47]

Those Indians remaining with Little Crow—nearly forty men—broke camp early the next day and immediately encountered a company of sixty-four Minnesota militia, commanded by Captain Richard Strout, en-

gaged in a march to Forest City. Although Strout put forward a good
skirmish line, the militia was quickly routed when the other Sioux party
came to the assistance of Little Crow's men. Strout fled back to Hutchinson
after suffering small losses. About forty or fifty Indians then marched
boldly into Forest City and looted and burned most of the town. Two
hundred refugees and forty armed men huddled behind the walls of the
stockade and watched with despair as their property went up in flames.
Meanwhile, Little Crow and sixty Indians moved south to Hutchinson
where similar scenes were enacted. The Big Woods campaign had not
altered the course of the war, but it produced a second exodus from
several central Minnesota counties. Whereas the Big Woods raids and
the Birch Coulee battle must have strengthened the Mdewakanton soldiers' basic belief that they could defeat the whites, this optimism quickly
faded when Little Crow returned to Hazelwood on September 7.

On the previous day, the major chiefs of the Sissetons and Wahpetons —
Scarlet Plume, Standing Buffalo, and Wanata — had arrived at Hazelwood.
Traveling Hail and others opposed to the war invited them to a council
where they reinforced the views of those Indians who remained friendly
to whites. Standing Buffalo, who spoke for the others, began by calling
the Mdewakantons "brothers" and "cousins," but then he noted that these
relatives had "cut our people's throats." He praised the Indians who
remained in Little Crow's camp for their opposition to the fighting, and
he said that he and his fellow chiefs would return to their buffalo ranges
and not get involved in the war. While the upper Indians had had dis-
agreements with the whites in the past, the adamant refusal of their chiefs
to support the war effort at this crucial time was a severe blow to the
Mdewakanton soldiers.[48]

The details of this discussion reached Little Crow at about the same
time that the chief received a curious note from Colonel Sibley. The
colonel had left the message attached to a stake at the Birch Coulee
battlefield, knowing full well that it would reach the Indian camp. When
it did, Little Crow called in Thomas A. Robertson to translate; Little
Crow's limited command of the English language forced him frequently
to rely on interpreters. The note, which asked Little Crow why the war
had been started, opened an interesting dialogue between the two camps.
Little Crow and Antoine Joseph Campbell, his secretary, composed a
detailed reply.[49]

In his response, Taoyateduta justified the war by reminding him that
the government had not lived up to its promises. Agent Galbraith, along
with the traders, was singled out for having made life itself unbearable

for the Indians. Little Crow realized that his warriors had "push[ed] the white man" with some degree of ferocity, but he argued that this was defensible. He ended his note by warning Sibley that he had a "great many prisoners women & children."[50] He seemed intent on using them as a shield or possibly as a bargaining tool sometime in the future.

Little Crow's reply reached Sibley via two mixed-blood couriers, Thomas Robinson and Thomas A. Robertson. These young men were able to enter Sibley's camp without incident and return the next day with an answer. In his response, Sibley simply ignored Little Crow's charges and instead insisted that the captives be released, whereupon, the colonel said, the two leaders could talk, man to man. Sibley, however, had no intention of negotiating in good faith with Little Crow and admitted as much in reports sent east.[51] A climate of hysteria gripped the white population of Minnesota, and this condition precluded any compromise settlement.

Once the reply reached Little Crow, and after the size of Sibley's army had been ascertained, the Mdewakanton soldiers decided to move farther north, departing on September 9. The two distinct camps negotiated the trip together, the caravan extending about five miles in length when en route. As the lead elements reached Red Iron's Wahpeton village, located ten miles below Lac qui Parle and near the mouth of the Chippewa River, commotion broke out. Red Iron's people, with their chief at their head, stopped the column and demanded that the Mdewakantons turn back. "You commenced the outbreak, and must do the fighting in your country," Red Iron exclaimed. Red Iron, Joseph Akipa Renville's brother, wanted no part of the war. Gunshots were fired by angry Indians on both sides, but no one was killed. During the confrontation, two mission Indians, one a close relative of Little Crow's, Lorenzo Lawrence, and the other an old schoolmate, Simon Anawangmani, gathered several white captives together and successfully fled to Fort Ridgely. As the turmoil subsided, considerable numbers of Mdewakantons, including Wabasha, Wakute, and Taopi, chose to leave the soldiers' camp and live with the friendly Sissetons and Wahpetons. They had been told by the various mixed- and full-blood messengers who had carried letters to Sibley that Indians who had not killed civilians would not be punished.[52]

The events at Red Iron's village had a sobering impact on Little Crow. In the two days that followed he spoke frequently with Susan Brown, who noted that the chief felt that he had lost any influence that he had once held over the young Mdewakanton soldiers. He realized by this time that many members of his band and even his own, close relatives had no intention of following his lead. Little Crow's anticipated role as a creator of tribal unification had ended in bitter disappointment. The optimism and unity, as well as the sense of daring that had existed in the early days of the war, had faded, the goals had been discarded, and all that remained was intertribal squabbling and violence. Consequently, at times in his discussions with Mrs. Brown, Little Crow lapsed into utter dispair, telling her that over the coming winter he intended to go to the "Green Lake region of the big woods" and kill as many whites as possible. He professed to care little if he, too, lost his life, but he did not want to be captured and hanged. Such a death had no dignity.[53]

While still committed to the war, Little Crow was driven by a sense of failure to feel Sibley out on the issue of peace. He broached the subject to the colonel in a letter written for him by Campbell on September 12. Short and to the point, Little Crow's message first mentioned the "one hundred and fifty five prisoners," reminding the colonel once more of this trump card. Little Crow also pointed out that they had been treated "just as well as us." Quickly, he turned to the issue at hand: "I want to know from you as a friend what way that I can make peace for my people." Little Crow hoped that the cordial relations that had existed between the two men in earlier years would now work in his favor. Even before an answer could be expected, however, the Mdewakanton soldiers found out about the offer. Stephen Return Riggs, who was serving with Sibley as a chaplain, learned from the messengers who brought the note that its contents had produced a "conspiracy" in the hostile camp to kill Little Crow.[54]

When Sibley received this unusual offer, he decided against giving Little Crow any encouragement. The colonel had learned from the mixed-blood messengers that the Indians were now hopelessly divided, and if he remained patient, the friendly Indians would solve the captive problem themselves. Sibley knew of the threats to Little Crow's life, and he was fully aware of every evolutionary step in the development of the friendly camp. Furthermore, Sibley believed that the opposition of such leaders as Wabasha, Wakute, and Taopi along with that of the Sissetons and Wahpetons made any continuation of the war on a large scale practically impossible. The friendly Mdewakanton chiefs also had smuggled to Sibley their own letter, which had been carried to the colonel at the time Little Crow made his offer of peace. They voiced strong opposition to the war and indicated a willingness to be of assistance to the American army.

Sibley replied positively, telling them that he came only to punish the guilty and encouraging them to maintain their separate camp and to fly a white flag.[55]

Over the next week, the two Indian camps contested for control of the captives—dancing, feasting, and continually singing war songs in characteristic displays of strength. Occasionally, this exuberance resulted in clashes as Mdewakanton soldiers frequently rode over to the friendly village and tipped over tepees and destroyed property. At the height of this skirmishing, Paul Mazakutemani made one last effort to convince the Mdewakantons to surrender the captives. "The Americans have given us money, food, clothing, ploughs, powder . . . and they have nourished us even as a father does his children," he said, trying once again to remind the Mdewakanton soldiers of the kinship bonds that had once existed between whites and Indians. Paul could not understand why the Mdewakantons had started such a war, and he wanted them now to give up the captives. A few soldiers, disenchanted with the war and probably influenced by Mazakutemani's efforts, did not resist when a small number of captives were led off to the friendly camp.[56]

This minor success led to an important council in the friendly camp on September 18. Some of the mission Indians wanted to take the few mixed-blood relatives and whites whom they had obtained from the Mdewakantons and flee to Fort Ridgely. Paul Mazakutemani openly opposed this, however, arguing that they ought to work to free all the captives. The next day, as members of the friendly village quietly tried to move more captives to their camp, a quarrel erupted in which threats and counter-threats were exchanged for most of the afternoon. That night rumors circulated indicating that Little Crow had urged his men to kill the captives. Whether valid or not, he had lost so much prestige in the intervening days and so many captives had been moved or were under the protection of friendly Indians that the warriors failed to respond.[57]

The struggle over the captives continued until the afternoon of September 21 when news reached the hostile camp that Colonel Sibley had arrived at a point just below Yellow Medicine, where he camped for the night on a plain about a mile south of the bluff that formed the riverbank about two or three miles east of Wood Lake. The soldiers' lodge immediately decided to attack the army, and the next morning a camp crier announced to the village that every able-bodied man must turn out to confront Sibley. The soldiers tried to whip up support for the assault by promising presents and honors to anyone who carried back to camp the scalps of Sibley, Brown, or the traders Forbes, Robert, and Nathan Myrick.

While about three hundred warriors responded favorably to this call to arms, that many more went under duress, and many men in the friendly camp refused to go at all or joined only to ensure that Sibley would not be surprised.[58]

Little Crow placed himself at the head of this army, as he had in the past, but most of the organizational effort and the tactics fell under the control of the soldiers' lodge and its leaders, which may have been an unfortunate decision. When the warriors reached the Yellow Medicine, Little Crow went up onto a bluff and carefully looked over the neatly ordered military camp. Tall grass made detection difficult on the camp's perimeter, and Little Crow immediately proposed to wait until nightfall and then surround the camp and "crawl" in upon the sleeping men. "We are many and strong," Little Crow asserted, "this plan will not only secure for us an easy victory but lots of plunder, especially provisions." Sibley had lost most of his cavalry when his volunteers returned home and through the losses suffered at Birch Coulee. Worse, he was really expecting to engage the Indians somewhere north of the Yellow Medicine River, nearer to Red Iron's village. He had very little information regarding the proximity of the Sioux, his soldiers were not well disciplined, and a surprise attack at night might have worked. But several friendly Indians on the scene argued against this plan, and a leading member of the soldiers' lodge joined them. Solomon Two Stars, son of the Sisseton Cloud Man and thus a close relative of Little Crow's, apparently made the strongest argument against the plan, saying it was "so cowardly as to be unworthy of a Dakota brave and of the great chief who proposed it." Accordingly, the assault, called thereafter the battle of Wood Lake, was opened the next morning in the Indian fashion of ambush.[59]

As Sibley's sixteen-hundred-odd soldiers prepared to break camp on the morning of September 23, a column of the Third Minnesota Volunteers veered off from the main road to harvest potatoes from nearby Indian fields. Traveling half a mile from camp, they were fired on by Indians lying in the grass directly in their path. A general engagement ensued, the Dakota ambush being sprung before it had a chance to operate. Chaos followed on both sides as Sibley's attempts to recall and reorganize his troops were ignored, and the Indians moved from side to side, seeking an advantage. After two hours of skirmishing, most of the shots being fired from long range, the Indians withdrew, leaving fourteen dead, among them chief Mankato who was killed by a cannonball. White soldiers seeking trophies scalped and mutilated the Indian corpses. Sibley's losses were seven killed and thirty-four wounded.[60]

As the fighting continued at Wood Lake, the friendly Indians recovered the majority of the captives still remaining in the hostile camp. They immediately went to work digging holes in the center of the lodges at the friendly village—which soon came to be called Camp Release—to use for protection. Everyone seemed to sense that regardless of the outcome of the Wood Lake battle, the Mdewakantons would return and destroy the friendly camp. As the defeated Indians straggled back to Little Crow's village, pandemonium broke out in both camps. Within hours, surely in a day or two, Sibley and his army would arrive.[61]

While a few Mdewakanton soldiers openly advised rushing the fortified friendly camp and Little Crow at first sympathized with them, he soon concluded that it would do no good to harm any more white civilians at this point, and besides, many of the full- and mixed-bloods involved in protecting them would be injured in the process. They were his relatives, and Little Crow wanted at all costs to avoid a tribal civil war.[62] Instead, as men and women scurried about him, the chief walked into the center of the hostile village and told his followers to pack their tents and flee with him out onto the plains. Yet his words were not entirely magnanimous, and a tone of bitterness crept into his departing speech. "To be sure," he concluded, "the whites had big guns and better arms than the Indians and outnumbered us . . . but that is no reason we should not have whipped them, for we are brave men while they are cowardly women." Little Crow could not help but charge that the defeat must have been engineered by "traitors in our midst."[63]

Heartbroken, despondent, knowing that all was lost, Little Crow ordered his wives to break camp. Before he departed, he asked to see his old friend and secretary, Antoine J. Campbell. Despite Campbell's personal assistance to Little Crow during the war, he had also been instrumental in organizing the friendly camp during the last few days before the Wood Lake battle. Indeed, Campbell had just returned from Sibley's camp and had been told to relay a message to Little Crow; Sibley wanted the chief to surrender, unconditionally. Campbell went to Little Crow's tent reluctantly, fearful for his life, yet convinced that it was his duty to see his old friend and relative. Once in front of Little Crow, however, the chief gave him a friendly greeting and asked if he could do anything for his friend before leaving with his followers. Campbell responded by dutifully asking Little Crow to surrender to Sibley. With a "derisive laugh," Taoyateduta said: "The long merchant Sibley would like to put the rope around my neck, but he won't get the chance." Campbell countered by suggesting that perhaps the whites would not hang anyone—"they never did before." But Little Crow again demurred. The chief pledged never to be taken alive.[64]

At that point, Campbell asked for the few remaining white captives still in Little Crow's camp. "Yes, you shall have them," Taoyaleduta responded, and the chief gave orders that all captives still in his camp— Campbell indicated that forty-six were surrendered—should be turned over to the friendly Indians who awaited Sibley's arrival.[65] A few soldiers protested this order, and at least a couple simply ignored it, keeping their captives for several months thereafter, but Taoyateduta shamed many into giving up the people they possessed. "Let them [the captives] alone," he scolded. "Too many women and children have been killed already. If you [the soldiers] had killed only men, we could make peace now."[66]

This discussion between Little Crow and his old friend Campbell must have been heartrending. Certainly it conjured up the good times that Taoyateduta had had with his many mixed-blood and full-blood relatives while hunting for deer in the eastern woodlands or exploring the strange alleys and boulevards of the nation's capital. But the war, merely thirty-six days old, had altered his life forever. Little Crow could not return to his homeland, nor could he expect to see many of his friends and relatives ever again. As he watched the camp break up and Campbell depart with his captives in tow, surely Little Crow pondered whether life under such conditions was worth continuing. Such thoughts probably lingered for only a brief moment; preparations had to be made to move the several hundred people who still wished to continue the war out of the way of Sibley's approaching army.

The next morning, September 24, as a bright sun arose, foreordaining the end of the struggle and drying the rain-drenched Minnesota prairie, Little Crow rode out of the valley of the Minnesota River, stopping for a few moments on a hilltop to look out over his old home. "We shall never go back there," he said loudly to his few companions, and then he turned to the plains beyond.[67]

9

The Last Campaign

THE RETREAT of Little Crow and his small band of refugees onto the forbidding northern plains came at the most difficult time of the year. By October the grass had turned brown, and the few trees that did border an occasional lake had begun to shed their leaves. The northern Great Plains winter was imminent, with its arctic winds and biting cold. Normally, the eastern Sioux had sought shelter in more wooded terrain during this part of the year, but Sibley's victory at Wood Lake now precluded such a choice. Little Crow and those Indians who followed him faced the broad, gray skies to the north fully aware of the trials that lay ahead. They talked of bringing the plains Sioux—the mighty Yanktons, Yanktonais, and Tetons—into the war and hoped also to obtain British support in Canada. A plains alliance seemed to be the last hope for salvaging the war.

Taoyateduta left the Minnesota valley with the intention of doing his best to bring these potential allies together, although he probably recognized all too well that many hurdles stood in the way of such an alliance.[1] The Yankton Sioux were receiving annuities from the government on the lower Missouri River and had little to gain from war. Moreover, the northern plains people lacked homogeneity, with many different cultural groups—Red River métis, or mixed-bloods, and their relatives, the various Cree, Assiniboin, and Ojibway tribes. Generally these groups saw the Sioux as enemies and as competitors for the buffalo, the major resource of the region. This antipathy also prevailed among the agriculturally oriented Mandan, Hidatsa, and Arikara, or Ree, peoples of the big bend of the Missouri. Finally, Sioux warfare evolved from the village, and an alliance of even the most closely related Dakota tribes had never lasted very long. The Mdewakantons had been unable to convince the majority of the Sissetons and Wahpetons to join them earlier; bringing the western Sioux tribes into the war could hardly have been viewed as an easy matter.

The problems that had prevented Little Crow from dominating the war at its outset also were magnified on the plains. Although two to three hundred Mdewakantons had fled the Minnesota valley with Little Crow, only a handful of the warriors were from his own band. Despite his position as the symbol of the rebellion to whites in the Upper Midwest, he had little control over the war and would have even less influence with the very groups he wanted to rally to the cause. Traditionally young Sioux warriors had many reasons for going to war, but the two strongest were to gain glory and to fulfill obligations to family members and bands. It seemed almost contradictory for Little Crow to ask others for aid when many of his own band members had defied him.

On the other hand, there were certain advantages to carrying on the war from the plains. The Mdewakantons had fought as allies of the British during the War of 1812, and Taoyateduta hoped that the people of Canada would, at the very least, offer the Sioux a sanctuary. Geography as a factor also worked for his plan; the eastern Dakota plains had never been penetrated by a large American army, and the Missouri River Yanktons and Yanktonais, who spent many months on the plains each year, would probably resist such an advance. Finally, the actions of Sibley's army on the upper Minnesota River would certainly be watched by the plains Sioux. If Sibley treated the Indians who surrendered liberally, Little Crow would find few Indian allies; harsh retribution, on the other hand, might provide a catalyst for an all-out plains war.

Unfortunately, Little Crow's decision to continue the war had not been unanimous. Many Mdewakantons believed that they would eventually starve on the Dakota plains, and despite the uncertainty of the army's retribution, large numbers of Dakota Indians decided to remain behind and trust in the benevolence of the Americans.[2] Mixed-bloods, who had contact with Sibley, had indicated since early September that the colonel intended to punish only those Indians who had killed white civilians.[3] Accordingly, when Sibley arrived at Camp Release on September 26, many warriors moved off to a safe distance and waited to see what would happen. To their surprise, Sibley marched his troops beyond the Indian camp, allowed the friendly Indians to turn over the white captives in an impressive ceremony, and did nothing else. With the exception of several dozen men who were arrested, Sibley did not even disarm the majority of the Indians at the friendly camp, some of whom had been involved in the fighting.[4] The belief that Sibley intended to treat the eastern Sioux liberally—at the very least as prisoners of war—and the fear of what would happen on the plains prompted many Indians to move quietly into Camp Release during the week after Sibley's arrival. The camp of most friendly

Indians increased from about 150 lodges on September 26 to 243 by early October. Three other scattered camps were captured by a handful of mounted men under Sibley's command; one contained Cut Nose, a major leader of the soldiers' lodge, and another was surrounded some seventy miles west of Camp Release.[5] The colonel's surprisingly benign policies had resulted in the concentration at Camp Release of about 2,200 people, mostly Mdewakantons, many of whom had been involved in the various battles and some of whom had killed civilians.

Sibley made no move to arrest the Dakota participants in the war until October 11 when he concluded that those who wanted to had surrendered. Troops then surrounded Camp Release, as well as a second compound of Indians relocated near Yellow Medicine. As the Dakota warriors surrendered, they were disarmed and brought in front of a military commission to be tried, a procedure that had never been used on Indians by the nineteenth-century American army. On some days, several dozen men appeared in court. Although the Dakotas did not realize it at the time, their simple admission to being at one of the battles and firing a gun constituted evidence of guilt. The vast majority of Indians so judged received the death penalty.[6] Log prisons had been built in the meantime, and chains had been brought up from St. Paul. By November 4 the tribunal had condemned 303 men, or three-fourths of the captured Mdewakantons, and moved them to Mankato to await execution.[7]

In the case of Little Crow's band, the trial records reveal that about half of the forty-odd men who served under the chief stayed behind rather than flee. Of those at Camp Release, seventeen faced the military commission; two were judged guilty of killing civilians and of rape. While twelve were convicted for participating in battles, the evidence against them was suspect at best. Three received aquittals, having played no part in the war, and six others were never brought to trial, surfacing as army scouts a year later. This left sixteen to eighteen men unaccounted for and presumably with the chief on the plains. Among those who left with Little Crow, most were undoubtedly close relatives. The group included his half-brothers, White Spider, Passing Daylight, and His Big End, his son Wowinape, and Heyoka, his son-in-law. His Sisseton brother-in-law, Peter Tapetatanka, apparently left with him and then returned to surrender.[8]

While the state military command had some reservations about the legality of trying Indians, or civilians, by a military tribunal and there was even a basic question of whether Sibley, as the commander in the field, had the right to organize the court, Sibley felt sure that he had acted properly and intended to execute the guilty en masse.[9] Washington officials, however, demanded to see the trial transcripts and soon discovered major flaws. Minnesota politicians had claimed on the floors of Congress that Dakota men had raped every white captive woman; the evidence, on the other hand, showed that only two had been assaulted.[10] In addition, many Indians argued that they had been compelled to go to the various battles by the soldiers' lodge and that they fought unwillingly, hurting no one. When it came to determining which Indians had actually killed civilians, only in a few cases could eyewitnesses be produced to verify such charges. After examining the flimsy evidence, often consisting of only a paragraph of testimony, Abraham Lincoln selected thirty-nine of the most obvious offenders and signed their death warrants. They received notice of their fate a few days before the actual execution, scheduled for December 26.[11]

Despite the increasing intemperate weather, the white citizenry of Minnesota flocked into Mankato days before the mass execution. A large square gallows had been erected to accommodate all the condemned men at once, making it the largest mass execution in American history. The army allowed the condemned Indians to prepare in whatever fashion they wanted, and many spent their final day painting their bodies. A last minute reprieve saved one man from the gallows; those less fortunate talked with missionaries and asked for cigars and pipes so that they might smoke. As they marched to the gallows, many started singing their death songs, while others, "deeply affected with the awful scene through which they were about to pass," attempted to brace themselves as soldiers put them on the scaffold and cinched the ropes around their necks. Once in place, the single rope holding the support mechanism under them was severed. While the vast crowd of spectators rose up in one long, protracted cheer at the scene before them, the long-awaited moment was soon over and the crowd dispersed. For many Minnesotans, the "Great Sioux War" had finally ended.[12]

Soon thereafter, the remaining Dakota Indians held in captivity were moved out of the state. The government sent 326 men to a prison in Davenport, Iowa. Housed in close quarters and fed from stores that most were unaccustomed to, more than one-third died over the three-year term of their imprisonment. Their dependents, initially quartered below Fort Snelling, suffered nearly as severely. The army tried to keep them separated from angry civilians but often failed. By spring, most were happy to learn that they would be moved to a barren location near Crow Creek on the upper Missouri River. Once there, many of these people died of starvation. The remnant received a more hospitable reservation farther down the Missouri near Santee, Nebraska, in 1866.[13]

The departure of the Indians left only an occasional Sioux scout in the

This photograph is identified only as Little Crow's wife and children and was taken at Fort Snelling in spring 1864. The woman is probably either Saiceyewin (Isabelle Wakeman) or Makatowin (Eva Rice). The identity of the children is not known.

Male Dakota captives, photographed at Fort Snelling in spring 1864: Otadan (Plenty), White Spider, Tachunkdahupa, Mahpiyakanhte, Wowinape, and unidentified

*Wowinape posed for
J. E. Whitney in
February 1864.*

*Once Little Crow's body had been identified, the state of
Minnesota paid Nathan Lamson a bounty of five hundred dollars.
Note the Indian who adorns the check.*

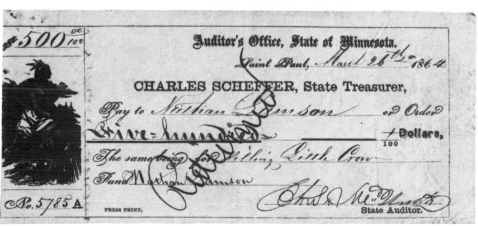

state working for the army. Sibley, Brown, and the missionaries had recruited Dakota scouts early in the war, and a formal organization, including several Renvilles, John Moore, Thomas A. Robertson, and a number of other former mission Indians or their relatives received commissions in February 1863. The scouts received the difficult task of preventing the Mdewakantons with Little Crow from causing more havoc on the Minnesota frontier. From the beginning, they tried to coax as many hostile Indians as possible into surrendering, one of their small parties reaching Little Crow's camp while Sibley was still assembling Mdewakanton Indians near Camp Release in October 1862. The scouting party found Little Crow camped with Standing Buffalo's band, made up mostly of Sissetons, about twenty miles north of Big Stone Lake. The scouts carried with them a letter from Sibley addressed to Standing Buffalo, calling upon him to refuse aid to Little Crow and surrender.[14]

Standing Buffalo's people debated the text of Sibley's letter as well as Little Crow's continued appeals to them for assistance. During the councils, Little Crow argued that Sibley would soon arrive at the head of a large army with the intention of annihilating all the Sioux people, including the Sissetons. His words provoked such fear that a few Sissetons who had not been involved in the war fled out onto the plains while the discussions were underway. Among those leaving was old Wakanmani, who had not participated in the fighting and whose sons, Gray Foot and Sounding Heavens, had studied in mission classes at Lac qui Parle with Little Crow.[15]

When the Sissetons finally reached a decision, Standing Buffalo summed up the consensus of his people in a speech that blamed Little Crow for the war. "You have already made much trouble for my people," Standing Buffalo told Little Crow. "Go to Canada or where you please, but go away from me and off the lands of my people." The reluctance of key Sisseton and Wahpeton leaders to join Little Crow hurt his chances for an alliance. The Mdewakantons then hesitantly agreed to move away from the Sisseton and Wahpeton camp. Even so, Standing Buffalo also refused Sibley's offer to surrender. Large numbers of Sissetons had participated in the second assault on Fort Ridgely; others briefly attacked Fort Abercrombie. While Standing Buffalo had not sympathized with the war effort, so many of his young men had been involved that he feared what the Americans would do. By early winter, most of the Sissetons and Wahpetons—nearly four thousand people—had moved their camps to the shores of Devil's Lake, hoping to avoid a confrontation.[16]

Little Crow and the Mdewakanton soldiers left the regions above Big Stone Lake in early October and headed in a northwesterly direction out onto the Dakota plains. Although their movements are difficult to trace, several white captives were with the party, and one boy of seventeen, John Euni, left a narrative of his odyssey with them. The camp, consisting of thirty lodges or about three hundred people, first halted southwest of Devil's Lake where the Mdewakantons stayed for a week. Little Crow and most of the men used the respite to travel to Devil's Lake to survey the political scene. Euni and nine lodges of people then turned southwest to the Missouri River where they camped, on and off, with over five hundred lodges of Yanktons, who were spread along the Missouri for fifty to a hundred miles above the fur-trade center of Fort Pierre. In early December, Little Crow rejoined the camp that contained Euni, increasing the Mdewakanton population on the Missouri to sixty lodges. Young Euni estimated that the chief had 135 men with him.[17]

Shortly after arriving on the Missouri, Little Crow once again took up the task of forming a coalition of plains tribes. He first made overtures to the Yanktons and Yanktonais. But these western relatives of the Mdewakantons showed little inclination to join Little Crow's rebellion even though they listened to the chief's arguments for nearly a month. A white observer reported that sometime just before Christmas, the Yanktons and Yanktonais broke camp and departed, some of them leaving in a bad humor. Apparently Little Crow had urged them to attack the trading post at Fort Pierre; some Yanktons responded by sending a large force to guard their traders from the Mdewakantons.[18]

This rebuff prompted Little Crow to move farther upriver, the Mdewakantons traveling for four days. They crossed into what is today North Dakota and established a camp at Painted Woods. The intention of this move was to open negotiations with the Mandan, Hidatsa, and Arikara peoples located roughly fifty miles above Little Crow's camp and near present-day Bismarck, North Dakota. While the Sioux had seldom sought peaceful ties with these river tribes and more frequently than not had raided their villages, Little Crow needed allies, and he soon sent his best envoys to treat for peace. They approached the Mandans in the accepted fashion for peace, as one account notes, "dancing, whooping, and firing of guns, and making as much bluster and noise as possible," all the time holding the peace pipe aloft, the sign to put past grievances away and establish friendly ties. Such actions had been employed for centuries in initiating commercial contact based upon the creation of temporary kinship bonds that were symbolized by various rituals, including the smoking of peace pipes. But the Mandans opened fire, and some Arikaras enveloped the delegation, nearly cutting off its retreat. Eight Mdewakan-

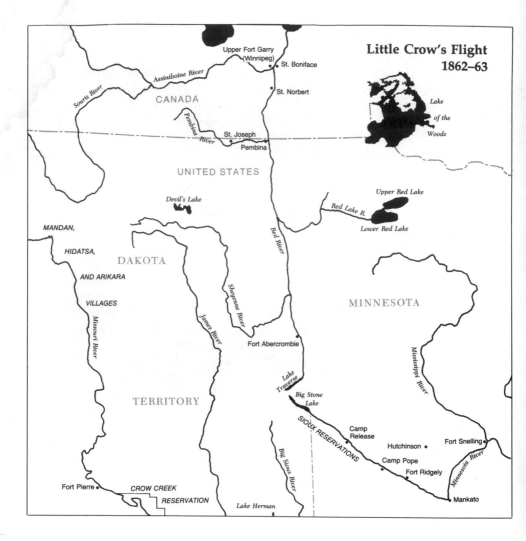

Little Crow's Flight
1862–63

tons were killed, and any chance of assistance from the river tribes quickly faded.[19]

Meanwhile, envoys from the Sisseton and Wahpeton tribes turned northeast to open negotiations with the British in Canada. During the fighting on the Minnesota River, the Mdewakantons had often expressed a belief that the British would come to their aid. Little Crow's grandfather had fought for the British during the War of 1812, and many of the traders who remained in Dakota lands after the war held strong sympathies toward Great Britain. Nevertheless, Little Crow was slow to test such long-neglected ties. He was also engaged in negotiations with Missouri River Indians, whom he thought would be more likely to support his cause. Thus Little Crow elected to stay behind when, in late December, a party of Standing Buffalo's people traveled to Fort Garry in Canada to see the British. About a dozen Mdewakantons went along to hear what the British would say.[20]

The Dakota delegation of eighty men and six women arrived at St. Norbert, south of Fort Garry, on December 27 and went into council with William McTavish, the governor of the Red River colony, and Alexander Grant Dallas, the governor of the Hudson's Bay Company. Bishop Taché, the leading cleric in the colony, also attended the conference and later preached a sermon to the delegation. While Dallas tried to convince the Indians to end their trip at St. Norbert, the Indians refused and went on to St. Boniface, spending one night inside the gates of Upper Fort Garry. The Sioux made few demands in their councils with Canadian officials, only pointing to the long-standing ties of friendship that had once existed between the British and the Sioux.[21] McTavish, however, suspected that the real purpose of their trip was to ferret out the views of the substantial métis population. The métis demonstrated concern over the Sioux visit, even brandishing arms at times, but they did not start trouble.[22]

The journey of Sioux Indians to Fort Garry came at a difficult time for the British colony. While Canadian officials told the leaders of the party upon their departure that it would be better for all concerned if the Indians did not return, they lacked military forces with which to enforce such a demand. The "Canadian rifles," a regular army force, had been withdrawn the year before, and British officials in the east soon concluded that the supposed Indian threat did not warrant their return. Nevertheless, the Indians, were they to remain, had to be fed and protected from the surrounding tribes, tasks that consumed resources. Food in the colony always had been precious—the métis did little farming—and the fears that the Cree and Ojibway Indians would attack the party and bring frontier war to the colony were very real.[23]

Rather than leave the British alone, however, after Christmas the eastern Sioux bands, both those still at war and those professing peace, turned increasingly to Canada for assistance. Standing Buffalo wrote Governor Dallas in February asking him to intercede with Sibley and obtain peace for the Sissetons. His Sisseton people still seemed divided over the war, no doubt fearful that if they surrendered they would be executed.[24] More importantly, a group of Mdewakanton soldiers from Devil's Lake began courting the Ojibway near and east of Pembina, old enemies who could hardly be expected to give them military assistance. Even so, when the Dakota Indians supplied presents in large numbers—the symbols of creating meaningful kinship ties—and even offered their women in marriage to the Ojibway to cement these ties, representatives of the Turtle Mountain and Leech Lake bands accepted. Formal ceremonies establishing friendly bonds followed, and for at least a short time the chances of developing an alliance improved. James Whitehead, a trader at Leech Lake, feared the outcome: "Whites might be driven out of northern Minnesota and southern Canada and trade between the two regions severed."[25]

The efforts to build friendly relations with Canada and its inhabitants went a step further when fifteen lodges of Sioux, mostly Mdewakantons, moved across the border in February 1863 and camped north of St. Joseph, a small métis village some thirty miles west of Pembina. Slowly, the number of Sioux increased to several hundred. The inhabitants of St. Joseph showed alarm over the incursion at first, but within a month they recognized that the Dakotas wanted only to trade for food. Father A. André, the parish priest at St. Joseph, visited their camp regularly and established a good relationship with the Mdewakantons.[26] By late spring he even found them willing to trade three white boys who had been adopted by the tribe as a result of the Minnesota war. Father André soon noticed, however, that the Mdewakantons had very little food, and if they stayed long, they would cause famine. The two traders at the village made no effort to conserve food, giving the Indians whatever they wanted in exchange for the plundered goods they still possessed.[27]

The rejection that Little Crow and his following received on the Missouri, coupled with the seemingly encouraging signs of support coming from Canada, convinced Little Crow to move back to Devil's Lake in early February, his camp of just over a hundred men taking up a militarily strong position on a peninsula on the north side of the lake near Burnt Island. While only little patches of snow hindered their progress and buffalo remained plentiful, the trip caused some hardship, and a few of Little Crow's followers decided against remaining with him. (Whether they rejected his leadership or simply reacted to the obvious difficulty of feeding large numbers of people on the plains during the winter is not clear.) Several British traders arrived in the vicinity of Devil's Lake by March and conducted a brisk trade, exchanging food for plundered goods. The Dakotas near the lake seemed to have sufficient meat, but they now lacked items that had become standard fare—flour, salt, tobacco, coffee, and ammunition. British and métis traders had no qualms about carrying such items to them.[28]

Because Little Crow was well aware of the importance to any alliance of these economic and social ties, he traveled to St. Joseph sometime in late April to open more formal negotiations with the British. In talks with Father André in early May, Little Crow indicated that he intended to ask the Canadians for land upon which to settle his people. To show loyalty, many of his men started wearing British medals bearing characterizations of George III, apparently given to the Mdewakantons after the War of 1812; for an ensign the tribe adopted the Union Jack. Little Crow spoke of the promises of assistance from the British and of the aid his people had offered during earlier wars. In addition, he left Father André with the clear impression that he wished to travel to Fort Garry and visit Hudson's Bay Company authorities.[29] To this effect, the chief sent two messengers to Governor Dallas in mid-May. A lower-ranking British official noted that these men professed "great friendship to the people [of the colony], but they vowed vengeance on the Americans."[30]

The efforts to move onto Canadian soil underscored a growing problem with the hoped-for alliance; while the Ojibway and métis seemed friendly, other Sioux tribes remained decidedly cool towards the Mdewakantons, making it difficult for Little Crow and his people to stay at Devil's Lake. Indeed, not long after the Mandans and Arikaras rejected them, Little Crow and his followers quarreled with a band of Yanktons. The Yanktons had come to visit the Mdewakantons from their hunting grounds to the south, but upon leaving Devil's Lake, they cut up several Mdewakanton lodges. These troubles encouraged Standing Buffalo and Sweet Corn, Sisseton and Wahpeton leaders, to speak forcefully for negotiating peace with Sibley. Standing Buffalo traveled to the Yanktons in order to advise them of his plans, while Indian scouts informed various plains Sioux groups of the new series of campaigns soon to be undertaken by the Americans. Sibley had been selected to command the one being organized on the upper Minnesota River to dislodge the Indians from Devil's Lake. Although Little Crow bragged that he would get behind the slow moving troops and attack the Minnesota frontier, many of the Sioux at or near Devil's Lake realized the truly serious nature of their situation. By May few Dakota Indians were listening to Little Crow or contemplating joining him.[31]

With his options fast dwindling, Little Crow turned to the British, hoping to receive from them the prestige and support necessary to build an alliance. On May 24, he reached Pembina with sixty men and about twenty women and announced his intentions of going on to Fort Garry. While at Pembina, the party camped near the Hudson's Bay Company post and opened negotiations with the Red Lake, Lake of the Woods, and Pembina Ojibway, some two hundred men in number. They openly discussed the war and emphasized the need of the Mdewakantons for a new country. Although details are sketchy, the delegates did attempt to agree upon a boundary separating the Sioux and Ojibway. Some Ojibway leaders remained aloof from the discussions, however, expressing a hatred for the Sioux that made any agreement difficult to enforce. The Pembina chief, Red Bear, was the most obstinate, meeting Little Crow while draped in an American flag. His mulish display was matched to some extent by several métis who lived near the post. They remained distant and constantly spread rumors among the Sioux, hoping to convince them to return to Devil's Lake.[32]

The Dakota delegation departed from Pembina for Fort Garry on May 27. Upon arriving two days later, they paraded into town aboard horses and mule-drawn wagons, dressed in all the finery they possessed. Most of the men wore "fine broadcloth coats and pants," spoils of war from the Minnesota frontier. The women appeared in "ladies' silk dresses and gaiters [leather leggings], and had parasols and umbrellas." Little Crow, though, upstaged the women, appearing in a black coat with velvet collar, a breechcloth of broadcloth, and deerskin leggings. He wore one fine shawl around his neck and another around his waist as a sash. As a sidearm, he carried a "seven shooter," a showy but delicate weapon. The firing mechanism broke while the party was at Fort Garry, and the chief discarded it.[33]

Little Crow, imposing and impressive in appearance by any standard, quickly made known to Canadian officials his reason for coming. He offered peace and friendship to the inhabitants of Canada, but he pledged warfare "to the knife" against the Americans. He told Governor Dallas that he and his people were "fighting with the rope around their necks," but he hoped that the British would provide them with arms and ammunition to carry on the war. The British, he said, had once promised such assistance when they had needed the help of the Sioux people. While Little Crow "hinted" at requesting a homeland, he never directly did so, perhaps realizing that the British had already decided against such a proposal.[34]

The presentation of these demands left many observers with the impression that Little Crow had acted in a "insolent, reckless and bold manner." At times he seemed to be testing Canadian authorities, as when Dallas refused a request for ammunition and guns; Little Crow responded haughtily that he did not need them anyway because he had plenty of firearms and ammunition with which to "kill Americans."[35] Likewise, the Sioux sensed that the Canadians could do little about their intended use of St. Joseph as a base of operation. This tough-minded facade on Little Crow's part, however, did not last throughout the three days of discussions, and before he departed, the chief asked Dallas if he might intercede with Sibley on behalf of the Mdewakantons.[36]

Little Crow had a brief opportunity to talk with newspaper reporters while at Fort Garry, a task that he clearly enjoyed. During these discussions, Little Crow made it obvious that he and his people knew of the treatment that Sibley afforded the Mdewakantons who stayed behind in October 1862. Little Crow had detailed information regarding the execution of the thirty-eight men at Mankato, and he had some understanding of what hardships the remainder of his people had undergone, including the detainment of the dependents at Fort Snelling and the imprisonment of their menfolk at Davenport, Iowa. The treatment of these people worried him, and he asked Governor Dallas if he would write Sibley and obtain the release of the prisoners. Little Crow argued that he had surrendered white prisoners at Camp Release without harming them, and he now hoped that Sibley would reciprocate. He even suggested that peace be negotiated, although he knew of the futility of such a gesture. While Dallas agreed to write the letter to Sibley, it did not result in any negotiations. It was, however, the one concession that Little Crow obtained, for upon leaving, he and his party received nothing more than a few presents and some food from the Canadians.[37]

Dallas was pleased to see the Sioux leave. He had no intention of helping them, although he pointed out to his superiors that the Indians had made no disturbances while in the colony. The governor's concerns stemmed no doubt from the delicate nature of relations between the United States and Canada over the Canadian West. Some Minnesota "expansionists" hoped to annex the lands governed by the Hudson's Bay Company, and an "American party" existed at Fort Garry that supported such a scheme. Nevertheless, Dallas also feared what the Algonquins (Crees and Ojibway), the Assiniboins, and the métis living near the fort might do. They distrusted the Sioux Indians much more so than did the Indians and mixed-bloods living near Pembina. Their young men had often clashed with the Dakotas in the past, and Dallas, disturbed over the likelihood that his Indians and mixed-bloods might start a general war, distributed large numbers of presents to Ojibway and Cree men to keep them quiet. When the Sioux departed, Dallas strongly suggested that they never return.[38]

Once back at St. Joseph, more disquieting news reached Little Crow and his people. Sibley was about to march, having massed his army on the upper Minnesota River at Camp Pope. The chief, with a small number of supporters, pushed on, leaving St. Joseph on June 4 for Devil's Lake, no doubt intending to try to persuade the Sioux there to join him. About twenty lodges of Mdewakantons decided to abandon Little Crow at this point, saying that they wanted, according to one account, "to give themselves up rather than to be caught in a trap with Little Crow." Since most of the people who fled with him were not of his band, Little Crow probably anticipated such desertions. Even so, he scoffed at this talk, telling several people before he took leave that he intended to attack the Minnesota frontier, and that, if Sibley wished to find him, he would be at "Yellow Medicine."[39]

More trouble for Little Crow surfaced at Devil's Lake where the non-Mdewakantons were hostile to him. The Sissetons and Wahpetons, although divided over the war, blamed Little Crow for their loss of annuities and for the approaching American threat. They feared that they might never be allowed to return to their planting grounds near Big Stone Lake and that Sibley intended to expand the war beyond the Minnesota River valley. More Mdewakantons also left Little Crow at this juncture, electing to stay with the Sissetons and Wahpetons.[40] Finding little or no assistance, Little Crow abandoned efforts for an alliance and decided to mount a raid on the Minnesota frontier, collecting several close associates and relatives. The group numbered seventeen men, including his son, Wowinape, and his son-in-law, Heyoka.[41] Although the identities of the remaining men are unknown, the number is nearly equal to the size of the contingent from his band that originally fled with him onto the plains the previous fall.

Little Crow never clearly explained why he wished to return to the settlements with so few warriors. He told several people that he intended simply to kill Americans. Yet he justified the raid to Wowinape by saying that he wished to steal a horse for each of his children—approximately

176

six were still living—before he died. A horse would be necessary for hunting buffalo if the Dakotas hoped to stay on the high plains, and virtually all of the animals taken out onto the plains the September before had perished during the winter.[42]

Nevertheless, such rationalizations disguise one other possible motivation for Little Crow's return to the Minnesota frontier. The previous fall, during the fighting near the agencies, Little Crow, in his several conversations with Susan Brown, revealed that he intended one day to return to the Big Woods for which he had so many pleasant memories. Even then Little Crow sensed that his return would result in his death. Yet he seemed unconcerned about such an outcome, secure in the fact that a better life awaited him.[43] As seen already by the generosity of leaders, self-sacrifice had always been a central motivating factor in the Dakota world view, and it often was manifested in the form of physical punishment necessary to obtain a vision, the direction gained from such visions benefiting the people as a whole. By extension, Dakota men saw death, the ultimate sacrifice, as a means to demonstrate one's commitment to assisting relatives. Blamed for the war by many Dakotas and now a source of divisiveness, Little Crow probably saw that the same destiny that had propelled him to a position of leadership demanded that he sacrifice his life.[44]

Seemingly aware that his final moments on earth were near at hand, Little Crow asked Wowinape to accompany him to Minnesota and "carry his [medicine] bundles." The ownership of such bundles ensured happiness and long life, and Dakota warriors who were about to face death often handed them down to close relatives.[45] The passing of the bundles also symbolized the transition in leadership from one generation to another.

The party of nineteen walked for many days before reaching the regions east of Yellow Medicine in late June. Two or three groups of men then broke off from the main party, one of them meeting and attacking the Amos Dustin family two miles north of Howard Lake and killing two people. Mrs. Dustin lived several hours after white neighbors found her. While one of the rescuers later indicated that she had identified Little Crow and his son as being in the party, the description of the attack brings the evidence into question. It does seem certain that Heyoka became involved in the killing of whites, however, as he later gave Little Crow a coat taken from a lone traveler, whose body was discovered sometime thereafter. Little Crow had the coat when he was killed.[46]

A day or two after the attack on the Dustins, the members of the party quarreled. Eight men went south and eight others, including Heyoka, went back to Canada. Little Crow refused to go with either group. Instead he stayed in the Big Woods with Wowinape, camping several miles north of Hutchinson. The berries had ripened, and Little Crow and his son spent many hours gathering them. Towards the evening of July 3, while busily engaged in picking, a sudden shot rang out, hitting Little Crow in the groin. Wowinape, much smaller and unarmed, hid in the brush, but his father grabbed the weapons lying on the ground beside him and returned fire. As he fired a second shot, a bullet instantaneously struck his weapon and lodged in his chest. The second bullet knocked him down, and he lay on his back in the raspberry patch. At that point, the shooting ended. But the wound in Little Crow's chest was mortal, and the Mdewakanton chief died shortly thereafter.[47]

Wowinape dressed his father in new moccasins for his trip into the afterlife, wrapped his body in a blanket, and departed. Little Crow had told his son to take both of the weapons as well as his medicine bundle and to locate his mother, who was camped near Devil's Lake. Traveling mostly at night, it took Wowinape a month to reach his destination. But when he arrived in early August, everyone was gone, having fled from Sibley's army. On August 10, scouts from the nearby army expedition captured the half-starved Wowinape. He had used his last bullet while hunting, and now weaponless, he surrendered peacefully. Before his imprisonment at Davenport, Iowa, he told authorities of his father's last days and death. Wowinape was released in 1866 and later lived near Redwood Falls, not far from where his father was killed.[48]

Meanwhile, the news of the killing of an Indian ten miles north of Hutchinson created a stir. The perpetrators of the deed, Nathan and Chauncey Lamson, became instant heroes, even though Chauncey had deserted his father—he later said that he assumed that the elder Lamson had been killed—and run back to Hutchinson with the news. When the news reached Hutchinson, a party of citizens and self-appointed militia went out to the scene of the killing and searched the area. They discovered Little Crow's body and promptly scalped him. Nathan Lamson later received an award of five hundred dollars from the state of Minnesota for the hair, and the trophy ultimately surfaced as a main attraction at the state historical society.[49] Minnesota's frontier population ignored the fact that whites had fired upon unidentified, seemingly unarmed people.

The death of Little Crow and the later dismemberment of his body symbolized in many ways the tragedy of his life and that of his nation. He wished to be memorialized as a great leader, but that dream ended when he and a handful of followers fled the Minnesota valley, leaving behind a fragmented and defeated people. Little Crow, however, should not be remembered as he was at this dark hour, defeated in battle, rejected by many of his own people, and destined for an ignoble death. His place in history should not depend solely upon his role in the war, a conflict that heaped little glory on any of the participants, Indian or otherwise. To portray him in such a light only perpetuates myths.

It is the obligation of historians to separate myth from reality and, in the case of Indian biography, to show how members of a minority group responded to acculturational pressures and tried to reshape them. While the white population of Minnesota came to see Little Crow as the symbol of the savagery inherent in the 1862 war, in reality he spent his entire adult life supporting a policy of accommodation that sought to avoid just such a war. His program propelled him into a position of leadership, and it provided him with the mechanism needed to reshape his society during a period when change was inevitable. Few Indian leaders possessed Little Crow's vision, and few understood the white man as well as he did. He realized the futility of war with the Americans and played a major role in defusing troubles in the 1850s. He negotiated treaties with the United States and patiently waited for the government to fulfill the terms of them. But this policy of accommodation failed because it ultimately required compromise and understanding on the part of white Americans and the federal government. Even after Washington bureaucrats lied to him and discredited him among his own people, he remained supportive of reservation officials and, above all, an advocate of peace. This is the tragedy of Little Crow's life.

Little Crow was a consistent spokesman for the Mdewakanton Sioux, a man who sought power and honors, as does any politician, but who had an accurate vision of what realistically was necessary in order to coexist with the advancing Americans. He supported as much as possible the traditional world view that went with being an Indian; yet he adopted from the white world whatever seemed necessary to survive. When forced to chose between the two worlds in which he tried to live, however, he elected to side with that of his ancestors, despite the possibility that a majority of his relatives would refuse to accept such a decision and oppose the war. For a Sioux Indian, no choice could have been more difficult; the agony of it brought him back to the Minnesota frontier where he sought death and an ultimate release from the earthly world that had been lost to him forever.

Epilogue:
The Final Journey

THROUGHOUT the three decades following his death, Little Crow's bones fell into the hands of various individuals who kept them as souvenirs. Frank Powell donated the skull to the Minnesota Historical Society in 1896.[1] It, along with the scalp lock, which the state already owned, and the forearms, which the society received at about the same time, were put on display in a case in the society's museum. As the frontier closed and Minnesota entered a new era, the curiosities became an embarrassment. The display was quietly dismantled in the early twentieth century, and the remains of Little Crow were placed on a shelf, ironically not more than a dozen miles from the place of his birth. Finally in 1971 at the request of Little Crow's grandson and with the support of the society, the remains were transported to South Dakota by Alan R. Woolworth of the society's staff and buried in a private family plot.[2] So passed from the scene one of the more remarkable Indian leaders of America's frontier, a man who had become an enigma to whites and Indians alike.

Appendix 1:
A Note on Little Crow's Genealogy

THE WRITING of Indian biography by necessity requires genealogical research. Historically, tribal societies like the Dakota placed a strong emphasis upon relationships, especially societies such as the eastern Sioux where very few families dominated bands and where members of those bands were forced to go outside their community (exogamy) in order to find mates. Put simply, kinship provided the socioeconomic glue that held early Dakota villages together, while ties outside the band provided the visibility that resulted in rising political influence. In other words, knowing the nature and extent of Little Crow's Dakota-white kinship network can prove helpful in determining his political motives and actions.

Any assessment of Dakota genealogy must unfortunately be prefaced with a cautionary word. Formed around the extended family and divided along lines of gender, the kinship structure of the Sioux people differed significantly from European patterns. Thus, terms equivalent to father, mother, brother, cousin, and so forth in European society had different meanings in the Sioux world. In Dakota, the term father could mean any of a number of men, including the biological father, his brothers, and his male parallel and cross-cousins. When using the Dakota term for elder brother, a Dakota male was probably referring to his biological brother for whom he held the deepest respect, while the term denoting younger brother brought a meaning of less importance that could even include the men who married sisters. The same seems to be true for other terms. For example, when the term "cousin" appears in nineteenth-century records, it could refer to a variety of relationships, including the male or female cross-cousin of an individual, meaning the offspring of father's sister's son, mother's brother's son, father's sister's daughter, or mother's brother's daughter.[1] It could also be employed when referring to a distant relative. Little Crow, for example, commonly called Antoine J. Campbell, a relative far removed from his lineage, "cousin." While the Dakota understood how their kinship system worked, modern researchers still find it difficult to comprehend. Cultural anthropologists working in the field in the 1970s discovered discrepancies, with Indian informants using "English" definitions when the researcher assumed the opposite.[2]

To add confusion, there is some question as to whether Dakota kinship definitions and usages have changed in the course of the last two centuries. Some cultural anthropologists, for example, argue that in Sioux society blood may have been less a factor in kinship ties than the feelings of solidarity that evolved from "fictive," or non-blood, relationships.[3] There may be much to this argument, but the type of evidence that exists, at least in the early nineteenth century, frequently precludes any assessment of this idea.

What insights can be gleaned from the sources suggest that Dakota men such as Little Crow listened carefully to their relatives, supported them when necessary, and often hunted with them. Affine relations, or those connecting men by blood, were always important; those developed by ceremony frequently depended upon how strongly individuals reinforced them. Furthermore, evidence shows that both parallel and opposite-sex relatives were highly esteemed by Dakota individuals, although friction and harassment could also characterize opposite-sex relationships.[4] Simply knowing the Little Crow genealogy, then, helps in understanding this man. Despite acknowledged problems with sources and working under the realization that many questions regarding kinship systems remain unanswered, it is important to attempt a reconstruction of Little Crow's kinship network.

There is a second reason for tracing the Little Crow genealogy. Much of the Indian history written has come from the pens of white historians. Understandably, Indians have frequently found fault with the interpretations offered, mostly because the authors write about Indians as a group, cultural or political, and fail to learn about Indians as people. The Dakotas believe that relationships are crucially important, and as much for their sake as any other, it is essential to learn as much as possible about the Little Crow family. Indeed, the discussion of lineage that follows, although it may at times seem antiquarian, will at least illustrate some understanding of the family and friends of the subject of this biography.

Genealogy also demonstrates the value of the tiyośpaye, or lodge group, in Dakota society. The evolution of a kinship network began for Little Crow at birth, as inhabitants of a Sioux village were interrelated in some fashion and belonged to the same lodge group. Thus if Taoyateduta's

father Big Thunder followed the general rules of exogamy accepted by
the Dakota people—evidence suggests that most men certainly did—then
he automatically looked for eligible mates among villages other than his
own, for it was unlawful to marry among close kin.[5] The first woman
whom he took as a wife was Miniokadawin, or Woman Planting in Water.
She came from the Wabasha band and likely was related to Wabasha,
suggesting that Big Thunder married well. She apparently left Big Thunder
at an early date, probably in the 1820s, after the Kaposia chief took two
more wives. She bore Big Thunder a son, who, as tradition dictated, was
initially called Caske, meaning first male born. This name would change
to Taoyateduta, or His Red Nation, at adulthood.[6] As a young man,
Taoyateduta spent a considerable amount of time hunting with Jack Frazer,
a mixed-blood member of Red Wing's band. Frazer's uncle was the chief,
Wakute. The Red Wing and Wabasha bands were very closely allied, the
former probably being a faction of the latter. Although no genealogical
evidence exists to demonstrate blood ties between the two young men,
they probably were closely related.[7]

Big Thunder's other two wives bore a large family. Taoyateduta had
ten half-brothers and ten half-sisters.[8] These children did not fare well
in life. Two half-brothers, Tamazawakan and Dowan, were killed during
a raid on the Ojibway in 1841. One of these men was likely the "son of
Little Crow" reported by agent Taliaferro as being married at Black Dog's
village in 1835. Some evidence suggests that Big Thunder had hopes that
one of these young men would succeed him as chief.[9] Such expectations
perhaps can be explained by Taoyateduta's early departure from the village, or even his mother's apparent abandonment of Big Thunder. Yet
another possible explanation is Taoyateduta's failure to demonstrate
leadership abilities early in life.

Sources reveal information on six of the other eight half-brothers. Two
tried to kill Little Crow in May 1846 at Kaposia and were killed shortly
thereafter at the new chief's orders.[10] Relatives of Little Crow writing at
the turn of the century never did know their names or their ages, but
simple chronology suggests that they, along with the two half-brothers
killed by the Ojibway, were the sons of Big Thunder's second wife. Such
an assumption seems warranted only because sources identify the chief's
third wife, a Wahpeton woman named Wikusauwin. One of her sons,
Unktomiska, or White Spider, later became an important ally of Little
Crow's, an unusual alliance had it been his full-brothers whom Little
Crow had ordered killed.[11]

The same rationale suggests that three other half-brothers of Little

Crow were sons of Wikusauwi*n*. These men were Su*n*kacisti*nn*a, or Little Dog, A*n*pahiyaye, or Passing Daylight, and Tai*n*kpaota, or His Big End. Little Dog sided with Little Crow in the dispute over the chieftainship in 1846, killing one of the half-brothers who attempted to depose Little Crow. Little Dog fled to the plains with Little Crow after the Mdewakanton defeat and was killed by Arikara Indians in December 1862.[12] Passing Daylight also fled with Little Crow out onto the plains, surrendered to United States authorities at Pembina in January 1864, served two years in prison at Davenport, Iowa, and ultimately farmed in Nebraska where he died in 1896. Sometime after the war, he adopted the name Moses Wakeman (not to be confused with the son of White Spider also called Moses Wakeman).[13] Little is known about His Big End other than that he surrendered with Passing Daylight and received a prison term.[14]

The best known of the half-brothers was U*n*ktomiska, or White Spider. He was born to Wikusauwi*n* in July 1831 and was still a boy when Little Crow became chief of his village. White Spider participated in the war, fighting bravely by the side of Taoyateduta. Even so, in a narrative written after the war he emphasized that he spent most of his time trying to save whites from the hostiles. He stayed with Little Crow on the plains for some months, but apparently refused to join the chief on his last raid into Minnesota. He surrendered at Pembina in 1864, having with him one wife and three children. After serving two years in prison at Davenport, Iowa, he converted to Christianity and settled at Flandreau, Dakota Territory, and later at Morton, Minnesota. Adopting the English name John C. Wakeman, he worked as a mail carrier for many years, dying at his home in April 1902.[15]

The Sioux emphasized the need of a brother to be loyal and helpful, especially in time of war. Given this premise, it is interesting to speculate on Little Crow's relationship with his many half-brothers. The fact that his mother left Kaposia early probably had an impact on how he was perceived by his close kin. Certainly the two young men who challenged him for the chieftainship showed little respect for his wishes. Such a struggle was notable in Sioux society, as indicated by the large number of sources that reported it. In addition, once Little Crow was established at Kaposia as chief his other, younger half-brothers accepted his authority without question and remained loyal. Of the four, at least three stayed at Kaposia and later lived in the Little Crow village at Redwood. White Spider and Little Dog appear on the annuity rolls in 1854, 1856, and 1857. A*n*pahiyaye, or Passing Daylight, shows up on the annuity roll of 1860, without dependents. Tai*n*kpaota never does appear on the Little

Crow roll, suggesting that he either married and left the band or was too young to be counted.[16]

Little Crow had at least one sister who married a leading elder in his band. Her name was Taśinaśapawin, or Her Black Shawl, or in English, Elizabeth Westman. She died at Morton, Minnesota, in 1890. Her Black Shawl became the wife of Makanahotonmani, who did not play an important role in the war but had signed the Treaty of Mendota in 1851. Wamditanka, or Big Eagle, was also the cousin (perhaps mother's brother's son) of White Spider. In addition, Big Eagle's brother was the Mdewakanton subchief Medicine Bottle, or Wakanoźanoźan.[17] Medicine Bottle led the Kaposia soldiers' lodge during the 1851 treaty negotiation and encouraged Little Crow to step forward and sign the treaty first. Makanahotonmani, Big Eagle, and Medicine Bottle were important Kaposia men who were related to Taoyateduta through marriage. All three, however, turned to farming, Makanahotonmani and Medicine Bottle leaving the Little Crow village for the "farmer band" led by White Dog in 1858 or 1859.[18]

Little Crow probably realized at an early age that Dakota men with political ambitions must attempt to build kinship networks outside of one's band and tribe. This explains why he turned to the Wahpekute tribe for a wife in the early 1830s. Very little information exists on the origins of the two women whom he took as wives among the Wahpekutes, except a suggestion in an early secondary source that they were the daughters of a leading chief of the Wahpekute people and that they produced two sons and a daughter. Later relatives of Little Crow who survived the war never knew the names of the wives or their children.[19]

The third marriage contracted by Little Crow was with Mazaiyaġewin, or Iron Cluster Woman, the eldest daughter of the Wahpeton (although he is usually identified as a Sisseton) chief Inyangmani of Lac qui Parle. The marriage took place in 1838, Little Crow being roughly twenty-six years of age.[20] Mazaiyaġewin, bore Taoyateduta seven children, only one of whom lived past infancy. The survivor was Wowinape.[21] Little Crow married three other daughters of Inyangmani. Inyangmani accepted Little Crow's offer for Saiceyewin, or Isabelle Wakeman in later life, according to one account, "while he was drunk, and she but ten years of age." This marriage produced two boys and three girls, for whom little information exists.[22] The third daughter taken was Makatowin, or Blue Earth. She was born about 1831 and later took the English name Eva Rice, living at least to the age of eighty-five. Eva became Little Crow's wife sometime between 1846 and 1853. She had five children by Little Crow, two of whom were living at the time of the war.[23] The fourth sister married by

Taoyateduta was Manikiyahewi*n*, who according to mission records was born in 1838. She went to live with Little Crow sometime after 1853 and bore him three children, none of whom survived. In 1864, Manikiyahewi*n* married David Wells, a prisoner at Davenport, Iowa. She died on March 3, 1900.[24]

These marriages produced only five children who survived the war. Three were girls, including Jane Williams, Hannah Redearth, and Eugenia La Moure. The two sons who survived were Wowi*n*ape, who was with Little Crow at his death, and Tateiyahnamani, later called Thomas Wakeman. Little Crow had at least one son-in-law, who went by the name Heyoka, or Clown. He married the daughter of Saiceyewin. Heyoka joined a war party in August 1862 that went into Ojibway country, and he later fled to Canada with his father-in-law. Heyoka was also with Little Crow on his last raid into Minnesota in June-July 1863. He returned from Canada in 1881 and was reported living on a farm on the Sisseton Reservation in 1915.[25]

Little Crow's marriage to the daughters of I*n*yangmani also made him a relative of the chief's two sons, called by the missionaries Peter Tapetata*n*ka and Henok Appearing Cloud. Little Crow became very close to Peter, as brother-in-laws were treated like cross-cousins. In other words, Peter would at least listen to Little Crow's advice, and vice-versa. This relationship helps to explain why Peter gave up teaching for the missionaries in the 1850s after Little Crow asked him to stop.[26]

The kinship ties that Little Crow developed outside his immediate family were valuable in a political sense and interesting in relation to what Little Crow came to think of whites. Some of the female members of Little Crow's family married whites or mixed-bloods. Such ties proved valuable when it came to negotiating with the United States government. The major link came through the marriage of Joseph Renville, Senior, to a granddaughter of Cetanwakanmani, Little Crow's grandfather. Although a full-blood Kaposia girl, Renville's wife took the name Mary Renville. Taoyateduta was Mary Renville's mother's brother's son, or male cross-cousin.[27] It is difficult to determine how cross-cousins responded to each other in Dakota society, but such a relationship was usually characterized by respect among males, and when members of the opposite sex were involved, sexual playfulness. Joseph and Mary Renville produced a large family, including eight surviving children: Joseph, Antoine, Michel, John B., Angeline, Rosalie, Madeline, and Marguerite. Four of these children— Joseph, Antoine, Angeline, and Rosalie—moved to Kaposia in the late 1840s and received annuities as part of Little Crow's band.[28] When necessary, then, the Renvilles considered themselves to be Mdewakantons and members of Little Crow's family.

The Renville connection took yet another curious line, which resulted in even stronger ties with the Little Crow family. Joseph Renville, Senior's, father, identified in the records as Joseph Rainville, took a woman from the Kaposia band, named Miniyuhe, who was of the Little Crow family. She was probably a daughter of Cetanwakanmani, or perhaps of his brother (he had a brother whom Taliaferro identified as "Estamuzza").[29] The marriage was no doubt possible since station was determined by the mother's lineage, meaning that Rainville's mother-in-law was from a band other than Kaposia. Such strong kinship ties made Taoyateduta even more welcome at Lac qui Parle in the 1830s and 1840s, and it strengthened his relationships with Renville's children.

Several other kinship ties evolved from the Renville connection that proved valuable for Little Crow. The most interesting involves the families of Old Eve and Catherine Totedutawin, two important women who converted to the Protestant faith at the Lac qui Parle mission. Old Eve's husband was the brother of Joseph Rainville's Kaposia-born wife.[30] Thus all of Old Eve's children were cross-cousins of Mary Renville and therefore related to Little Crow. They included Wamdiokiya, Fearful Face, Maȟpiyawicaṡta, or Cloud Man, and Paul Mazakutemani. On the other hand, since Old Eve's husband was of the Little Crow family (see discussion of Rainville's wife), perhaps even a son of Cetanwakanmani, there is a strong possibility that Wamdiokiya, Fearful Face, Mazakutemani, and Cloud Man were all Little Crow's parallel cousins.[31] Either tie, through Mary Renville or Old Eve's husband, would help explain Little Crow's interest in the mission school at Lac qui Parle, since so many of his relatives were enrolled, and further explains his desire to preserve peace with the friendly Sioux and their spokesman, Paul Mazakutemani, during the war.

Catherine Totedutawin's relationship with Little Crow is interesting because it was her son, Lorenzo Lawrence, who stood by the chief's side when he was shot in 1846. Lorenzo also killed one of Little Crow's half-brothers shortly thereafter, thus helping Taoyateduta secure his position as chief.[32] Lorenzo's relationship with Little Crow comes through his mother's marriage with Left Hand, who was Mary Renville's brother and Little Crow's cross-cousin. Although this tie is not found in any records, it can be substantiated from the published books and correspondence of the American Board missionaries at Lac qui Parle. Catherine Totedutawin converted to Christianity in 1837 and was an active member of the Dakota

Christian community until her death. When her husband Left Hand applied for admission in 1841, however, the missionaries refused him based upon his polygamous marriage. Shortly after Left Hand's death in 1847, missionary Riggs wrote that one of his wives "has well maintained the character of a sincere disciple of Jesus," and that of his children, some "have become educated and conformed to the customs and habits of civilized men." The wife mentioned was clearly Catherine. In turn, all of Catherine's children were tied to the mission. They included Lorenzo, Joseph Kawanke, and Sarah. Lorenzo and Joseph became farmers in the 1850s and helped save whites during the war.[33]

One other close relative of Little Crow's who warrants some consideration is Joseph Napeśniduta. Although no information exists on his father, his mother was Mary Renville's sister. He remained a member of the Little Crow band throughout the 1840s and 1850s, being one of the first band members to adopt farming. Riggs suggested that he formed the "*nucleus* of the party of progress" at Kaposia.[34]

The importance of cousins in Little Crow's kinship network is difficult to assess. The chief seemed at times to listen carefully to such relatives and receive assistance from them. His interest in the mission school and Christianity at Lac qui Parle clearly evolved from his ties with the likes of Lorenzo Lawrence, Left Hand, and Mary and Joseph Renville. And Wamdiokiya was the premier scholar of the school, acting at times as a teacher. Once the missionaries received the support of Joseph Renville, then, it followed that Renville's relatives would listen to the missionaries, since they were obligated to heed the advice of Renville. Little Crow, who arrived at Lac qui Parle in about 1837, seemed to fit this pattern, being perhaps eager to learn about a new religion but also wanting to please his relatives who came to support Christianity.

Several people important in Little Crow's life have blood lines that reach the chief through rather torturous paths. Indeed, sometimes genealogical ties can only be surmised. Perhaps the most interesting is Antoine Joseph (A. J.) Campbell. He was often identified by Little Crow as "cousin." His father was Scott Campbell, the well-known interpreter at the St. Peter's Agency who worked for so many years with agent Taliaferro. The elder Campbell was the son of Archibald John Campbell, who had married a Dakota woman. Little is known of this woman other than that she was a Wahpeton, suggesting that her father was of the Little Crow family.[35]

Better evidence exists tying Smokey Day, Little Crow's companion of the 1840s, to the chief's family circle. Smokey Day was the son of

Maḣpiyawicaśta, or Cloud Man, a Mdewakanton who helped to found the Lake Calhoun village in 1830. Cloud Man's close companion at Lake Calhoun, a man who most likely is his cousin, or perhaps even his brother, was "Keiyah," or more correctly Keya. Philander Prescott married Keya's full-blood daughter, Mary, and had several children, including Lucy Prescott Pettijohn. On one occasion, Lucy identifies Catherine Totedutawi*n* as her "grandmother." In the 1850s, Lucy adopted Lorenzo Lawrence's stepson, further confirming kinship ties with the children of Little Crow's cross-cousin Left Hand. Such ties help explain Little Crow's close relationship with Smokey Day.[36]

One final series of kinship ties connect Little Crow to the family of Joseph R. Brown, Indian agent for the eastern Sioux between 1857 and 1861. In 1840 Brown married a mixed-blood Dakota woman named Susan Frenier who was the daughter of Winona, a full-blood Sisseton woman and Narcisse Frenier. Frenier died about 1831, but by this time Winona had already married Victor Renville, who was to be killed by the Ojibway in 1833. She then married Joseph Akipa Renville. Akipa Renville was neither a Renville nor a Mdewakanton. He was a full-blood Wahpeton Indian whose brothers were the noted chiefs Mazamani, or Iron Walker, and Mazaśa, or Red Iron. But Akipa developed strong fictive kinship ties with the Renvilles and even adopted their name. He raised Susan Frenier along with several of his own children whom he had with Winona, Susan's mother. Among these children were Thomas and Charles Crawford. Victor Renville, Winona's second husband, was the brother of Joseph Renville of Lac qui Parle and also the father of Gabriel Renville. Gabriel, an important figure in the war, also played a major role in Dakota affairs after 1862.[37]

There are several conclusions that arise from the genealogical information available on Little Crow's life. First, most of his closest relatives, particularly his half-brothers, were quite young; the four half-brothers who were already dead by 1846 were much closer to the chief's own age. Accordingly, relationships outside the immediate family seemed at times to be more important to Taoyateduta. Parallel cousins, cross-cousins, and their children were often the chief's companions, and they stood by him, as in the case of Lorenzo Lawrence, even to the point of placing themselves in mortal danger. Yet by the time of the war, many of these relatives had joined the farmer bands and supported the organization of the friendly camp. Rather than fight, they tried to secure white captives from the Dakota soldiers. Such a situation made it difficult for Little Crow to pursue the war; indeed, this split with many of his relatives may have been the most tragic event in the chief's life.

Explanations exist for the failure of so many of Little Crow's close relatives to come to his support in 1862. Part of kinship obligation involved constant reinforcement, in the form of feasts and companionship. After Little Crow returned to Kaposia in 1846, he cut himself off from many of his Lac qui Parle relatives. They in turn settled on the upper reservation after 1853, rather than at Redwood. While Little Crow obviously tried to maintain ties with the people on the upper reservation, this was not always possible. Indeed, during the latter 1850s, the size of his village diminished every year, a decline that undoubtedly influenced the way in which the Sioux looked upon obligation and even kinship relations.

Appendix 2:
Genealogy of Little Crow

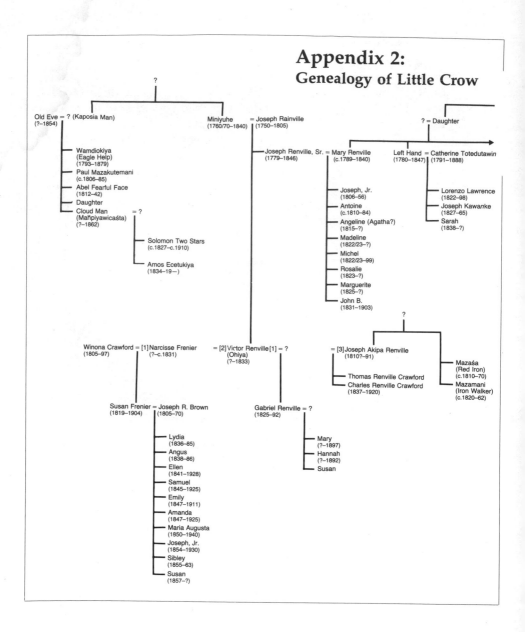

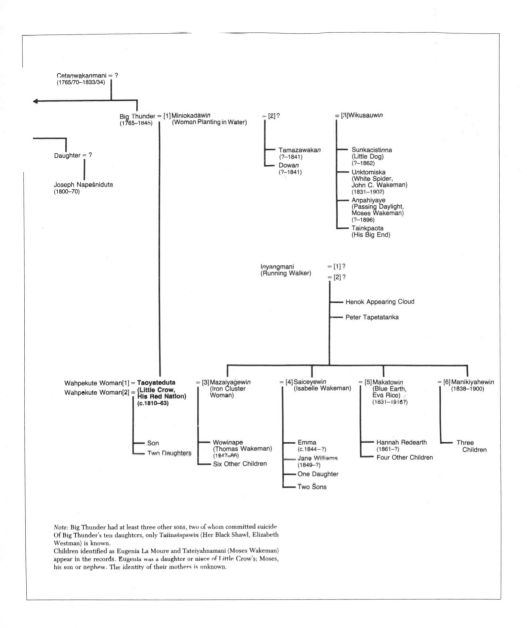

Cetanwakanmani = ?
(1765/70–1833/34)

Big Thunder = [1] Miniokadawin
(1765–1845)   (Woman Planting in Water)

Daughter = ?

Joseph Napeśniduta
(1800–70)

= [2] ?

Tamazawakan
(?–1841)
Dowan
(?–1841)

= [3] Wikusauwin

Sunkacistinna
(Little Dog)
(?–1862)
Unktomiska,
(White Spider,
John C. Wakeman)
(1831–1902)
Anpahiyaye
(Passing Daylight,
Moses Wakeman)
(?–1896)
Tainkpaota
(His Big End)

Inyangmani
(Running Walker)

= [1] ?
= [2] ?

Henok Appearing Cloud

Peter Tapetatanka

Wahpekute Woman[1] = Taoyateduta
Wahpekute Woman[2] = (Little Crow,
                      His Red Nation)
                      (c.1810–63)

= [3] Mazaiyagewin
(Iron Cluster
Woman)

= [4] Saiceyewin
(Isabelle Wakeman)

= [5] Makatowin
(Blue Earth,
Eva Rice)
(1831–1918?)

= [6] Manikiyahewin
(1838–1900)

Son
Two Daughters

Wowinape
(Thomas Wakeman)
(1847–86)
Six Other Children

Emma
(c.1844–?)
Jane Williams
(1849–?)
One Daughter
Two Sons

Hannah Redearth
(1861–?)
Four Other Children

Three
Children

Note: Big Thunder had at least three other sons, two of whom committed suicide
Of Big Thunder's ten daughters, only Taśinaśapawin (Her Black Shawl, Elizabeth
Westman) is known.
Children identified as Eugenia La Moure and Tateiyahnamani (Moses Wakeman)
appear in the records. Eugenia was a daughter or niece of Little Crow's; Moses,
his son or nephew. The identity of their mothers is unknown.

193

Notes

Introduction

[1] Alvin M. Josephy, Jr., *The Patriot Chiefs: A Chronicle of American Indian Resistance* (New York: Viking Press, 1961; New York: Penguin Books, 1980), xiii–xiv.

[2] See, for example, William Watts Folwell, *A History of Minnesota* (St. Paul: Minnesota Historical Society, 1921–30), 2:286; Roy W. Meyer, *History of the Santee Sioux: United States Indian Policy on Trial* (Lincoln: University of Nebraska Press, 1967), 135.

[3] A good example would be Dee Brown who entitles his chapter on the war, "Little Crow's War"; see Brown, *Bury My Heart at Wounded Knee: An Indian History of the American West* (New York: Holt, Rinehart and Winston, 1970; New York: Bantam Books, 1972), 37–65.

[4] Folwell to Jane Williams, June 22, 1916, William W. Folwell Papers, MHS; Folwell, *History of Minnesota*, 2:286.

Prelude

[1] Here and below, Marion P. Satterlee, "Narratives of the Sioux War; The Killing of Chief Little Crow," *Collections of the Minnesota Historical Society* (hereafter *Minnesota Collections*) 15(1915):368–69; Walter N. Trenerry, "The Shooting of Little Crow: Heroism or Murder?" *Minnesota History* 38 (September 1962):150–53.

[2] For a complete list of white casualties, see William W. and Marion P. Satterlee Papers, Minnesota Historical Society (hereafter MHS).

[3] *St. Paul Daily Press*, July 10, August 6, 21, 1863; *Hutchinson Leader*, January 6, 1893, October 6, 1905, p. 3.

[4] *St. Paul Daily Press*, August 21, 1863; *St. Paul Pioneer*, August 20, 1863.

Chapter 1. A Dakota Childhood

[1] Taoyateduta's age is the subject of speculation. While some sources suggest that he was born as late as 1814 or even 1818, missionaries who had him as a pupil listed his age as thirty-four in 1844. It is also clear that he served as a warrior in the Sioux contingent that fought in the Black Hawk War in 1832. Thus it seems likely that he was born just prior to the War of 1812. See Asa W. Daniels, "Reminiscences of Little Crow," *Minnesota Collections* 12(1908):514; Return I. Holcombe, *Minnesota as a Territory*, vol. 2 of *Minnesota in Three*

Centuries, 1655-1908, eds. Lucius F. Hubbard, William P. Murray, James H. Baker, and Warren Upham (Mankato: Publishing Society of Minnesota, 1908), 2:266; Henry Hastings Sibley, *Iron Face: The Adventures of Jack Frazer, Frontier Warrior, Scout, and Hunter,* eds. Theodore C. Blegen and Sarah A. Davidson (Chicago: Caxton Club, 1950), 149; "School reports," 1844, American Board of Commissioners for Foreign Missions (hereafter ABCFM) Papers, transcriptions, MHS.

[2] Ruth Landes, *The Mystic Lake Sioux: Sociology of the Mdewakantonwan Santee* (Madison: University of Wisconsin Press, 1968), 5–7.

[3] For a discussion of the term Dakota, see Stephen Return Riggs, *Dakota Grammar, Texts, and Ethnography,* in *Contributions to North American Ethnology,* ed. James Owen Dorsey (Washington, D.C.: Government Printing Office, 1893), 9:156.

[4] Gary Clayton Anderson, *Kinsmen of Another Kind: Dakota-White Relations in the Upper Mississippi Valley, 1650–1862* (Lincoln: University of Nebraska Press, 1984), 1–3, 60; Gary Clayton Anderson, "Early Dakota Migration and Intertribal Warfare: A Revision," *Western Historical Quarterly* 11(January 1980):17–36. For a discussion of the James River trade fairs, see W. Raymond Wood, "Plains Trade in Prehistoric and Protohistoric Intertribal Relations," in *Anthropology on the Great Plains,* ed. W. Raymond Wood and Margot Liberty (Lincoln: University of Nebraska Press, 1980), 98–107.

[5] Anderson, *Kinsmen of Another Kind,* 1–3, 24, 80–81.

[6] Benjamin O'Fallon made a tour of all the Mdewakanton villages in May 1818 and left a census of the number of warriors in several of the bands. His account can be supplemented by the recently edited journals of Stephen H. Long, who was on the upper Mississippi in 1817 and the upper Minnesota in 1823. Other data on population and village locations is found in Zebulon Montgomery Pike's journal, Thomas Forsyth's journal, and Lawrence Taliaferro's journals. Consult O'Fallon to William Clark, May 20, 1818, in *The Territorial Papers of the United States,* ed. Clarence E. Carter and John P. Blum (Washington, D.C.: Government Printing Office, 1934-), 15:407-13; Donald Jackson, ed., *The Journals of Zebulon Montgomery Pike* (Norman: University of Oklahoma Press, 1966), 1:220-22; Lucile M. Kane, June D. Holmquist, and Carolyn Gilman, eds., *The Northern Expeditions of Stephen H. Long: The Journals of 1817 and 1823 and Related Documents* (St. Paul: Minnesota Historical Society Press, 1978), 57–67, 78–81, 149, 157–60; Lawrence Taliaferro Journals, 1820-39, Lawrence Taliaferro Papers, MHS (hereafter Taliaferro Journals); Thomas Forsyth, "Journal of a Voyage from St. Louis to the Falls of St. Anthony, in 1819," *Collections of the State Historical Society of Wisconsin* (hereafter *Wisconsin Collections*), 6(1872):204–7, 217.

[7] Jackson, ed., *Pike Journals,* 1:35; Kane, Holmquist, and Gilman, eds., *Northern Expeditions,* 67. For a description of the bark house, see Philander Prescott, "Contributions to the History, Customs, and Opinions of the Dacota Tribe," in *Historical and Statistical Information Respecting the History, Condition, and Prospects of the Indian Tribes of the United States* (hereafter *Historical and Statistical Information*), ed. Henry R. Schoolcraft (Philadelphia: J. B. Lippincott, 1865), 2:191–92.

[8] Prescott, "Contributions to the History, Customs, and Opinions of the Dacota Tribe," in *Historical and Statistical Information,* 2:191–92; Samuel William Pond, "The Dakotas or Sioux in Minnesota as They Were in 1834," *Minnesota Collections* 12(1908):353–55, reprint, St. Paul: Minnesota Historical Society Press, 1986.

[9] Pond, "The Dakotas . . . as They Were in 1834," *Minnesota Collections* 12(1908):365–66. Pond's account of the Dakota hunting-gathering cycle is the most complete, but it should be compared with the information in Taliaferro's journals. The children's shouts varied depending on the kind of animal killed.

[10] Pond does not describe a buffalo hunt, since by 1834 these animals no longer could be found in numbers in Minnesota, and the Mdewakanton Sioux turned increasingly to hunting muskrats. Twenty years before, however, buffalo still roamed along the Buffalo River, a tributary of the Mississippi, in the Blue Earth River valley, and even in the Minnesota River valley. Consult Pond, "Dakotas . . . as They Were in 1834," *Minnesota Collections* 12(1908):369–75; Kane, Holmquist, and Gilman, eds., *Northern Expeditions*, 60–61, 295; Alan R. Woolworth and Nancy L. Woolworth, "Eastern Dakota Settlement and Subsistence Patterns Prior to 1851," *Minnesota Archaeologist* 39(May 1980):78–80.

[11] Pond states that "the greater portion of their subsistence was obtained by hunting and fishing" (p. 345). Pond, "Dakotas . . . as They Were in 1834," *Minnesota Collections* 12(1908):342–46; Woolworth and Woolworth, "Eastern Dakota Settlement and Subsistence," *Minnesota Archaeologist* 39(May 1980):80–85.

[12] Anderson, *Kinsmen of Another Kind*, 11–12; Pond, "Dakotas . . . as They Were in 1834," *Minnesota Collections* 12(1908):382–85.

[13] Landes, *Mystic Lake Sioux*, 78–79. Considerable confusion exists with the Little Crow genealogy. Perhaps it never will be solved to anyone's satisfaction, but available sources seem to suggest that three men bore the name Little Crow in the nineteenth century before Taoyateduta. The eldest, a man of considerable age, died in 1827, the death being reported by the Indian agent Lawrence Taliaferro in the following fashion: "Petit Corbeau [Little Crow] great medicine man died last night." This apparently was Little Crow II, who handed over the mantle of leadership to Cetanwakanmani sometime prior to 1805 when Zebulon Montgomery Pike arrived at the Little Crow village and dealt with "Chatewaconamani." Taliaferro suggests that Cetanwakanmani, or Little Crow III, was born about 1764, putting him in the prime of life, and certainly eligible to be chief, in 1805. Cetanwakanmani continued in power throughout the 1820s, turning over the name and mantle of leadership to his son, Big Thunder, or Wakinyantanka, in the early 1830s. He apparently died sometime during the winter of 1833–34, depending upon the source of reference. Big Thunder, in turn, died in October 1845, leaving the chieftainship to his eldest son, Taoyateduta. For further information consult Taliaferro Journals, September 21, 28, 1821, November 6, 1827, March 8, September 24, 1829, August 25, 1835, February 11, 1836; Doane Robinson, *A History of the Dakota or Sioux Indians* (N.p.: South Dakota Historical Society, 1904; Minneapolis: Ross and Haines, 1956), 109–18, 340–42; Pond, "The Dakotas . . . as They Were in 1834," *Minnesota Collections* 12(1908):324; Thomas Hughes, *Indian Chiefs of Southern Minnesota* (Mankato: Free Press Co., 1927; Minneapolis: Ross and Haines, 1969), 52–58; Stephen R. Riggs, "Dakota Portraits," *Minnesota History Bulletin* 2 (November 1918):492–93; Jackson, ed., *Pike Journals*, 2:37–39, 220. At least one account suggests that an early Ojibway chief gave the name "Little Crow" to Taoyateduta's grandfather. Consult Col. Hankins, *Dakota Land; or, The Beauty of St. Paul. An Original, Illustrated Historical and Romantic Work on Minnesota, and The Great North-west*, 2nd ed. (New York: Hankins & Son, Publishers, 1869), 380–81. For a fictionalized account of how Cetanwakanmani gained distinction, consult "The Fortunes of Mendokaychennah," *The New-England Magazine* 3(July–December 1832):290–96, probably written by William Joseph Snelling.

[14] Landes, *Mystic Lake Sioux*, 128–29; Raymond J. De Mallie, "Change in American Kinship Systems: The Dakota," in Robert E. Hinshaw, ed., *Currents in Anthropology: Essays in Honor of Sol Tax, Studies in Anthropology* (The Hague and New York: Mouton, 1979), 3:221–41. See also Appendix I.

[15] Kinship competition existed, especially between cross-cousins; see Landes, *Mystic Lake Sioux*, 118–28. Consult also Ella C. Deloria, *Speaking of Indians* (New York: Friendship

Press, 1944), 24–26; Pond, "The Dakotas . . . as They Were in 1834," *Minnesota Collections* 12 (1908):485–89. For an excellent discussion of how social structure developed in nonliterate societies, see Sam D. Gill, *Beyond "The Primitive": The Religions of Nonliterate Peoples* (Englewood Cliffs, N.J.: Prentice-Hall, Inc., 1982), 17.

[16] For information on Mdewakanton religious beliefs, consult Prescott, "Contributions to the History, Customs, and Opinions of the Dacota Tribe," in *Historical and Statistical Information*, 2:170–78, 229, 230–33; Gideon H. Pond, "Powers and Influences of Dakota Medicine-men," in *Historical and Statistical Information*, 4:641–51; James W. Lynd, "The Religion of the Dakotas," *Minnesota Collections* 2(1860–67):150–74; Gideon H. Pond, "Dakota Superstitions," *Minnesota Collections* 2(1860–67):216–31; Samuel Pond, "Dakotas . . . as They Were in 1834," *Minnesota Collections* 12(1908):401–12, 425–28; Landes, *Mystic Lake Sioux*, 57–59. See also William K. Powers, *Oglala Religion* (Lincoln: University of Nebraska Press, 1975); James R. Walker, *Lakota Belief and Ritual*, eds. Raymond J. De Mallie and Elaine A. Jahner (Lincoln: University of Nebraska Press, 1980).

[17] For a discussion of religion and childhood, consult Stephen R. Riggs to David Greene, September 10, 1839, ABCFM Papers; Charles A. Eastman, *Indian Boyhood* (New York: McClure, Phillips and Co., 1902; New York: Dover Publications, 1971), 41–50.

[18] Eastman, *Indian Boyhood*, 41–46, 73–83; Prescott, "Contributions to the History, Customs, and Opinions of the Dacota Tribes," in *Historical and Statistical Information*, 2:229.

[19] Eastman, *Indian Boyhood*, 87–96; Deloria, *Speaking of Indians*, 24–26.

[20] Charles A. Eastman, *Indian Heroes and Great Chieftains* (Boston: Little, Brown and Co., 1918), 45; Bertha L. Heilbron, ed., *With Pen and Pencil on the Frontier in 1851: The Diary and Sketches of Frank Blackwell Mayer* (St. Paul: Minnesota Historical Society, 1932; reprint, 1986), 149, 202; Pond, "Dakotas . . . as They Were in 1834," *Minnesota Collections* 12(1908):485–87.

[21] Eastman, *Indian Boyhood*, 41–46.

[22] Lynd, "Religion of the Dakotas," *Minnesota Collections* 2(1860–67):161–62; Pond, "Dakotas . . . as They Were in 1834," *Minnesota Collections* 12(1908):439–40.

[23] Lynd, "Religion of the Dakotas," *Minnesota Collections* 2(1860–67):161–62; Gill, *Beyond "The Primitive"*, 28–29, 77–81. For a discussion of Little Crow's adoption of the crow as his sacred animal, see Hughes, *Indian Chiefs*, 31; Daniels, "Reminiscences of Little Crow," *Minnesota Collections* 12(1908):516.

[24] The medicine dance is discussed in Samuel Pond, "Dakotas . . . as They Were in 1834," *Minnesota Collections* 12(1908):409–12; Gideon Pond, "Dakota Superstitions," *Minnesota Collections* 2(1860–67):219–28; Prescott, "Contributions to the History, Customs, and Opinions of the Dacota Tribes," in *Historical and Statistical Information*, 2:170–75, 230–31.

[25] Interestingly, a portrait sketched of Taoyateduta in 1851 has the name "Wakinyantanka" attached to it, which is the name of Taoyateduta's father. Although the artist, Frank Blackwell Mayer, may have erred, the use of the father's name may reflect Taoyateduta's initiation into the medicine society. The original sketch is found in the Newberry Library, Chicago. See also, Gill, *Beyond "The Primitive"*, 28–32.

[26] Views on death are found in Lynd, "Religion of the Dakotas," *Minnesota Collections* 2(1860–67):169; Pond, "Dakotas . . . as They Were in 1834," *Minnesota Collections* 12(1908):426–29; Prescott, "Contributions to the History, Customs, and Opinions of the Dacota Tribes," in *Historical and Statistical Information*, 2:229.

[27] See Anderson, *Kinsmen of Another Kind*, 58–76; Joseph Tassé, *Les Canadiens de l'Ouest* (Montreal: Berthiaume et Sabourin, 1882), 1:293, 310, 316, 318, 323–24; Mixed-blood

genealogies, "Indian Reserve Papers," National Archives Record Group (hereafter NARG), 75.

Chapter 2. The Formula for Leadership

[1] Anderson, *Kinsmen of Another Kind,* 77–149; Landes, *Mystic Lake Sioux,* 95–160; Raymond J. De Mallie, "Teton Dakota Kinship and Social Organization" (Ph.D. diss., University of Chicago, 1971), 41–42; Marcel Mauss, *The Gift: Forms and Functions of Exchange in Archaic Societies* (New York: W. W. Norton, 1967), 3–35; Robin Fox, *Kinship and Marriage: An Anthropological Perspective* (Harmondsworth, England: Penguin Books, 1976), 20–43.

[2] E. T. Langham to Taliaferro, August 19, 1828, Taliaferro Papers; Taliaferro Journals, September 23, 1838; Charles A. Eastman to H. M. Hitchcock, September 8, 1927, Edward A. Ayer Collection, Newberry Library, Chicago; Satterlee cards on participants in the Sioux War, Satterlee Papers. For more on Cloud Man, see Appendix I.

[3] See Taliaferro Journals, entries for the 1820s; John S. Wozniak, *Contact, Negotiation, and Conflict: An Ethnohistory of the Eastern Dakota, 1819–1839* (Washington, D.C.: University Press of America, 1978); Joseph Epes Brown, ed., *The Sacred Pipe: Black Elk's Account of the Seven Rites of the Oglala Sioux* (Norman: University of Oklahoma Press, 1953), 102–15; Edward M. Bruner, "Mandan," in *Perspectives in American Indian Culture Change,* ed. Edward M. Spicer (Chicago: University of Chicago Press, 1961), 201.

[4] See Taliaferro Journals, entries for the 1820s.

[5] "Auto-Biography of Maj. Lawrence Taliaferro," *Minnesota Collections* 6(1894):204. Thomas Forsyth, a trader and Indian agent, mistakenly informed Washington that Little Crow had been killed by Sac and Fox Indians; see Forsyth to Calhoun, August 24, 1824, Thomas Forsyth Papers, State Historical Society of Wisconsin.

[6] Taliaferro Journals, June 23, July 26, August 7, 1827, May 5, 1828, September 24, 1829.

[7] Taliaferro Journals, May 1821-September 1822, October 19, 1827, May 5, 7, 1828, June 15, 1829.

[8] Taliaferro Journals, May 24, 1826, May 3, 7, 1829; John H. Case, "Historical Notes of Grey Cloud Island and its Vicinity," *Minnesota Collections* 15(1915):373.

[9] Taliaferro Journals, February 19, 1826, June 18, December 6, 1827, May 3, 5, 1829, April 30, 1831; John Marsh to E. T. Langham, September 6, 1826, Taliaferro Papers; Colonel Josiah Snelling to the Adjutant General, January 2, 1825, NARG 94, LR, Office of Adjutant General (hereafter AGO).

[10] Taliaferro to Clark, May 25, 1829, NARG 75, LR, St. Peter's Agency; Clark to Taliaferro, April 22, 1833, Taliaferro Papers; Taliaferro Journals, May 30, 1826; "Auto-Biography of Maj. Lawrence Taliaferro," *Minnesota Collections* 6(1894):200–25; Francis Paul Prucha, *American Indian Policy in the Formative Years: The Indian Trade and Intercourse Acts, 1790–1834* (Cambridge: Harvard University Press, 1962; Lincoln: Bison Books, 1970), 213–49; "Council Notes" of Prairie du Chien treaty, August 1825, St. Louis Superintendency correspondence, William Clark Papers, Kansas State Historical Society; "Council Notes" of Prairie du Chien treaty, July 1830, NARG 75, Documents Relative to the Negotiation of Ratified and Unratified Treaties (hereafter DRNRUT).

[11] Cetanwakanmani made this argument for the first time in 1819. See Forsyth, "Journal of a Voyage," *Wisconsin Collections* 6(1908):213; Taliaferro Journals, September 24, 1823, March 8, June 15, August 1, 1829, August 11, 1830.

[12] Taliaferro Journals, May 24, 1826, May 3, June 3, 1829, April 30, 1831, May 19, 1836; Taliaferro to Clark, September 1, 1834, Taliaferro to Major John Bliss, July 17, 1835, NARG 75, LR, St. Peter's Agency.

[13] Scattered "returns" from the upper Mississippi brigades are found in the American Fur Company Papers, Burton Collection (hereafter AFCP-Burton), Detroit Public Library.

[14] See returns for April 28, 29, May 9, 1820, June 23, July 11, 1827, AFCP-Burton; "Fur returns," compiled by Taliaferro, September 1831, LR, St. Louis Superintendency, Clark Papers.

[15] Taliaferro Journals, November 10, 1827, June 17, August 1, 1829, June 2, August 9, 14, 1831, May 24, June 2, 10, 1832; Joseph Rolette to Alexis Bailly, May 1, 1833, Bailly "credit" lists, Alexis Bailly Papers, MHS; Taliaferro "Notice" on credit, July 12, 1833, Henry Hastings Sibley Papers, MHS; Bailly to Major John Bliss, January 1, 1834, Taliaferro Papers.

[16] Taliaferro Journals, August 1, 1829.

[17] Taliaferro Journals, June 2, 1831. See also March 25, 1829, August 30, 1831, June 11, 14, 1832.

[18] Taliaferro Journals, April 10, 1828; Pond, "The Dakotas . . . as They Were in 1834," *Minnesota Collections* 12(1908):324–25; E. J. Pond to H. M. Hitchcock, December 16, 1931, Miscellaneous Correspondence, MHS.

[19] Pond, "The Dakotas . . . as They Were in 1834," *Minnesota Collections* 12(1908):325.

[20] Taliaferro Journals, July 27, October 2, 5, 1835, July 26, August 10, 1836; Taliaferro to Clark, August 2, 1833, NARG 75, LR, St. Peter's Agency; Bliss to Major General E. P. Gaines, March 1, 1835, NARG 393, LR, Jefferson Barracks, 1831–1835.

[21] Taliaferro Journals, May 1, 9, 1836. Taliaferro indicated that he had approached the major Mdewakanton leaders regarding a land sale and found only "some opposition."

[22] See Gary Clayton Anderson, "The Removal of the Mdewakanton Dakota in 1837: A Case for Jacksonian Paternalism," *South Dakota History* 10(Fall 1980):310–33.

[23] Chauncey Bush kept a word-by-word journal of the negotiation, which is found in the Bentley Historical Library, Michigan Historical Collections, Ann Arbor, Mich. See discussions for September 21, 23, 27, 1837.

[24] Taliaferro portrait list, no date [1837], NARG 75, LR, St. Peter's Agency. See also Herman J. Viola, *The Indian Legacy of Charles Bird King* (Washington, D.C.: Smithsonian Institution Press and Doubleday and Co., Inc., 1976), 107–9.

[25] Scott Campbell to Taliaferro, December 7, 1837, NARG 75, LR, St. Peter's Agency.

[26] Taliaferro Journals, June 9, 20, July 8, August 10, 24, 1838; Holcombe, *Minnesota in Three Centuries*, 2:262–64; Stephen R. Riggs, "Protestant Missions in the Northwest," *Minnesota Collections* 6(1894):137-38; Edward D. Neill, "Occurrences in and around Fort Snelling, from 1819 to 1840," *Minnesota Collections* 2(1860–67):133.

[27] Taliaferro Journals, October 21, 1838; Anderson, "Removal of the Mdewakanton Dakota in 1837," *South Dakota History* 10(Fall 1980):330–33.

[28] Taliaferro Journals, June 16, 17, 1839; Anderson, "Removal of the Mdewakanton Dakota in 1837," *South Dakota History* 10(Fall 1980):330–33; Thomas Pope to Sibley, May 22, 1839, Sibley Papers. See also Pope to Taliaferro, August 24, 1838, Taliaferro Papers.

[29] Taliaferro Journals, June 16, 17, July 15, 17, August 10, October 24, 1839; Amos Bruce to T. Hartley Crawford, November 26, 1844, NARG 75, LR, St. Peter's Agency; R[ichard] G. Murphy to Major Thomas H. Harvey, October 9, 1848, *House Executive Documents* (hereafter *HED*), no. 1, 30th Congress, 2d session, serial 537, p. 474–75; Nathaniel Fish Moore, "Journal by Way of Buffalo and the Lakes to the falls of St. Anthony & return . . .

by Way of St. Louis and the Ohio River in the autumn of 1845," Ayer Collection, Newberry Library.

[30] Pope to Sibley, May 22, 1839, Sibley Papers; Bruce to Robert Lucas, November 6, 1840, Bruce to Crawford, October 30, 1841, NARG 75, LR, St. Peter's Agency; Crawford to Taliaferro, June 1, 1839, NARG 75, LS, Office of Indian Affairs; Riggs, "Protestant Missions," *Minnesota Collections* 6(1894):142.

[31] Neill, "Occurrences in and around Fort Snelling," *Minnesota Collections* 2(1860–67):133; J. Fletcher Williams, *A History of the City of Saint Paul to 1875* (St. Paul: *Minnesota Collections,* vol. 4, 1876; St. Paul: Minnesota Historical Society Press, Borealis Reprints, 1983), 64–69, 85–88; Andrew Drips to D. D. Mitchell, January 2, 1844, Drips to Thomas H. Harvey, October 25, 1844, December 6, 1845, Drips Papers, Bancroft Library, Berkeley, Calif.; Martin McLeod to Sibley, January 29, 1846, Sibley Papers; Captain G. Dearborn to Brigadier General R. Jones, May 6, 1842, NARG 94, LR, AGO.

[32] Pond, "The Dakotas . . . as They Were in 1834," *Minnesota Collections* 12(1908):325 (quotation). There is some question as to whether Big Thunder actually led the party. See Pond, above, and E[dward] D. Neill, "Battle at Lake Pokeguma," *Minnesota Collections* 1(1852; reprint, 1902):141–45. Also consult Holcombe, *Minnesota in Three Centuries,* 2:170–75; Dearborn to Jones, March 25, 1842, Dearborn to AGO, June 18, 1842, NARG 94, LR, AGO; Bruce to Chambers, June 20, 1842, NARG 75, LR, St. Peter's Agency.

[33] See Donald Dean Parker, ed., *The Recollections of Philander Prescott: Frontiersman of the Old Northwest, 1819–1862* (Lincoln: University of Nebraska Press, 1966), 175–76; Holcombe, *Minnesota in Three Centuries,* 2:175–79; August L. Larpenteur, "Recollections of the City and People of St. Paul, 1843–1898," *Minnesota Collections* 9(1901):374–75; Treaty, enclosed with Lieutenant H. J. Wilson to Jones, November 28, 1843, NARG 94, LR, AGO; Captain Electus Backus to Major L. Cooper, July 27, 1843, NARG 94, LR, AGO; Bruce to Chambers, August 4, 12, 1843, NARG 75, LR, St. Peter's Agency.

[34] Bruce to Crawford, September 1, 1841, Bruce's annual report, September 1, 1843, NARG 75, LR, St. Peter's Agency; Hercules L. Dousman to Sibley, September 16, November 4, 1842, Sibley Papers.

[35] Big Thunder offered considerable advice on the kinds of goods his people needed. See Remarks of chiefs, September 25, 1839, NARG 75, LR, St. Peter's Agency; Bruce to Chambers, April 3, 1843, NARG 75, LR, St. Peter's Agency; Anderson, "Removal of the Mdewakanton Dakota in 1837," *South Dakota History* 10(Fall 1980):330–33; Parker, ed., *Recollections of Philander Prescott,* 215.

[36] Remarks of chiefs, September 25, 1839, NARG 75, LR, St. Peter's Agency; Taliaferro Journals, September 25, 1839.

[37] The trader and later Minnesota governor, Henry Hastings Sibley, in a memoir that he wrote approximately thirty years after the incident, described a meeting between Big Thunder and Taoyateduta just before the chief's death. Although Sibley had a penchant for fiction, it seems unlikely that he would have created the story and then published it as a historical tract. More than likely, Sibley did not know the sons very well in 1845, and he actually described the meeting between Big Thunder and the younger son whom the chief sanctioned to follow him. White Spider, Little Crow's younger brother, seemed to suggest that his father lived only a few hours after the accident, and other sources strongly suggest that Taoyateduta remained at Lac qui Parle that fall. Consult Sibley, "Reminiscences of the Early Days of Minnesota," *Minnesota Collections* 3(1870–80):251–52; Holcombe, *Minnesota in Three Centuries,* 2:180–83; Riggs and Gideon H. Pond to David Greene, September 10,

1846, ABCFM Papers; Daniels, "Reminiscences of Little Crow," *Minnesota Collections* 12(1908):515–16; *St. Paul Pioneer Press*, October 24, 1897; Daniel Buck, *Indian Outbreaks* (1904; Minneapolis: Ross and Haines, 1965), 46–47.

Chapter 3. The Price of Leadership

[1] Holcombe, *Minnesota in Three Centuries*, 2:180.

[2] Little Crow's friendship with Jack Frazer, who was certainly considered to be disreputable by many Dakotas, is a good example; see Sibley, *Iron Face*, 58, 97–98, 100, 149. See also Martin McLeod's comments on the company that young Little Crow kept; McLeod to Sibley, February 25, March 30, 1848, Sibley Papers.

[3] See Andrew Drips to D. D. Mitchell, January 2, 1844, Drips to Thomas H. Harvey, October 25, 1844, December 6, 1845, Drips Papers, Bancroft Library; McLeod to Sibley, January 29, 1846, February 25, March 30, 1848, Sibley Papers; Sibley to McLeod, January 27, 1848, Martin McLeod Papers, MHS.

[4] For first quotation, see Daniels, "Reminiscences of Little Crow," *Minnesota Collections* 12(1908):514. See also Note on "Little Crow," 1841, John Fletcher Williams Papers, MHS.

[5] See, for example, Andrew Robertson to Charles Flandrau, April 1, 1857, Charles E. Flandrau Papers, MHS.

[6] Riggs and Gideon Pond to David Greene, September 10, 1846, Williamson to Greene, June 30, 1844, ABCFM Papers; Gideon Pond, Diary, August 2–3, 1837, Gideon H. and Samuel W. Pond Papers, MHS; Nancy Aiton to J. F. Aiton, March 7, 1849, John F. Aiton Papers, MHS.

[7] Oscar Garrett Wall, *Recollections of the Sioux Massacre: An Authentic History of the Yellow Medicine Incident, of the Fate of Marsh and his Men, of the Siege and Battles of Fort Ridgely, and of Other Important Battles and Experiences. Together with a Historical Sketch of the Sibley Expedition of 1863* (Lake City, Minn.: Home Printery, 1908), 184–85.

[8] Lynd quotation is in James W. Lynd, "History of the Dakotas," *Minnesota Collections* 2(1860–67):147. For the quotation on popularity, see Williamson to Greene, February 17, 1847, ABCFM Papers. For a good example of Little Crow's dress, see the description of him at the 1851 treaty in Holcombe, *Minnesota in Three Centuries*, 2:307.

[9] See, for example, the descriptions and interviews in the *Minnesota Pioneer* (St. Paul), May 27, 1852, May 5, 1854.

[10] Pond, "The Dakotas . . . as They Were in 1834," *Minnesota Collections* 12 (1905-08):325; Daniels, "Reminiscences of Little Crow," *Minnesota Collections* 12 (1905–08):515; Williamson to Greene, June 30, 1844, ABCFM Papers.

[11] Daniels reported that Taoyateduta took a daughter of "the chief of the [Wahpekute] band." Robinson suggests that he actually took as wives two sisters of the tribe and had three children by them. Since Tasagye was the only recognized chief of the Wahpekutes during this period, it seems likely that the women were his daughters. Tasagye was killed by members of his own band in 1839. See Daniels, "Reminiscences of Little Crow," *Minnesota Collections* 12(1905–08):515; Robinson, *A History of the Dakota*, 342–43; Riggs, "Dakota Portraits," *Minnesota History Bulletin* 2(November 1918):500; *St. Peter Tribune*, July 29, 1863.

[12] The best description of Wahpekute troubles is found in the Taliaferro journals, especially the agents' councils with Tasagye. See also the report of Lieutenant E. R. Williams to Captain W. R. Jouett, November 28, 1831, NARG 393, LR, Jefferson Barracks, 1831–53.

[13] Inyangmani had apparently married a Sisseton woman, as some sources identify his daughters as Sissetons. See Miscellaneous notes, Satterlee Papers; Thomas A. Robertson, Reminiscences, MHS; Thomas A. Robertson to Marion P. Satterlee, November 1, 1922, Satterlee Papers.

[14] Stephen Return Riggs, *Tah-koo Wah-kan; or, The Gospel among the Dakotas* (Boston: Congregational Publishing Society, 1869), 25.

[15] E[dward] D. Neill, "Dakota Land and Dakota Life," *Minnesota Collections* 1(1853, reprinted, 1902):226; Riggs and Gideon Pond to Greene, September 10, 1846, ABCFM Papers.

[16] Riggs, "Dakota Portraits," *Minnesota History Bulletin* 2(November 1918):535–36.

[17] There is contradictory evidence regarding Mary Renville's relationship to Taoyateduta, but the best evidence suggests that Mary was a cross-cousin of Taoyateduta's. See Hughes, *Indian Chiefs*, 31, 77; Riggs, "Dakota Portraits," *Minnesota History Bulletin* 2(November 1918):532, 552. Renville's lineage also originates in the Mdewakanton band. See Riggs, *Tah-koo Wah-kan*, 154–55; Wozniak, *Contact, Negotiation and Conflict*, 46–47; Tassé, *Canadiens de l'Ouest*, 1:293. Left Hand headed the soldiers' lodge; information on his life is found in Riggs, "Dakota Portraits," *Minnesota History Bulletin* 2(November 1918):532–37; Lieutenant Jefferson Vail to William Clark, March 4, 1833, NARG 94, LR, AGO. Napešniduta was at one time a "principal man" of Little Crow's village; see T. S. Williamson, "Napehshneedoota: The First Male Dakota Convert to Christianity," *Minnesota Collections* 3(1880):188–91; Riggs and Gideon Pond to Greene, September 10, 1846, ABCFM Papers. A good description of Renville's lodge is found in Edmund C. Bray and Martha Coleman Bray, trans. and eds., *Joseph N. Nicollet on the Plains and Prairies: The Expeditions of 1838–39 with Journals, Letters, and Notes on the Dakota Indians* (St. Paul: Minnesota Historical Society, 1976), 106–8.

[18] Old Eve's ties to Renville are found in Bray and Bray, trans. and eds., *Joseph N. Nicollet*, 279–80. Williamson provided corroborating evidence by identifying Cloud Man, or "Petit Fusee," as a "relative of Mr. Renvilles," while Riggs indicated that Cloud Man and Abel Fearful Face were "closely allied" to Renville, which undoubtedly suggests kinship ties; see Riggs, "Dakota Portraits," *Minnesota History Bulletin* 2(November 1918):547–52; Williamson to Amos Bruce, August 5, 1840, NARG 75, LR, St. Peter's Agency. For a complete discussion of kinship relations, see Appendix I.

[19] Although the relationship is difficult to document, there appears to be no doubt that Catherine Totedutawin, the mother of Lorenzo Lawrence and Joseph Kawanke, was one of the two wives of Left Hand. For further details, consult Appendix I and the following sources: Stephen R. Riggs, *Mary and I: Forty Years with the Sioux* (Boston: Congregational Sunday-School and Publishing Society, 1880), 50–51, 71; Riggs, "Dakota Portraits," *Minnesota History Bulletin* 2 (November 1918):532–37, 543–45; Riggs, *Tah-koo Wah-kan*, 180–81.

[20] Williamson to Greene, May 4, 1836, January 2, 1846, ABCFM Papers; Riggs, *Mary and I*, 28–52.

[21] Riggs, "Dakota Portraits," *Minnesota History Bulletin* 2(November 1918): 532–37, 544; Williamson, "Napehshneedoota," *Minnesota Collections* 3(1880):188–91; Riggs, *Mary and I*, 139–41; Riggs, *Tah-koo Wah-kan*, 165–69; Riggs to Greene, December 31, 1840, Williamson to Greene, January 2, 1846, Riggs and Gideon Pond to Greene, September 10, 1846, Williamson to Treat, April 1, 1853, ABCFM Papers.

[22] Riggs, "Dakota Portraits," *Minnesota History Bulletin* 2(November 1918): 561–63; Williamson to Greene, January 2, 1846, Sioux missionaries to the American Board, August 31, 1848, ABCFM Papers.

[23] Riggs and Gideon Pond to Greene, September 10, 1846, Williamson to Greene, June 30, 1844, ABCFM Papers; Gideon Pond, Diary, August 2–3, 1837, Pond Papers.

[24] McLeod to Sibley, January 29, 1846, February 25, March 30, 1848, Joseph La Framboise to Sibley, February 21, 1847, Sibley to McLeod, January 27, 1848, Sibley Papers; A. J. Campbell to Scott Campbell, April 12, 1848, Scott Campbell Papers, MHS. See also Andrew Drips to D. D. Mitchell, January 2, 1844, Drips to Thomas H. Harvey, October 25, 1844, December 6, 1845, Drips Papers, Bancroft Library.

[25] Holcombe, *Minnesota in Three Centuries*, 2:180–81; Prescott, "Contributions to the History, Customs, and Opinions of the Dacota Tribes," in *Historical and Statistical Information*, 2:183.

[26] Holcombe, *Minnesota in Three Centuries*, 2:181–82 (quotations). See also Prescott, "Contributions to the History, Customs, and Opinions of the Dacota Tribes," in *Historical and Statistical Information*, 2:183; Moore, "Journal by Way of Buffalo and the Lakes to the Falls of St. Anthony," Ayer Collection, Newberry Library; F. V. Lamare-Picquot, "Minnesota as Seen by Travelers: A French Naturalist in Minnesota, 1846," *Minnesota History* 6(September 1925), 275–76.

[27] Prescott, "Contributions to the History, Customs, and Opinions of the Dacota Tribes," in *Historical and Statistical Information*, 2:183; Robertson to Satterlee, November 1, 1922, Notes on individuals tried by the Sioux Commission, "Little Dog," Satterlee Papers; Thomas A. Robertson, Reminiscences.

[28] Gideon Pond to Robert Murphy, August 27, 1849, Ramsey to Brown, June 15, 1850, NARG 75, LS, Minnesota Superintendency (hereafter MS); *Minnesota Pioneer*, June 13, 1850.

[29] Pond, "Dakotas . . . as They Were in 1834," *Minnesota Collections* 12(1908):390; Landes, *Mystic Lake Sioux*, 136–37.

[30] Holcombe, *Minnesota in Three Centuries*, 2:180, 184 (quotation); Williams, *History of the City of Saint Paul*, 162; Samuel Pond to Greene, March 18, 1845, Gideon Pond to Sibley, February 12, 1849, Sibley Papers; J. F. Aiton to Treat, June 21, 1849, Williamson to Greene, January 28, 1847, ABCFM Papers; Bruce to Sibley, August 30, 1842, Sibley Papers; Anderson, *Kinsmen of Another Kind*, 172.

[31] Riggs and Gideon Pond to Greene, September 10, 1846 (quotation), Riggs to Greene, July 1, 1846, Williamson to Greene, November 30, 1846, ABCFM Papers; Riggs, *Mary and I*, 100–1.

[32] Riggs, *Mary and I*, 100; Riggs and Gideon Pond to Greene, September 10, 1846, Sioux missionaries to the American Board, August 31, 1848, Williamson to Greene, November 30, 1846, ABCFM Papers; Annuity roll for Mdewakanton tribe, 1847[?], Sibley Papers.

[33] Williamson to Greene, January 28, February 17, 1847, ABCFM Papers.

[34] Williamson to Greene, January 28, July 12, 1847, Williamson to S. B. Treat, June 5, 1848, Annual Reports, August 31, 1848, September 1849, ABCFM Papers; Williamson to Sibley, January 26, 1849, Sibley Papers.

[35] Medill to Harvey, January 7, August 28, 1847, NARG 75, LS, Office of Indian Affairs (hereafter OIA); Williamson to Greene, January 28, 1847, ABCFM Papers.

[36] T. H. Harvey to Medill, July 17, 1848, Sibley and Ramsey to Orlando Brown, December 10, 1849, NARG 75, LR, St. Peter's Agency; Nathaniel McLean to Ramsey, December 8, 1849, NARG 75, LR, MS.

[37] Taliaferro to T. Hartley Crawford, September 30, 1839, NARG 75, LR, St. Peter's Agency; J. D. Stevens to Greene, March 23, June 29, 1839, Williamson to Treat, August 1,

1848, ABCFM Papers; Crawford to Robert Lucas, September 18, 1839, August 15, 1841, Crawford to John Chambers, July 13, 1841, NARG 75, LS, OIA.

[38] Williamson report, September 1, 1849, NARG 75, LR, MS.

[39] Medill to Williamson, June 29, 1848, NARG 75, LS, OIA; Luke Lea to Ramsey, August 7, 1849, NARG 75, LR, MS.

[40] "Boarding School Students," 1847–59, Riggs Papers; Williamson to McLean, August 27, 1851, *Senate Executive Documents* (hereafter *SED*), no. 1, 32d Congress, 1st session, serial 613, p. 437–39.

[41] Lorenzo Lawrence to Ramsey, February 13, 16, 1850, NARG 75, LR, MS.

[42] See Parker, ed., *Recollections of Philander Prescott*, 176–79; Sibley to McLeod, January 27, 1848, McLeod Papers; McLeod to Sibley, February 25, March 30, 1848, Sibley Papers.

[43] La Framboise to Sibley, February 21, 1847, Sibley Papers.

[44] McLeod to Sibley, March 30, 1848, Sibley Papers.

[45] Memorial of Sioux farmers, July 1849, Prescott's farm report, September 23, 1850, NARG 75, LR, MS.

[46] Brown to Ramsey and Chambers, August 25, 1849, *HED*, no. 5, 31st Congress, 1st session, serial 570, p. 979–80; Sibley to Ramsey, September 15, 1849, Alexander Ramsey Papers, MHS; Riggs to Sibley, September 7, 1849, Sibley Papers.

[47] Brown to Ramsey and Chambers, August 25, 1849, *HED*, no. 5, 31st Congress, 1st session, serial 570, p. 979–80.

[48] Riggs to Ramsey, November 5, 1849, Lea to Ramsey, November 8, 1849, NARG 75, LR, MS; Riggs to Treat, November 12, 1849, ABCFM Papers.

[49] Sibley to Ramsey, September 15, 1849, Instructions to Ramsey and Lea, May 16, 1851, Ramsey Papers; Sibley to McLeod, December 16, 1849, Sibley Papers.

[50] Riggs to Ramsey, October 13, November 5, 1849, Petition of "Upper" Indians to President Zachary Taylor, November 2, 1849, NARG 75, LR, MS.

[51] "Journal of Proceedings," September 29, 1849, NARG 75, DRNRUT.

[52] Ramsey and Chambers to Brown, October 18, 1849, NARG 75, LR, St. Peter's Agency.

[53] Sibley to McLeod, December 16, 1849, Sibley Papers.

[54] Sibley to McLeod, June 23, 1850, McLeod Papers; McLeod to Sibley, August 22, September 16, 1850, Sibley to McLeod, October 24, 1850, Fred Sibley to Henry Sibley, June 27, 1850, Fred Sibley to Pierre Chouteau, September 14, 1850, Sibley Papers; *Minnesota Pioneer* (St. Paul), January 2, 1850.

[55] Fred Sibley to Henry Sibley, June 27, 1850, Sibley Papers; "Journal of Proceedings," September 29, 1849, NARG 75, DRNRUT; Alexis Bailly to Sibley, December 6, 1849, Sibley Papers.

[56] "Outline of a Plan for Civilizing the Dakotas, Adopted at a Meeting of the Dakota Mission held at Kaposia," 1850, NARG 75, LR, MS.

[57] McLean to Ramsey, September 25, 1850, Ramsey to Lea, October 21, 1850, Lea to A. H. H. Stuart, November 27, 1850, *HED*, no. 1, 31st Congress, 2d session, serial 595, p. 103–7, 75, 35–36.

[58] Contradictory opinions exist on the population of Pig's Eye. See Patricia C. Harpole and Mary D. Nagle, eds., *Minnesota Territorial Census, 1850* (St. Paul: Minnesota Historical Society, 1972), 59–60; E. S. Seymour, *Sketches of Minnesota, The New England of the West. With Incidents of Travel in that Territory During the Summer of 1849* (New York: Harper and Brothers, 1850), 92-93, 95, 99; Prescott to Sibley, March 4, 1850, Franklin Steele to Sibley, March 12, 1850, Sibley Papers.

[59] McLean to Ramsey, May 12, 14, 1850, NARG 75, LR, MS; Ramsey to Sibley, April 10, 1850, Alexander Faribault to Sibley, April 11, 1850, Prescott to Sibley, April 24, 1850, Sibley Papers.

[60] Brown to Ramsey, April 22, 1850, R. W. Kirkham to Ramsey, May 15, 1850, Ramsey to Brown, June 15, 1850, Lea to Ramsey, August 26, 1850, Ramsey to Lea, September 7, 1850, NARG 75, LR, MS; Ramsey to Sibley, June 15, 1850, Fred Sibley to Chouteau, June 26, 1850, Sibley Papers; *Minnesota Pioneer*, June 13, 1850.

[61] *Minnesota Pioneer*, November 14, 1850.

[62] Lorenzo Lawrence to Ramsey, February 13, 15, 1850, NARG 75, LR, MS. Lawrence's views were considered to be very progressive, and Ramsey informed him through the agent that he and any other Indian who adopted farming and accepted white dress could stay in the soon-to-be ceded land; see Ramsey to McLean, April 6, 1851, NARG 75, LR, MS.

Chapter 4. Sale of a Homeland

[1] See the letters of McLeod to Sibley, especially January 21, April 26, 1851, Sibley Papers; Andrew Robertson, Report on Farmer Society, August 17, 1851, NARG 75, LR, MS.

[2] Williamson to Treat, February 10, 1851, Riggs to McLeod, February 12, 1851, Samuel Pond to Treat, June 23, 1851, ABCFM Papers; McLeod to Sibley, April 26, 1851, Sibley Papers; *Minnesota Pioneer*, June 5, 1851.

[3] Wabasha was opposed to the treaty negotiation from the beginning, speaking out strongly against it in 1849 and in discussions with traders; see the Sibley correspondence for the period 1849–51, Sibley Papers.

[4] Sibley to McLeod, May 6, 1851, Sibley Papers. Sibley was concerned about possible influencing of the Indians "by sundry persons on the other side of the Mississippi [east bank] who . . . have endeavored to infuse into the minds of the principal men suspicions unfavorable to the traders." See Sibley to Dousman, May 14, 1851, Hercules L. Dousman Papers, State Historical Society of Wisconsin. For an account of the traders' role in the treaty process, consult Lucile M. Kane, "The Sioux Treaties and the Traders," *Minnesota History* 32(June 1951):65–80.

[5] McLeod to Sibley, April 26, 1851, Sibley Papers; Sibley to McLeod, May 19, 1851, McLeod Papers.

[6] For particulars on the negotiation with the eastern Sioux, see "Journal of the Joint Commission to Treat with the Sioux," 1851, NARG 75, DRNRUT; W[illiam] G[ates] Le Duc, *Minnesota Year Book for 1852* (St. Paul: W. G. Le Duc, [1852]), 23–70; *Minnesota Pioneer*, June–August 1851; Heilbron, ed., *With Pen and Pencil on the Frontier*, 149–63.

[7] "Journal of the Joint Commission," July 12, 1851, NARG 75, DRNRUT; Le Duc, *Minnesota Year Book for 1852*, 40 (quotation).

[8] *Minnesota Pioneer*, July 3, 7, 10, 1851; Heilbron, ed., *With Pen and Pencil on the Frontier*, 149–71.

[9] Heilbron, ed., *With Pen and Pencil on the Frontier*, 125. The exquisite drawing of Little Crow, shown on page 119 of Heilbron, is in the Ayer Collection, Newberry Library.

[10] Heilbron, ed., *With Pen and Pencil on the Frontier*, 125 (quotation), 149; *Minnesota Pioneer*, July 17, 1851.

[11] "Journal of the Joint Commission," July 9, 1851, NARG 75, DRNRUT.

[12] "Journal of the Joint Commission," July 21, 1851, NARG 75, DRNRUT.

[13] "Journal of the Joint Commission," July 22–23, 1851, NARG 75, DRNRUT.

[14] A. H. H. Stuart to Ramsey and Lea, May 16, 1851, NARG 75, LR, St. Peter's Agency; Le Duc, *Minnesota Year Book for 1852*, 64–65.

[15] *Minnesota Pioneer*, July 31, 1851.

[16] "Journal of the Joint Commission," July 29, 1851, NARG 75, DRNRUT; Le Duc, *Minnesota Year Book for 1852*, 70–73.

[17] "Journal of the Joint Commission," July 29, 1851, NARG 75, DRNRUT; Sibley to Pierre Chouteau, July 11, 1851, Sibley Papers.

[18] "Journal of the Joint Commission," July 30, 1851, NARG 75, DRNRUT.

[19] "Journal of the Joint Commission," July 31, 1851, NARG 75, DRNRUT; Holcombe, *Minnesota in Three Centuries*, 2:307–8; Le Duc, *Minnesota Year Book for 1852*, 77–81.

[20] Holcombe, *Minnesota in Three Centuries*, 2:308–10; "Journal of the Joint Commission," August 5, 1851, NARG 75, DRNRUT.

[21] Here and below, "Journal of the Joint Commission," August 5, 1851, NARG 75, DRNRUT; Holcombe, *Minnesota in Three Centuries*, 2:310–16 (quotation, 314–15); Ramsey and Lea report, August (1851?), LR, MS; Joseph W. Hancock, "Missionary Work at Red Wing, 1849 to 1852," *Minnesota Collections* 10 (1900-04):177; Lea to Stuart, August 6, 1851, *SED*, no. 1, 32d Congress, 1st session, serial 613, p. 279; Le Duc, *Minnesota Year Book for 1852*, 81–87.

[22] "Journal of the Joint Commission," August 5, 1851, NARG 75, DRNRUT; Charles J. Kappler, comp. and ed., *Indian Affairs, Laws, and Treaties* (Washington, D.C.: Government Printing Office, 1904), 2:591–93; McLean to Ramsey, September 1, 1851, *SED*, no. 1, 32d Congress, 1st session, serial 613, p. 434; Williamson to Treat, August 7, 1851, ABCFM Papers; Ramsey to Lea, April 22, 1852, NARG 75, LR, St. Peter's Agency.

[23] Newton H. Winchell first described the 1851 treaties as a "monstrous conspiracy." Roy W. Meyer used the term as a title for his chapter on the treaty negotiations; see Meyer, *History of the Santee Sioux*, 87.

[24] This document is found in several collections, but the original, dated July 23, 1851, appears to be in the Sibley Papers. The sum of $210,000 was determined by the traders and Ramsey. For an interesting discussion of the "traders' paper" controversy, consult McLean to Ramsey, September 1, 1850 [1852], *SED*, no. 1, 32d Congress, 2d session, serial 658, p. 351.

[25] Three copies of the Wahpekute "traders' paper" exist, all dated August 5, 1851, in the Ramsey Papers, Sibley Papers, and in NARG 75, LR, St. Peter's Agency. See also Sibley to Dousman, October 6, 1851, Dousman Papers; Sibley to Chouteau, November 1, 1851, Sibley Papers.

[26] Sweetzer to George Ewing, October 26, 29, 1851, William G. and George W. Ewing Papers, MHS; Sibley to McLeod, November 24, 28, 1851, Sibley to Joseph La Framboise, November 23, 1851, McLeod to Fred Sibley, December 20, 1851, and Fred Sibley to La Framboise, April 20, 1852, Sibley Papers; Sibley to Dousman, December 29, 1851, Dousman Papers; Sioux Petition, December 6, 1851, NARG 75, LR, St. Peter's Agency.

[27] McLean to Lea, August 19, 1851, NARG 75, LR, St. Peter's Agency; McLean to Ramsey, January 15, 1852, NARG 75, LR, MS; Lee to Captain Irwin McDowell, August 20, 1851, NARG 393, LR, Jefferson Barracks, 1831–1853; *Minnesota Pioneer*, May 27, 1852.

[28] Ramsey to Lea, May 1, 1852, NARG 75, LR, MS.

[29] *Minnesota Pioneer*, May 27, 1852.

[30] Kappler, comp. and ed., *Indian Affairs, Laws, and Treaties*, 2:591–93; Sibley to Dous-

man, June 23, 1852, Dousman Papers; Sibley to Ramsey, June 26, 1852, Ramsey Papers; Fred Sibley to Chouteau, June 17, 1852, Sibley Papers.

[31] Fred Sibley noted that the upper Indians were now desperate and "look to their annuities as their only hope of salvation." See Fred Sibley to Chouteau, July 11, 1852, Sibley Papers. See also Williamson to S. B. Treat, July 30, 1852, S. W. Pond to Treat, August (n.d.), 1852, ABCFM Papers.

[32] Riggs to Treat, July 31, 1852, ABCFM Papers.

[33] Lee to McDowell, August 7, 1852, NARG 94, LR, AGO; Ramsey to Lea, August 28, 1852, NARG 75, LR, MS.

[34] Ramsey to Lea, August 28, 1852, NARG 75, LR, MS; Stuart to the Sioux, October 2, 1852, NARG 75, Selected Documents from the Office of Indian Affairs Regarding the Treaty of 1851, microfilm copies in MHS.

[35] Ramsey to Lea, September 10, 1852, NARG 75, LR, MS; Ramsey to Lea, January 15, 1853, *SED*, no. 61, 33d Congress, 1st session, serial 699, p. 7–9 (hereafter Ramsey Investigation); Affadavit of Philander Prescott, August 29, 1853, Ramsey Papers. Prescott's account of the Indian response suggests that Bad Hail acted as orator. After being asked to give up all lands, including those designated for reservations, he supposedly said: "Father, we fear that our Great Father at Washington wishes to drive us to some country to starve us to death"; Parker, ed., *Recollections of Philander Prescott*, 185–86. Information regarding Little Crow's role in the negotiation is found in Treaty with the Mdewakanton, Wahpekute, Sisseton, and Wahpeton Sioux, April 9, 1858, NARG 75, DRNRUT.

[36] Here and below, see Ramsey Investigation, 7–9, 76, 81–82, 124–25, 169, 171–72, 189–90, 277. See also Thomas Hughes, *Old Traverse des Sioux* (St. Peter, Minn.: Herald Publishing Co., 1929), 3–5.

[37] Fred Sibley to Chouteau, November 16, 1852, Sibley Papers.

[38] Ramsey Investigation, 170–71, 172–74, 177; Mdewakanton "receipt," November 9, 1852, "receipt" of Mdewakanton chiefs for $2,857.14 (apiece), November 11, 1852, Ramsey Papers.

[39] Hughes, *Old Traverse des Sioux*, 3–5; Ramsey Investigation, 7–9, 86–87, 93–94, 102–3, 139–40, 152–53, 156–61, 275–76, 281–82; Ramsey to Lea, January 15, 1853, NARG 75, LR, St. Peter's Agency.

[40] Ramsey Investigation, 34–35; Gorman to George Manypenny, June 1, August 27, September 6, 8, 1853, NARG 75, LR, MS; Antoine Freniere to McLeod, April 23, 1853, McLeod Papers. The flour and pork contracts amounted to seventeen thousand dollars for the Mdewakantons. Unfortunately it soon became obvious that Ramsey had allowed the contractors bidding on the contract to work together, resulting in a cost per barrel that was nearly twice as high as it should have been. See Manypenny to Gorman, February 3, 25, 1854, NARG 75, LR, MS; Gorman to Manypenny, September 6, 1853, February 21, 1854, NARG 75, LS, MS; Ramsey to Manypenny, February 27, 1854, NARG 75, LR, St. Peter's Agency.

[41] Gorman to Manypenny, May 27, June 1, 1853, NARG 75, LR, MS.

[42] Gorman to Manypenny, June 12, 24, August 31, 1853, NARG 75, LR, MS; Jane Williamson to Andrew Robertson, March 29, 1853, Jane Williamson to John Aiton, April 1, 1853, Thomas S. Williamson Papers, MHS.

[43] McLean to Ramsey, May 10, 1853, J. W. Hancock to Gorman, July 1, 1853, Bailly to Murphy, October 9, 1853, Bailly to Gorman, October 27, 1853, NARG 75, LR, MS; Gorman to Alex Faribault, June 18, 1853, NARG 75, LS, MS; Fred Sibley to Chouteau, April 18, 1853, Sibley Papers; Hancock to Treat, June 14, 1853, ABCFM Papers; R[obert] G. Murphy, Agent's Report, *SED*, no. 1, 33d Congress, 1st session, serial 690, p. 314.

[44] Murphy to Gorman, September 3, 1853, Gorman to the Commissioner of Indian Affairs (hereafter CIA), November 28, 1853, NARG 75, LR, St. Peter's Agency; Prescott to Murphy, September 1, 1853, Gorman to CIA, September 14, 1853, *HED*, no. 1, 33d Congress, 1st session, serial 710, p. 319, 296; Gorman to CIA, September 7, October 4, November 15, 1853, NARG 75, LR, MS; Riggs to Treat, June 22, September 19, December 15, 1853, Williamson to Treat, July 18, 1853, Samuel Pond to Treat, November (n.d.), 1853, ABCFM Papers; Prescott to Alex Faribault, August 1, 1853, Sibley Papers; *Minnesota Pioneer*, December 8, 1853.

[45] Gorman to CIA, September 14, 1853, *HED*, no. 1, 33d Congress, 1st session, serial 710, p. 296; Charles Mix to Gorman, September 27, 1853, NARG 75, LR, MS.

[46] Gorman to CIA, November 28, 1853, NARG 75, LR, St. Peter's Agency; Manypenny to Gorman, November 9, 1853, NARG 75, LR, MS, Gorman to CIA, November 15, 1853, NARG 75, LS, MS.

[47] Murphy to Gorman, March 4, 1854, NARG 75, LR, St. Peter's Agency; Gorman to CIA, January 9, 1854, NARG 75, LR, MS.

[48] Gorman was ordered to investigate Ramsey in May 1853, and he and his assistant, Richard M. Young, gathered testimony throughout the summer. Their report did not reach the Senate until late fall. It listed three main charges of fraud: Ramsey received the treaty money in gold and changed it to paper notes, apparently pocketing a profit; Ramsey and his secretary, Hugh Tyler, took a fee of 10 to 15 percent for acting as attorneys for the claimants in the treaty; and the commissioners "again and again" refused the demands of the Indians that the money be put into their hands so that they could distribute it. See Gorman to Manypenny, August 27, 1853, NARG 75, LR, St. Peter's Agency; Mix to Gorman, May 28, 1853, NARG 75, LR, MS; Secretary of the Interior to CIA, January 11, 1853, June 17, 1853, NARG 48, LR, Indian Division of the Department of the Interior. For the efforts of Sibley and Ramsey to defend themselves, consult Sibley to Ramsey, December 7, 23, 1853, Ramsey Papers; Ramsey to Sibley, December 23, 1853, Sibley statement to Congress, January (n.d.), 1853, Sibley Papers. For the Senate findings, see *Senate Report*, February 24, 1854, no. 131, 33d Congress, 1st session, serial 706.

[49] *Daily Union* (Washington, D.C.), April 8, 1854. For Belland's ties to the Kaposia band consult "A Scout For Forty Years," Henry Belland, Sr., MHS Scrapbook No. 1; Elizabeth Jeffries obituary, *Iape Oaye/The Word Carrier*, January 1888.

[50] *National Intelligencer* (Washington, D.C.), April 10, 1854; *Daily Union*, April 9, 1854; Anderson, *Kinsmen of Another Kind*, 121, 152–54.

[51] *National Intelligencer*, April 10, 1854; *Daily Union*, April 8, 9, 1854.

[52] Secretary of the Interior to the President, April 5, 1854, NARG 48, LR, Indian Division of the Department of the Interior; Gorman to Manypenny, March 27, 1855, NARG 75, LR, St. Peter's Agency; *Daily Union*, April 22, 1854.

[53] Secretary of the Interior to Manypenny, April 13, 1854, NARG 48, LR, Indian Division of the Department of the Interior; Treat to the Dakota Mission, April 5, 1854, ABCFM Papers; Joseph R. Brown to W[illiam] J. Cullen, September 10, 1859, *SED*, no. 2, 36th Congress, 1st session, serial 1023, p. 451–53.

[54] *Daily Minnesota Pioneer* (St. Paul), May 5, 1854; *Minnesota Democrat* (St. Paul), May 3, 1854.

[55] *Daily Minnesota Pioneer*, May 5, 1854; *Minnesota Democrat*, May 3, 1854; Treaty with the Mdewakanton, Wahpekute, Sisseton, and Wahpeton Sioux, May 25, 1858, NARG 75, DRNRUT; Gorman to Manypenny, August 22, 1855, NARG 75, LR, St. Peter's Agency. The Senate amendment included a section that expanded the eastern Sioux reservations

down to the Little Cottonwood River. Obviously, Little Crow left after the Senate had acted but did not realize the need for the president's signature on the legislation. See *Daily Minnesota Pioneer*, May 8, 1854; *Minnesota Weekly Democrat* (St. Paul), May 10, 1854. Little Crow apparently thought that the $20,035 was part of sums held back in the past, but it actually came out of funds due in 1854; see Murphy to Manypenny, September 20, 1855, NARG 75, LR, St. Peter's Agency.

[56] *Daily Union*, April 9, 27, 28, 29, 1854.

[57] *Daily Minnesota Pioneer*, June 3, 1854; *Weekly Minnesotian* (St. Paul), May 13, 1854; Viola, *Indian Legacy of Charles Bird King*, 114–18.

[58] *Daily Union*, April 9, 22, 1854.

Chapter 5. Spokesman for the Sioux

[1] The Mdewakantons initially thought that the money came from the 1837 education fund, but it apparently came from other sources. While the Sioux eventually received the sum, they still thought that the government owed them fifteen thousand dollars more, and a new controversy erupted over this money in 1855. See Murphy to Manypenny, September 20, 1855, Gorman to Murphy, October 20, 1855, NARG 75, LR, St. Peter's Agency.

[2] *Daily Minnesota Pioneer*, May 5, 1854 (quotation). See also J. Travis Rosser to Andrew Robertson, May 12, 1854, NARG 75, LR, MS.

[3] *Daily Minnesota Pioneer*, May 5, 1854; Daniels, "Reminiscences of Little Crow," *Minnesota Collections* 12(1905–08):520. Regarding promises made in Washington, see also Treaty with the Mdewakanton, Wahpekute, Sisseton, and Wahpeton Sioux, May 25, 1858, NARG 75, DRNRUT.

[4] Daniels, "Reminiscences of Little Crow," *Minnesota Collections* 12(1905–08):520–21; Philander Prescott to Gorman, June 27, 1854, NARG 75, LR, MS; Lieutenant Colonel Francis Lee to Major Francis N. Page, June 30, 1854, NARG 393, Department of the West and Western Department, 1853–1861; *St. Paul Pioneer Press*, October 24, 1897.

[5] Charles Mitchell, "Our Interpreter's Story," *Iape Oaye/The Word Carrier*, April 2–3, 1887.

[6] Mitchell, "Our Interpreter's Story," *Iape Oaye/The Word Carrier*, April 2–3, 1887.

[7] Daniels, "Reminiscences of Little Crow," *Minnesota Collections* 12(1905–08):522–23; Lee to Page, June 30, 1854, NARG 393, LR, Department of the West and Western Department, 1853–1861. The seven Ojibway warriors were quietly released in September after civil authorities refused to incure the expense necessary to try them; see Lee to Page, July 8, September 19, 1854, Gorman to Page, August 10, 1854, NARG 393, LR, Department of the West and Western Department, 1853–1861.

[8] Samuel Pond to Treat, August 14, October 19, 1854, Riggs to Treat, August 3, November 13, 1854, ABCFM Papers; Francis Huebschmann to Manypenny, June 28, 1856, Moses N. Adams to Manypenny, August 3, 1854, NARG 75, LR, St. Peter's Agency; *Daily Pioneer and Democrat* (St. Paul), June 26, 1856. Gorman requested that dragoons be stationed at Fort Ridgely to stop the intertribal warfare, but his request was denied. See Secretary of the Interior to Secretary of War, August 4, 1854, NARG 48, LS, Indian Division of Department of the Interior; Jefferson Davis to R. McClelland, August 11, 1854, Charles E. Mix to Gorman, August 18, 1854, NARG 75, LR, MS.

[9] Secretary of the Interior to the President, April 5, 1854, NARG 48, LS, Indian Division

of the Department of the Interior; Manypenny to Gorman, April 19, 1854, Gorman to Murphy, June 15, 1854, Prescott to Gorman, June 16, 1854, Gorman to Manypenny, July 18, 1854, Gorman's annual report, September 30, 1854, Mix to Gorman, August 22, 1854, NARG 75, LR, MS; Prescott to Murphy, October 10, 1854, *SED*, no. 1, 33d Congress, 2d session, serial 746, p. 282; *Daily Minnesota Pioneer*, June 1, 1854; Prescott to Murphy, September 3, 1856, Manypenny to Huebschmann, November 20, 1856, *SED*, no. 5, 34th Congress, 3d session, serial 875, p. 606–11, 612.

[10] *Daily Minnesota Pioneer*, March 9, 23, 1854; Riggs to Treat, March 9, August 3, 26, 1854, January 11, 1855, Williamson to Treat, March 28, 1854, June 13, 1855, ABCFM Papers; Murphy to Gorman, September 3, 1853, NARG 75, LR, St. Peter's Agency.

[11] Prescott to Murphy, October 10, 1854, *SED*, no. 1, 33d Congress, 2d session, serial 746, p. 282.

[12] Sioux contractors Culver and Farmington to Gorman, September 6, 1854, NARG 75, LR, MS; Gorman to Manypenny, December 7, 1854, *SED*, no. 26, 33d Congress, 2d session, serial 751, p. 4–6; Lee to Page, July 8, 1854, NARG 393, LR, Department of the West and Western Department, 1853–1861. Lee concluded: "The Sioux are not at all satisfied as a body with their treaty and I am convinced that if proper measures are not promptly taken to conciliate them . . . which can only be done by their agent living among them . . . there will certainly . . . be an Outbreak on this frontier."

[13] Major H. Day to Murphy, October 19, 1854, NARG 393, Letterbook, Fort Ridgely, June 1854–November 1858 (quotation). See also Captain J. Hayden to Lieutenant A. F. Bond, November 18, 1854, NARG 393, LR, Fort Ridgely, 1853–1859; Brown to Gorman, October 28, 1854, Prescott to Gorman, December 2, 1854, NARG 75, LR, MS.

[14] Gorman to Manypenny, October 31, 1855, Murphy to Gorman, September 22, 1855, Prescott to Murphy, September 10, 1855, *HED*, no. 1, 34th Congress, 1st session, serial 840, p. 368–70, 378–81, 384–85; Huebschmann to Manypenny, October 15, 1856, Murphy to Huebschmann, September 24, 1856, *SED*, no. 5, 34th Congress, 3d session, serial 875, p. 588–89, 604–6; Murphy to Gorman, April 7, May 17, July 5, 1855, NARG 75, LR, MS; Gorman to Manypenny, April 19, 1855, Murphy to Manypenny, May 25, 1855, NARG 75, LR, St. Peter's Agency; Gorman to CIA, July 12, 1855, NARG 75, LS, MS.

[15] Daniels, "Reminiscences of Little Crow," *Minnesota Collections* 12 (1905–08):518; Gorman to Murphy, April 30, 1855, NARG 75, LS, MS.

[16] Prescott to Gorman, December 2, 1854, NARG 75, LR, MS (quotation). Sixteen lodges of Little Crow's band spent the winter of 1854–55 in the St. Croix River valley. See Henry Belland to Gorman, January 22, 1855, Murphy to Gorman, August 22, 1855, NARG 75, LR, MS; Gorman to Murphy, September 5, 1855, NARG 75, LS, MS; Gorman to CIA, May 30, December 5, 1855, NARG 75, LR, St. Peter's Agency.

[17] Riggs, *Mary and I*, 132–33; Williamson to Treat, February 17, 1854, Riggs to Treat, August 26, 1854, January 30, May 23, 1855, July 31, 1856, ABCFM Papers; Riggs to Murphy, September 1, 1854, *SED*, no. 1, 33d Congress, 2d session, serial 746, p. 274–75.

[18] Riggs, "Dakota Mission," *Minnesota Collections* 3(1870-80):124 (quotation); Mix to Gorman, October 6, 1854, NARG 75, LR, MS; Riggs to Treat, May 11, 1853, August 26, 1854, January 30, February 19, 1855, ABCFM Papers; Thomas A. Robertson, Reminiscences.

[19] Huebschmann to Manypenny, June 20, 28, 1856, NARG 75, LS, Northern Superintendency (hereafter NS); Williamson to Treat, June 24, 1856, ABCFM Papers.

[20] Huebschmann to Manypenny, June 28, 1856, NARG 75, LS, NS.

[21] *Daily Pioneer and Democrat*, June 26, 1856; Huebschmann to Manypenny, June 28, 1856, NARG 75, LS, NS.

[22] Huebschmann to Manypenny, June 28, 1856, NARG 75, LS, NS.

[23] *Daily Pioneer and Democrat*, November 19, 29, 1855, January 7, 1856; Testimony of James Wells, March 6, 1855, NARG 75, LR, St. Peter's Agency; Theodore E. Potter, "Captain Potter's Recollections of Minnesota Experiences," *Minnesota History Bulletin* 1(November 1916):426–28.

[24] Major H. Day to Assistant Adjutant General, January 26, 1855, NARG 393, LR, Department of the West and Western Department, 1853–1861.

[25] The debate over what to do with the Sioux prisoners is a classic example of the difficulty reservation officials faced in stopping intertribal warfare. No individual or government agency wished to take responsibility for punishing Indians. See Colonel E. B. Alexander to the Assistant Adjutant General, July 22, 1856, Alexander to Huebschmann, August 18, 1856, Lieutenant Henry E. Magruder to Assistant Adjutant General, September 1, 1856, NARG 393, Letterbook, Fort Ridgely, June 1854–November 1858; Captain Daniel Shaw to Manypenny, July 16, 1856, NARG 75, LS, NS; Order of J. J. Nash, U.S. Commissioner, September 16, 1856, Murphy to Alexander, August 14, 1856, NARG 393, LR, Fort Ridgely, 1853-59; Lieutenant Robert Hunter to Lieutenant G. D. Ruggles, June 30, 1856, Huebschmann to Manypenny, August 22, 1856, Magruder to the Marshal at St. Paul, August 31, 1856, Alexander to CIA, September 15, 1856, NARG 75, LR, St. Peter's Agency.

[26] M. M. Hayden to Gorman, October 28, 1854, Petition of New Ulm Farmers, August 1855, NARG 75, LR, MS; Captain T. Steele to Day, August 8, 1855, Gorman to Day, August 13, 1855, NARG 393, LR, Fort Ridgely, 1853–59; Petition of Settlers at Scotch Lake, August 27, 1855, NARG 75, LR, St. Peter's Agency; Alexander Berghold, *The Indians' Revenge; or, Days of Horror. Some Appalling Events in the History of the Sioux* (San Francisco: P. J. Thomas, 1891), 26–51. See also Hildegard B. Johnson, "The Germans," in June D. Holmquist, ed., *They Chose Minnesota: A Survey of the State's Ethnic Groups* (St. Paul: Minnesota Historical Society Press, 1981), 165.

[27] Unaddressed Flandrau letter, September 22, 1857, NARG 75, LR, NS.

[28] See, for example, Day to Assistant Adjutant General, January 26, April 16, 1855, Lee to Page, July 8, 1854, NARG 393, Letterbook, Fort Ridgely, June 1854–November 1858; Prescott to Day, March 18, 1855, NARG 393, LR, Fort Ridgely, 1853–59.

[29] Thomas Hughes, "Causes and Results of the Inkpaduta Massacre," *Minnesota Collections* 12(1905–08):264–72; Abbie Gardner-Sharp, *History of the Spirit Lake Massacre and Captivity of Miss Abbie Gardner* (Des Moines: Iowa Printing Co., 1885), 35–273; Riggs, *Mary and I*, 138–39; Lucius F. Hubbard and Return I. Holcombe, *Minnesota as a State, 1858–1870*, vol. 3 of *Minnesota in Three Centuries, 1655–1908*, 3:217–23; Kintzing Pritchette Report, October 15, 1857, NARG 75, LR, St. Peter's Agency. For information on the government response to the Lott killings, see Major Samuel Woods to Gorman, February 9, 1854, Gorman to CIA, March 2, 1854, NARG 75, LR, Upper Missouri Agency.

[30] There is conflicting testimony over whether Inkpaduta's people ever received annuities. Flandrau states that the band as a whole was turned away from the annuity table. Even so, the government claimed that they were annuity Indians. See minutes of examination of Ta-te-yah-he, no date, Alexander Faribault affadavit, February 19, 1860, W. J. Cullen to J. W. Denver, July 26, 1857, NARG 75, LR, St. Peter's Agency; Flandrau, Official Account, April 11, 1857, *SED*, no. 11, 35th Congress, 1st session, serial 919, p. 357–59; Hubbard and Holcombe, *Minnesota in Three Centuries*, 3:253.

[31] Flandrau to Huebschmann, April 16, 1857, Huebschmann to Denver, May 8, 1857, Pritchette Report, October 15, 1857, NARG 75, LR, St. Peter's Agency; Adjutant General

to Commanding Officer at Fort Snelling, May 5, 1857, NARG 393, LR, Department of the West and Western Department, 1853–1861; Alexander to Assistant Adjutant General, May 23, 1857, NARG 393, Letterbook, Fort Ridgely, June 1854–November 1858; Hubbard and Holcombe, *Minnesota in Three Centuries*, 3:242–49, 255–56; Riggs, *Mary and I*, 142.

[32] Alexander to Assistant Adjutant General, May 15, 1857, NARG 393, Letterbook, Fort Ridgely, June 1854–November 1858.

[33] Cullen to Denver, July 15, 1857, *SED*, no. 11, 35th Congress, 1st session, serial 919, p. 362–63.

[34] Captain Bernard Bee to Major W. W. Morris, July 2, 1857, NARG 393, LR, Fort Ridgely, 1853-59; Hubbard and Holcombe, *Minnesota in Three Centuries*, 3:255–56.

[35] Cullen to Denver, July 26, 1857, Pritchette Report, October 15, 1857, NARG 75, LR, St. Peter's Agency; *Henderson Democrat*, July 16, 1857.

[36] Sherman to Colonel John Abercrombie, July 16, 1857, NARG 393, LR, Fort Ridgely, 1853–59 (quotation). See also Cullen to Denver, July 26, 1857, Pritchette Report, October 15, 1857, NARG 75, LR, St. Peter's Agency; Riggs, *Mary and I*, 142–43.

[37] Sherman to Abercrombie, July 16, 1857, NARG 393, LR, Fort Ridgely, 1853–59.

[38] Cullen to Denver, July 26, 1857, NARG 75, LR, St. Peter's Agency (quotation). See also Sherman to Abercrombie, July 16, 1857, NARG 393, LR, Fort Ridgely, 1853–59; Abercrombie to Assistant Adjutant General, July 20, 1857, NARG 393, Letterbook, Fort Ridgely, June 1854–November 1858; Riggs to Treat, July 22, 1857, ABCFM Papers; Hubbard and Holcombe, *Minnesota in Three Centuries*, 3:261–63.

[39] Inyangmani's band is often identified as being of the Sisseton tribe, probably because of the tribal affiliation of his wife. See also the discussion of Little Crow's relatives at Lac qui Parle in Appendix 1.

[40] Denver to Pritchette, July 22, 1857, *SED*, no. 11, 35th Congress, 1st session, serial 919, p. 365.

[41] Cullen to Denver, July 26, 1857, NARG 75, LR, St. Peter's Agency.

[42] Sherman to Lieutenant James Hunter, July 22, 1857, NARG 393, LR, Fort Ridgely, 1853–59 (quotation). See also Cullen to Denver, July 26, 1857, NARG 75, LR, St. Peter's Agency; Hubbard and Holcombe, *Minnesota in Three Centuries*, 3:263–66; Riggs, *Mary and I*, 142–44; List of Indians on Little Crow Expedition, "Inkpaduta File," 1857, NARG 75, LR, NS; Riggs to Treat, August 13, 1857, ABCFM Papers. Antoine J. Campbell later claimed that he was in charge of the expedition, but he apparently did so in order to secure claims for expenses; see "Claims for goods and services as furnished in the Expedition against Inkpadutah in 1859," NARG 75, Special Files, no. 132.

[43] Cullen to Denver, July 26, 1857, NARG 75, LR, St. Peter's Agency.

[44] Captain Alfred Sully to Hunter, August 2, 1857, NARG 393, LR, Fort Ridgely, 1853–59; Abercrombie to Assistant Adjutant General, August 8, 1857, NARG 393, Letterbook, Fort Ridgely, June 1854–November 1858; A[ntoine] J. Campbell, Report, August 1857, *SED*, no. 11, 35th Congress, 1st session, serial 919, p. 376; Hubbard and Holcombe, *Minnesota in Three Centuries*, 3:264–66; Riggs to Treat, August 13, 1857, ABCFM Papers.

[45] Abercrombie to Assistant Adjutant General, August 8, 1857, NARG 393, Letterbook, Fort Ridgely, June 1854–November 1858; Sully to Hunter, August 6, 1857, NARG 393, LR, Fort Ridgely, 1853–59.

[46] Minutes of Cullen Council, included in Pritchette Report, October 15, 1857, NARG 75, St. Peter's Agency. See also Pritchette to Denver, August 5, 1857, *SED*, no. 11, 35th Congress, 1st session, serial 919, p. 374.

[47] Pritchette to Denver, August 16, 1857, Cullen to Denver, August 20, 1857, NARG 75, St. Peter's Agency; Mix to Pritchette, August 25, 1857, *SED*, no. 11, 35th Congress, 1st session, serial 919, p. 383.

[48] Abercrombie to Captain H. C. Pratt, August 30, 1857, NARG 393, Letterbook, Fort Ridgely, June 1854–November 1858; Andrew Robertson to Abercrombie, August 30, 1857, Pratt to Abercrombie, September 15, 1857, NARG 393, LR, Fort Ridgely, 1853–59.

[49] Abercrombie to Pratt, September 16, 1857, NARG 393, Letterbook, Fort Ridgely, June 1854–November 1858.

Chapter 6. The Broken Promise

[1] Pritchette Report, October 5, 1857, NARG 75, LR, St. Peter's Agency. Pritchette sent an earlier report that, in part, dealt with Indian leadership. Although he did not discuss individuals, he did allude to the difficulties that leaders had in maintaining influence, concluding that the eastern Sioux were "divided into separate bands under their own chiefs, without any common allegiance consequently there can be no union of action to a common end." See Pritchette to J. W. Denver, August 16, 1857, NARG 75, LR, St. Peter's Agency.

[2] Gideon H. Pond, Diary, August 2–3, 1837, Pond Papers; E. Dudley Parson, Letter to Editor, *Minneapolis Journal*, undated clipping, Alan Woolworth files, MHS.

[3] *Henderson Democrat*, June 5, 1856.

[4] *Henderson Democrat*, August 14, 1856.

[5] Riggs to Treat, July 31, November 30, 1856, ABCFM Papers; *Daily Pioneer and Democrat*, August 18, 1856.

[6] Williamson to Treat, March 17, 1857, ABCFM Papers; *Henderson Democrat*, August 14, 1856.

[7] Williamson to Treat, November (n.d.), 1857, ABCFM Papers; Receipts from purchase of food from Indians, November 17, 1856–March 31, 1857, Flandrau Papers; John H. Case, "Historical Notes of Grey Cloud Island and Its Vicinity," *Minnesota Collections* 15(1915):376; James Magner, Farm Report, September 24, 1857, *SED*, no. 11, 35th Congress, 1st session, serial 919, p. 349.

[8] There is some disagreement over the location of the Redwood Agency villages prior to the war. It is possible, indeed probable, that they moved from time to time. Consult Folwell, *History of Minnesota*, 2:226; Hubbard and Holcombe, *Minnesota in Three Centuries*, 3:273; Miscellaneous correspondence in the Satterlee Papers. Although Folwell uses a loose definition of "village," his locations are accurate.

[9] Cullen to Denver, September 28, 1857, *SED*, no. 11, 35th Congress, 1st session, serial 919, p. 339.

[10] Pritchette Report, October 5, 1857, NARG 75, LR, St. Peter's Agency; *Henderson Democrat*, June 5, 1856; Cullen to Denver, September 28, 1857, Flandrau to Cullen, September 24, 1857, *SED*, no. 11, 35th Congress, 1st session, serial 919, p. 339, 347–48.

[11] See "Nathan Myrick and others, claims against the Sioux of Minnesota for goods and supplies furnished in 1861–62," 1882–1886 (hereafter "Sioux claims"), NARG 75, Special Files no. 274.

[12] The petition is included in Gorman to CIA, January 16, 1856, J. Shields to Manypenny, February 12, 1856, NARG 75, LR, St. Peter's Agency. See also the unsigned report (presumably by Murphy) on the traders' role in the affair, (n.d.) 1856, NARG 75, LS, NS.

[13] "Sioux Papers," 1856, NARG 75, LS, NS. See also Huebschmann to CIA, April 2, 1856,

NARG 75, LS, NS; Murphy and Gorman to CIA, January 16, 1856, NARG 75, LR, St. Peter's Agency; Riggs to Treat, March 4, 1856, ABCFM Papers.

[14] Flandrau to Cullen, September 24, 1857, SED, no. 11, 35th Congress, 1st session, serial 919, p. 347–48. On land speculation, see contracts for Gorman and Nathan Hill, May 27, 1854, Flandrau Papers; Brown Family Petition, August 3, 1861, NARG 75, LR, St. Peter's Agency.

[15] Andrew Robertson to Flandrau, April 1, 1857, Flandrau Papers; Riggs to Treat, August 13, 1857, ABCFM Papers.

[16] Cullen to Denver, November 26, December 24, 1857, NARG 75, LR, St. Peter's Agency; Captain Alfred Sully to Cullen, October 12, 1857, Denver to Cullen, November 10, 1857, NARG 75, LR, NS.

[17] All information and quotations on the treaty negotiation of 1858 found in the pages to follow are in "Treaty with the Mdewakanton, Wahpekute, Sisseton, and Wahpeton Sioux," March 15–June 21, 1858, NARG 75, DRNRUT. See also *Henderson Democrat*, March 3, 1858.

[18] The Sioux held the Germans in general contempt; see Anderson, *Kinsmen of Another Kind*, 240–43, 263–67.

[19] *St. Paul Pioneer Press*, October 24, 1897; *Mankato Weekly Independent*, July 10, 1858; *Minneapolis Journal*, December 6, 1916, p. 1; Brown to Mix, July 2, 1858, Brown to Cullen, September 1, 1858, February 6, April 15, 1860, NARG 75, LR, St. Peter's Agency. Little Crow's daughter, Jane Williams, tried in 1916 to retrieve the money that her father deposited in a St. Paul bank, but no account was discovered.

[20] *Washington Union*, March 16, 1858.

[21] *Washington Union*, March 20, 28, 1858. One other mention of the Sioux delegation appears in *Washington Union*, May 28, 1858, describing a picnic that the Indian leaders had south of the capital at "Arlington Spring."

[22] Eastman, *Indian Heroes*, 47–48; Riggs to Treat, March 21, April 11, 1859, ABCFM Papers; *Washington Union*, April 7, 17, 1858. Riggs noted that while in Washington the entire delegation had difficulty heeding the commandment regarding adultery, especially Otherday, who "signalized himself in debauchery, for they [the delegation] had white men along to teach them." Besides Otherday's companion, two other women went back to Minnesota with the delegation, but apparently they failed to remain on the reservation. *Washington Union*, April 10, 1858, reported that a major social event, a costume ball, occurred at Senator William Gwin's residence on the evening of April 8. President James Buchanan, Secretary of the Interior Jacob Thompson, more than twenty senators and their wives, and many other dignitaries were in attendance. This ball was probably the one that Little Crow attended.

[23] "Auto-Biography of Maj. Lawrence Taliaferro," *Minnesota Collections* 6(1894):253–54.

[24] Brown to Cullen, September 1, 1858, NARG 75, LR, St. Peter's Agency; Antoine Freniere, Letter to Editor, *St. Paul Pioneer*, December 14, 1862. One Washington newspaper reported that the delegation was pleased with the result of the negotiation. It is possible that some delegates, especially those inclined to farming, did not find fault with the negotiation. See *Washington Union*, June 23, 1858.

[25] Brown to Cullen, September 1, 1858, NARG 75, LR, St. Peter's Agency; Freniere, Letter, *St. Paul Pioneer*, December 14, 1862.

[26] *St. Paul Pioneer Press*, October 24, 1897.

[27] Return I. Holcombe, ed., "A Sioux Story of the War: Chief Big Eagle's Story of the Sioux Outbreak of 1862," *Minnesota Collections* 6(1894):384.

[28] Red Owl's rise to power began in 1857, as agent Flandrau reported that he was "ap-

pointed captain of Police." But evidence to date this transition in power from Little Crow's leadership to Red Owl's is slight. Red Owl was acting as tribal spokesman in 1861. See Major W. Wilson to CIA, January 12, 1860, NARG 393, LS, Fort Ridgely, 1858–1860; Flandrau to Huebschmann, October 12, 1857, NARG 75, LR, NS; *Minnesota Pioneer*, August 23, 1849; *Weekly Pioneer and Democrat* (St. Paul), June 28, 1861; Thomas J. Galbraith to Clark W. Thompson, July 24, 1861, NARG 75, LR, St. Peter's Agency.

[29] Brown had been a candidate for agent several times in the past; see "One Who Knows" to Secretary of War, March 5, 1842, Brown to Cullen, February 4, 1858, NARG 75, LR, St. Peter's Agency; Williamson to Treat, January 18, 1858, ABCFM Papers.

[30] Brown to Cullen, February 4, August 30, 1858, Cullen to Mix, March 3, September 18, 1858, Manypenny to Secretary of the Interior, April 8, 1856, NARG 75, LR, St. Peter's Agency.

[31] Brown to Cullen, September 30, 1858, *SED*, no. 1, 35th Congress, 2d session, serial 974, p. 402; *Henderson Democrat*, October 1, 1858.

[32] See Petition for Schools, February 15, 1856, Brown to Cullen, February 4, 1858, NARG 75, LR, St. Peter's Agency; Robertson to Brown, September 29, 1858, *SED*, no. 1, 35th Congress, 2d session, serial 974, p. 409–10; Riggs to Treat, November 2, 1858, Williamson to Treat, November 18, 1858, ABCFM Papers; *Henderson Democrat*, June 16, 1858; Brown to Cullen, September 10, 1859, S[amuel] Brown to Joseph Brown, September 6, 1859, *SED*, no. 2, 36th Congress, 1st session, serial 1023, p. 459, 464–66.

[33] Samuel Brown to Joseph Brown, September 25, 1858, Joseph Brown to Cullen, September 30, 1858, *SED*, no. 1, 35th Congress, 2d session, serial 974, p. 411–13, 402; Cullen to Joseph Brown, September 6, 1859, Joseph Brown to Cullen, September 10, 1859, *SED*, no. 2, 36th Congress, 1st session, serial 1023, p. 466–69, 448–57; Joseph Brown to Cullen, March 28, 1859, Brown to Indian Office, April 18, 1859, Cullen to CIA, August 13, 1859, NARG 75, LR, St. Peter's Agency; Riggs to Treat, August 24, 1859, ABCFM Papers; Frederick P. Leavenworth, Diary, 1858–59, Frederick P. Leavenworth Papers, MHS.

[34] Brown to Cullen, September 30, 1858, *SED*, no. 1, 35th Congress, 2d session, serial 974, p. 401–2.

[35] Riggs to Treat, November 27, 1858, ABCFM Papers; Cullen to A. B. Greenwood, August 15, September 15, 1859, *SED*, no. 2, 36th Congress, 1st session, serial 1023, p. 435, 420–22.

[36] Cullen to Greenwood, August 15, September 15, 1859, *SED*, no. 2, 36th Congress, 1st session, serial 1023, p. 435, 420–22.

[37] The changes that occurred near both agencies were remarkable. Besides the government documents, several travel accounts describe them. Consult Potter, "Captain Potter's Recollections," *Minnesota History Bulletin* 1(November 1916):426–27; Leavenworth, Diary, 1858–59.

[38] *Henderson Democrat*, August 4, 1858; Gideon Pond, Diary, August 2, 1837; E. Dudley Parson, Letter to Editor, *Minneapolis Journal*, undated clipping, Alan Woolworth files.

[39] Leavenworth, Diary, October 1–3, 1859; Receipts from purchase of food, 1856–57, Flandrau Papers.

[40] Daniels, "Reminiscences of Little Crow," *Minnesota Collections* 12(1905–08):524; Sioux annuity rolls, 1857, 1860, NARG 75.

[41] Williamson gives an account of the discussion in Williamson to Treat, November 18, 1859, ABCFM Papers.

[42] Williamson to Treat, October 17, 1862, ABCFM Papers.

[43] Riggs to Treat, January 21, 1858, ABCFM Papers.

[44] Williamson to Treat, November 18, 1859, ABCFM Papers. See also Prescott, "Contributions to the History, Customs, and Opinions of the Dacota Tribes," in *Historical and Statistical Information*, 2:189; Pond, "Powers and Influences of Dakota Medicine-men," in *Historical and Statistical Information*, 4:641–51.

[45] Prescott, "Contributions to the History, Customs, and Opinions of the Dacota Tribes," in *Historical and Statistical Information*, 2:189; Andrew Robertson to Flandrau, April 4, 1857, Flandrau Papers; Brown to Cullen, September 10, 1859, *SED*, no. 2, 36th Congress, 1st session, serial 1023, p. 453.

[46] *Henderson Democrat*, April 20, 1859; Helen M. Tarble, "The Story of My Capture and Escape during the Minnesota Indian Massacre of 1862," in *The Garland Library of Narratives of North American Indian Captivities* (hereafter *Garland Library*), ed. Wilcomb E. Washburn (1904; New York: Garland Publishing Co., 1976), 105·14–17; Williamson to Treat, April 30, 1860, ABCFM Papers.

[47] Thomas J. Hendricks to Denver, January 15, 1859, Francis Bansen to Secretary of the Interior, February 2, 1859, Abercrombie's proclamation, May 11, 1859, Cullen to Greenwood, June 7, 1859, Henry M. Rice to Jacob Thompson, June 15, 1859, Thompson to Greenwood, July 5, 1859, W. G. Dodge to Cyrus Aldrich, December 13, 1859, NARG 75, LR, St. Peter's Agency; Abercrombie to Assistant Adjutant General, February 20, 1859, Mix to Thompson, April 23, 1859, Assistant Adjutant General to Colonel E. V. Sumner, July 19, 1859, NARG 393, LR, Department of the West and Western Department, 1853–1861; *Henderson Democrat*, May 11, 1859.

[48] *Henderson Weekly Democrat*, January 14, 1860.

[49] See Sioux claims in NARG 75, LR, St. Peter's Agency.

[50] Brown to Cullen, July 7, 1860, NARG 75, LR, St. Peter's Agency; Major W. Wilson to Bvt. Major J. C. Pemberton, June 29, 1860, NARG 393, LS, Fort Ridgely, 1858–1860; Thompson to Governor of Minnesota, July 17, 1860, NARG 48, LS, Indian Division of the Department of the Interior; Abercrombie to Assistant Adjutant General, September 6, 1860, NARG 393, LR, Department of the West and Western Department, 1853–1861.

[51] Brown to Captain G. A. DeRussy, August 10, 1860, DeRussy to Assistant Adjutant General, September 2, 1860, Morris to Assistant Adjutant General, September 12, 1860, NARG 393, LR, Department of the West and Western Department, 1853–1861; Thomas Russell to CIA, July 3, 1861, NARG 75, LR, St. Peter's Agency; *Minnesota Statesman* (St. Peter), August 30, 1861; Aldrich to William P. Dole, December 21, 1861, NARG 75, LR, St. Peter's Agency.

[52] Army patrols were finally sent into the regions east of the Sioux reservations in summer 1860. See Major W. Wilson to Bvt. Major J. C. Pemberton, June 29, 1860, NARG 393, LS, Fort Ridgely, 1858–1860. Brown's policies can be found in Brown to Cullen, October 25, 1860, *SED*, no. 1, 36th Congress, 2d session, serial 1078, p. 283–85; Brown to Cullen, February 6, July 7, 1860, NARG 75, LR, St. Peter's Agency.

[53] The best discussion of the compensation issue is in Folwell, *History of Minnesota*, Appendix 9, 2:398–99. See also *The Sisseton and Wahpeton Bands of Sioux Indians vs. the United States*, 1901–07, Court of Claims docket no. 22524, bound testimony in MHS (hereafter Sisseton-Wahpeton Claims, docket no. 22524), p. 306–8.

[54] Testimony of Nathan Myrick, 1886, Sioux claims, NARG 75, Special Files no. 274.

[55] Cullen, Council notes, December 1, 3, 1860, NARG 75, LR, St. Peter's Agency (quotations). See also Testimony of Myrick, 1886, Sioux claims, NARG 75, Special Files no. 274; Henry Benjamin Whipple, *Lights and Shadows of a Long Episcopate* (New York: Macmillan, 1912), 138; Folwell, *History of Minnesota*, 2:399.

[56] Charles A. Eastman, interview by William W. Folwell, May 24, 1919 (quotation), Folwell Papers. George Decker to CIA, October 26, 1861, NARG 75, LR, St. Peter's Agency; Testimony of Myrick, 1886, Sioux claims, NARG 75, Special Files no. 274.

[57] Decker to CIA, October 26, 1861, NARG 75, LR, St. Peter's Agency; Testimony of Myrick and Testimony of White Spider, Sioux claims, NARG 75, Special Files no. 274.

[58] Holcombe, ed., "Chief Big Eagle's Story," *Minnesota Collections* 6(1894):385.

[59] Galbraith to Thompson, October 1, 1861, *SED*, no. 1, 37th Congress, 2d session, serial 1117, p. 704; Sarah F. Wakefield, *Six Weeks in the Sioux Tepees: A Narrative of Indian Captivity* (Shakopee, Minn.: Argus Book and Job Printing Co., 1864), 6–7.

[60] *Weekly Pioneer and Democrat*, June 28, 1861.

[61] Galbraith to Thompson, July 24, 1861, NARG 75, LR, St. Peter's Agency. See also Thompson to Dole, August 6, 1861, NARG 75, LR, St. Peter's Agency.

[62] Most of the correspondence in NARG 75, LR, St. Peter's Agency for the years 1859–61 covers the growing problems at Yellow Medicine. For quotation from Galbraith, see Aldrich to Dole, July 16, 1861, NARG 75, LR, St. Peter's Agency. See also Anderson, *Kinsmen of Another Kind*, 232–48; Thompson to Major William H. Dyke and Galbraith to Lieutenant Colonel James George, September 5, 1861, NARG 393, LR, Fort Ridgely, 1853–1861.

[63] *Minnesota Statesman*, August 30, 1861; *Daily Pioneer and Democrat* (St. Paul), October 16, 1860.

[64] Galbraith to Thompson, January 27, 1863, *HED*, no. 1, 38th Congress, 1st session, serial 1182, p. 383.

[65] *Hutchinson Leader*, September 27, 1912, p. 1. Lake Judson was drained in about 1900.

[66] *Hutchinson Leader*, September 27, 1912, p. 1.

Chapter 7. The Failure of Accommodation

[1] Mrs. N. D. [Urania] White, "Captivity Among the Sioux, August 18 to September 26, 1862," *Minnesota Collections* 9(1901):396–97; Mrs. J. E. [Jannette] De Camp Sweet, "Mrs. J. E. De Camp Sweet's Narrative of Her Captivity in the Sioux Outbreak of 1862," *Minnesota Collections* 6(1894):355–57; Tarble, "The Story of My Capture and Escape," in *Garland Library*, 105:21–22; *Hutchinson Leader*, January 6, 1893, September 27, 1912, p. 1.

[2] Galbraith to Thompson, January 27, 1863, *HED*, no. 1, 38th Congress, 1st session, serial 1182, p. 398 (quotation), 403. Some sources suggest that the soldiers' lodge at Redwood was formally organized during the summer. A Nathan Myrick letter, however, shows that it was functioning by early May and probably operated intermittently throughout the several years prior to the war. Galbraith's policy of giving food to farmer Indians and denying hunters annuities was deliberate and reported by many farmer Indians in later testimony. For information on events in spring 1862, see Testimony of Wakanhdikaha, Mahpiyawakunza, and Wakanwaśte and Andrew Myrick to Nathan Myrick, May 18, 1862, Sioux claims, NARG 75, Special files no. 274; Galbraith to Thompson, June 4, August 27, 1861, NARG 75, LR, St. Peter's Agency; Winifred W. Barton, *John P. Williamson: A Brother to the Sioux* (New York: Fleming H. Revell Co., 1919), 47; Hubbard and Holcombe, *Minnesota in Three Centuries*, 3:283–85; Isaac V. D. Heard, *History of the Sioux War and Massacres of 1862 and 1863* (New York: Harper and Brothers, 1864), 48; Berghold, *Indians' Revenge*, 77; Whipple, *Lights and Shadows*, 106–7; *Missionary Papers. By the Bishop Seabury Mission. Number Twenty-three* (Faribault, Minn.: Alex. Johnson Book and Job Printer, Statesman Office, 1862).

[3] Captain Alfred Sully to Cullen, October 12, 1857, NARG 75, LR, NS.

[4] Thomas A. Robertson, Reminiscences.

[5] Galbraith to Thompson, August 27, 1861, NARG 75, LR, St. Peter's Agency; Jeremiah Chester Donahower, Journal, July 1861, Jeremiah C. Donahower Papers, MHS.

[6] Galbraith to Thompson, August 27, 1861, NARG 75, LR, St. Peter's Agency; Donahower, Journal, July 1861, Donahower Papers.

[7] Andrew Myrick to Nathan Myrick, May 18, 1862, Sioux claims, NARG 75, Special files no. 274 (quotation). See also Galbraith to Thompson, January 27, 1863, NARG 75, LR, St. Peter's Agency; Hubbard and Holcombe, *Minnesota in Three Centuries*, 3:285; Heard, *History of the Sioux War*, 48; Berghold, *Indians' Revenge*, 77; Williamson to Treat, October 17, 1862, ABCFM Papers; Holcombe, ed., "Chief Big Eagle's Story," *Minnesota Collections* 6(1894):387–88.

[8] Wakefield, *Six Weeks in the Sioux Tepees*, 6–7, 9–10. See also Testimony of Sioux Indians in Sioux claims, NARG 75, Special files no. 274; Indian Credit Book, Louis Robert Papers, MHS.

[9] Henry B. Whipple, "Civilization and Christianization of the Ojibways in Minnesota," *Minnesota Collections* 9(1901):132; Whipple, *Lights and Shadows*, 107–8.

[10] Bishop Whipple noted that the war party was from Shakopee's soldiers' lodge and concluded that some of its members were responsible for the Acton murders; see Whipple, *Lights and Shadows*, 107–8. See also Holcombe to Satterlee, April (n.d.), 1915, Satterlee Papers; Hughes, *Indian Chiefs*, 16–31; Heard, *History of the Sioux War*, 52; Testimony of David Weston (Tunkanwanyakapi), Sisseton-Wahpeton Claims, docket no. 22524, p. 310; Pond, "The Dakota . . . as They Were in 1834," *Minnesota Collections* 12(1905–08):329; Holcombe, ed., "Chief Big Eagle's Story," *Minnesota Collections* 6(1894):388–89.

[11] At least two oral history sources suggest that Little Crow was acting as speaker when the election took place in the late spring of 1862. Yet Red Owl clearly performed these duties in 1861 (see Chapter 5, above), and there is no evidence to suggest that another election had occurred after Red Owl's death. See Testimony of David Weston and Testimony of Thomas Williamson (Mahpiya-śotodan), Sisseton-Wahpeton Claims, docket no. 22524, p. 310, 288, 291, 294; Elizabeth W. Lawrence, Reminiscences, April 27, 1965, MHS; *Minnesota Statesman*, August 30, 1861; "As Red Men Viewed It: Three Indian Accounts of the Uprising: Account of George Quinn," ed. Kenneth Carley, in *Minnesota History* 38(September 1962): 147; Holcombe, ed., "Chief Big Eagle's Story," *Minnesota Collections* 6(1894):386.

[12] For Galbraith's views on "making chiefs," consult Galbraith to Riggs, February 17, 1862, Riggs Papers, MHS. See also Testimony of David Weston, Sisseton-Wahpeton Claims, docket no. 22524, p. 310; Elizabeth Lawrence, Reminiscences; Hubbard and Holcombe, *Minnesota in Three Centuries*, 3:285.

[13] Galbraith to Thompson, January 27, 1863, *HED*, no. 1, 38th Congress, 1st session, serial 1182, p. 387; *St. Paul Pioneer Press*, October 24, 1897; Elizabeth Lawrence, Reminiscences.

[14] Holcombe, ed., "Chief Big Eagle's Story," *Minnesota Collections* 6(1894):386.

[15] See Testimony of Antoine J. Campbell, Samuel B. Hinman, Galbraith, Nathan Myrick, Nahpidinja, Oyatekokipapi, Tukanwicaśta, Wakanhdikaha, White Spider, Good Thunder, Mahpiyawakunza and Andrew Myrick to Nathan Myrick, May 18, 1862, Sioux claims, NARG 75, Special files no. 274.

[16] Andrew Myrick to Nathan Myrick, July 20, 1862, Sioux claims, NARG 75, Special files no. 274 (quotation). See also Testimony of Antoine J. Campbell, Mahpiyawakunza, Galbraith, Noah Sinks, and Samuel B. Hinman, Sioux claims, NARG 75, Special files no. 274.

[17] Galbraith to Thompson, January 27, 1863, *HED*, no. 1, 38th Congress, 1st session, serial 1182, p. 388–89; Testimony of Galbraith, Sioux claims, NARG 75, Special files no. 274.

[18] The best account of the problems at Yellow Medicine is in Timothy J. Sheehan, Diary, June 24–November 6, 1862, Timothy J. Sheehan Papers, MHS. Sheehan also left extensive testimony in Sisseton-Wahpeton Claims, docket no. 22524, p. 271–82.

[19] Sheehan, Diary, July 8, 1862 (quotation). Consult also Anderson, *Kinsmen of Another Kind*, 244; Traders' claims papers, NARG 75, Special files no. 274; Galbraith to Thompson, July 31, 1861, NARG 75, LR, St. Peter's Agency; White, "Captivity Among the Sioux," *Minnesota Collections* 9(1901):396; Galbraith to Thompson, January 27, 1863, *HED*, no. 1, 38th Congress, 1st session, serial 1182, p. 402; Holcombe, ed., "Chief Big Eagle's Story," *Minnesota Collections* 6(1894): 384–85; Heard, *History of the Sioux War*, 31, 48–49; Berghold, *Indians' Revenge*, 77.

[20] Sheehan, Diary, August 4, 1862; Galbraith to Thompson, January 27, 1863, *HED*, no. 1, 38th Congress, 1st session, serial 1182, p. 389.

[21] Testimony of Robert Hake waśte and Testimony of Sheehan, Sisseton-Wahpeton Claims, docket 22524, p. 358–59, 274; Galbraith to Thompson, January 27, 1863, *HED*, no. 1, 38th Congress, 1st session, serial 1182, p. 389; Sheehan, Diary, August 4, 1862; S[tephen] R. Riggs, Letter to Editor, *St. Paul Daily Press*, August 20, 1862; Riggs, *Mary and I*, 151–52.

[22] Little Crow's speech and Myrick's comments are found in Barton, *John P. Williamson*, 48–50. Another less descriptive account is in Testimony of Sheehan, Sisseton-Wahpeton Claims, docket no. 22524, p. 274. Determining the exact sequence of events and the location where Little Crow made his speech and Myrick his comments poses some problems. Earlier historians have incorrectly assumed that it occurred two or three days before the war, possibly on August 15. But young Williamson left the agency for Ohio on August 11, and since he played a major role in the discussion and the description of the confrontation comes from his daughter, it had to have occurred prior to that date. Scholars have also assumed that it happened at the Lower Agency, which again does not fit the Williamson description of the council recorded by his daughter. In all the accounts depicting the confrontations at Redwood in early July, Galbraith, Little Crow, and Williamson are never mentioned. Finally William R. Shelley, Galbraith's clerk at Yellow Medicine, distinctly remembered in later testimony that during the troubles at the agency warehouse in early August, Galbraith requested that the traders give assistance to the Indians. Galbraith later confirmed this, stating that he asked the traders to hand out food during the enrollment. Thus the dialogue must have occurred in early August at Yellow Medicine.

The day of the discussion is more difficult to ascertain since Riggs, who attended the negotiations at Yellow Medicine on August 5, does not mention it, and Sheehan's account also is silent regarding the event. But since Captain Marsh arrived at Yellow Medicine at 1:30 in the afternoon on August 6 and promptly took an active part in the negotiations, it seems likely that the comments of Little Crow and Myrick occurred that morning. Sheehan's account does make it clear that councils occurred regularly for a four-day period, beginning on August 5. See Riggs, *St. Paul Daily Press*, August 20, 1862; Gary Clayton Anderson, "Myrick's Insult: A Fresh Look at Myth and Reality," *Minnesota History* 48(Spring 1983):198–206; Affidavit of William R. Shelley and Testimony of Galbraith, Sioux claims, Special files no. 274; Folwell, *History of Minnesota*, 2:232–33. For information on Little Crow's trading activities with Myrick, see Henry Belland to Forbes, August 13, 1860, Cory-Forbes Papers, MHS.

[23] Sheehan, Diary, August 6–9, 1862; Testimony of Sheehan, Sisseton-Wahpeton Claims,

docket 22524, p. 274; Testimony of Galbraith, Myrick, and Sinks, Sioux claims, NARG 75, Special files no. 274.

[24] Sheehan, Diary, August 9–18, 1862; Testimony of Sheehan, Sisseton-Wahpeton Claims, docket no. 22524, p. 274; Galbraith to Thompson, January 27, 1863, *HED*, no. 1, 38th Congress, 1st session, serial 1182, p. 387, 390; *Redwood Falls Gazette*, October 16, 1907, p. 2.

[25] Holcombe, ed., "Chief Big Eagle's Story," *Minnesota Collections* 6(1894):387 (quotation). See also Galbraith to Thompson, January 27, 1863, *HED*, no. 1, 38th Congress, 1st session, serial 1182, p. 387–90.

[26] Holcombe, ed., "Chief Big Eagle's Story," *Minnesota Collections* 6(1894):387; Charles S. Bryant and Abel B. Murch, *A History of the Great Massacre by the Sioux Indians, in Minnesota* (Cincinnati: Rickey and Carroll, 1864), 72.

[27] Holcombe, ed., "Chief Big Eagle's Story," *Minnesota Collections* 6(1894):384–85; Testimony of Indian farmers, Sioux claims, NARG 75, Special files no. 274.

[28] See testimony in Sioux claims, NARG 75, Special files no. 274; Holcombe, ed., "Chief Big Eagle's Story," *Minnesota Collections* 6(1894):390; Heard, *History of the Sioux War*, 49; Berghold, *Indians' Revenge*, 77; Testimony of Robert Hake waśte, Sisseton-Wahpeton Claims, docket no. 22524, p. 358–59; Hubbard and Holcombe, *Minnesota in Three Centuries*, 3:285; Wakefield, *Six Weeks in the Sioux Tepees*, 9–10; Anderson, *Kinsmen of Another Kind*, 226–60.

[29] Holcombe, ed., "Chief Big Eagle's Story," *Minnesota Collections* 6(1894):385.

[30] The fishing incident and the quotation are in Wilhelmina ("Minnie") B. Carrigan, *Captured by the Indians: Reminiscences of Pioneer Life in Minnesota* (Forest City, S.D.: Forest City Press, 1907), 7. See also Testimony of Myrick, Sioux claims, NARG 75, Special files no. 274.

[31] Carrigan, *Captured by Indians*, 7 (quotation). See also Anderson, *Kinsmen of Another Kind*, 240–43, 263–67.

[32] Riggs, *Mary and I*, 152–53; Marion P. Satterlee, *A Detailed Account of the Massacre by the Dakota Indians of Minnesota in 1862* (Minneapolis: Marion P. Satterlee, 1923), 10–13; Heard, *History of the Sioux War*, 52–58; Holcombe, ed., "Chief Big Eagle's Story," *Minnesota Collections* 6(1894):389; Holcombe to Satterlee, April 1915, Satterlee Papers. Folwell is less inclined to accept the argument that Jones was a whiskey trader; see Folwell, *History of Minnesota*, 2:415–17.

[33] Holcombe, ed., "Chief Big Eagle's Story," *Minnesota Collections* 6(1894):388–90.

[34] Three detailed accounts of this discussion exist, all of which originate with members of the Little Crow family. See H[anford] L. Gordon, *The Feast of the Virgins and Other Poems* (Chicago: Laird and Lee, Publishers, 1891), 341–44; Mr. and Mrs. Harry Lawrence, "The Indian Nations of Minnesota: The Sioux Uprising," in *Minnesota Heritage: A Panoramic Narrative of the Historical Development of the North Star State*, ed. Lawrence M. Brings (Minneapolis: T. S. Denison and Co., 1960), 80–82; "Taoyateduta Is Not a Coward," *Minnesota History* 38(September 1962):115. See also Riggs, *Mary and I*, 153; Elizabeth Lawrence, Reminiscences; *St. Paul Pioneer Press*, October 24, 1897.

[35] Galbraith to Thompson, January 27, 1863, *HED*, no. 1, 38th Congress, 1st session, serial 1182, p. 387; *St. Paul Pioneer Press*, October 24, 1897; Mr. and Mrs. Harry Lawrence, "Indian Nations of Minnesota," in *Minnesota Heritage*, 80–82.

[36] Joseph Fortier, Reminiscence, December 8, 1892, Joseph Fortier Papers, MHS.

Chapter 8. War

[1] The best account of the outbreak is Folwell, *History of Minnesota*, 2:109–241. See also Heard, *History of the Sioux War*, 59–295; Bryant and Murch, *History of the Great Massacre*, 83–274, 414–85; Harriet E. Bishop, *Dakota War Whoop: Or, Indian Massacres and War in Minnesota of 1862–3* (St. Paul: D. D. Merrill, 1863; Minneapolis: Ross and Haines, 1970), 17–195; Hubbard and Holcombe, *Minnesota in Three Centuries*, 3:269–410; Kenneth Carley, *The Sioux Uprising of 1862* (St. Paul: Minnesota Historical Society, 1976). While Congress appropriated only $71,000 for annuities on August 8, Major E. A. C. Hatch indicated that he had charge of $84,000 in gold when he reached Fort Ridgely on August 18. The money had been delayed because Washington bureaucrats, supposedly headed by Commissioner of Indian Affairs Charles Mix, had tried to substitute greenbacks, which had depreciated in value, for the gold coin. See Samuel D. Hinman to Henry Benjamin Whipple, June 19, 1862, Henry B. Whipple Papers, MHS; Barton, *John P. Williamson*, 47; Hatch to his sister, September 24, 1862, Edwin A. C. Hatch and Family Papers, MHS; Folwell, *History of Minnesota*, 2:238. For information on conditions at the agency on the morning of August 18, see George Spencer's account, in Bishop, *Dakota War Whoop*, 32–34; Mrs. Celia Stay, "The Massacre at the Lower Sioux Agency, August 18, 1862," typescript, Manitoba Provincial Archives, Winnipeg, Canada.

[2] Heard, *History of the Sioux War*, 62 (quotation); Satterlee, *A Detailed Account of the Massacre*, 14–20; Hubbard and Holcombe, *Minnesota in Three Centuries*, 3:312–13; Folwell, *History of Minnesota*, 2:110.

[3] One of the apocryphal stories of the outbreak deals with Myrick's death. In an account recorded two decades after the war, Big Eagle claimed that Indians killed Myrick and "stuffed his mouth full of grass." This was done supposedly to make amends for the cruel comments made by the trader. Mrs. Celia Campbell Stay corroborated Big Eagle's account of the incident, indicating that the head of Myrick had been severed from the body and the mouth stuffed with grass. Nevertheless, the two contemporary accounts of Myrick's burial failed to mention grass, a curious omission considering their thoroughness. Heard indicated that Myrick was found "with a scythe and many arrows sticking in his body." In addition, Major Hatch wrote his sister that Nathan Myrick had gone to the agency to retrieve his brother's body, and Nathan indicated that his brother "had an arrow in his arms [*sic*] and an old burned scythe thrust through [*sic*] him." Finally there is also some question as to who killed Myrick. While Mrs. Stay indicated that a brother of Myrick's first Dakota wife was responsible, Antoine J. Campbell believed that the Winnebago, Little Priest, fired the lethal shot. See Holcombe, ed., "Chief Big Eagle's Story," *Minnesota Collections* 6(1894):390; Heard, *History of the Sioux War*, 62; Hatch to his sister, September 24, 1862, Hatch Papers; Bishop, *Dakota War Whoop*, 25; *Independent Press* (Madison), May 18, 1906; *Mankato Weekly Record*, February 21, 1863.

[4] Satterlee, *A Detailed Account of the Massacre*, 14–15.

[5] Satterlee, *A Detailed Account of the Massacre*, 15–20; John Ames Humphrey, "Boyhood Remembrances of Life among the Dakotas and the Massacre in 1862," *Minnesota Collections* 15(1909–14):339–45; Minnesota Valley Historical Society, *Sketches Historical and Descriptive of the Monuments and Tablets Erected by the Minnesota Valley Historical Society in Renville and Redwood Counties, Minnesota* (Morton: Minnesota Valley Historical Society, 1902), 11–13; Wakefield, *Six Weeks in the Sioux Tepees*, 12–14; Folwell, *History of Minnesota*, 2:109–11. The ferryman is frequently incorrectly identified as Jacob Mauley. See Hubbard

and Holcombe, *Minnesota in Three Centuries*, 3:313; Joseph Connors, "The Elusive Hero of Redwood Ferry," *Minnesota History* 34(Summer 1955):233–38.

[6] Quotation in *Missionary Papers. By the Bishop Seabury Mission. Number Twenty-three*, n.p.; Heard, *History of the Sioux War*, 65–67.

[7] Bishop, *Dakota War Whoop*, 32–37; Testimony of White Spider, Sioux claims, NARG 75, Special files no. 274.

[8] Satterlee, *A Detailed Account of the Massacre*, 48–50; Riggs to Treat, August 24, 1862, ABCFM Papers; Riggs, *Mary and I*, 154–63; Minnesota Valley Historical Society, *Sketches Historical and Descriptive*, 64–66; Holcombe, ed., "Chief Big Eagle's Story," *Minnesota Collections* 6(1894):390; Heard, *History of the Sioux War*, 76–77.

[9] Satterlee, *A Detailed Account of the Massacre*, 20; John F. Bishop, "Battle of Redwood," *Minnesota in the Civil and Indian Wars, 1861–1865* (St. Paul: Pioneer Press Co., 1891), 2:166–70; Heard, *History of the Sioux War*, 71–74, 79–80; Minnesota Valley Historical Society, *Sketches Historical and Descriptive*, 20–27.

[10] Folwell, for example, wrote: "Friendly relations had been established with many settlers, who had exchanged pork and flour with them [Indians] for their game and fish." Certainly some friendly barter occurred, but the Sioux simply had little game with which to buy anything, and many Indians blamed white settlers for taking their lands. See Folwell, *History of Minnesota*, 2:111; Carrigan, *Captured by Indians*, [8]; Tarble, "Story of My Capture and Escape," in *Garland Library*, 105:18–22; Sweet, "Mrs. J. E. De Camp Sweet's Narrative," *Minnesota Collections* 6(1894):355; Anderson, *Kinsmen of Another Kind*, 239–43.

[11] Quotation in Samuel J. Brown, "In Captivity: The Experience, Privations and Dangers of Sam'l J. Brown, and Others, while Prisoners of the Hostile Sioux, during the Massacre and War of 1862," in *Garland Library* ([1900?]; New York: Garland Publishing Co., 1977), 76:n.p. Brown gives Shakopee's cry in the Dakota language and provides the following translation: "The Dutch have made me so angry, I will butcher them alive." A more literal translation is used by the author in the text. See also George G. Allanson, "Stirring Adventures of the Joseph R. Brown Family," in *Garland Library* ([1930?]; New York: Garland Publishing Co., 1976), 103:n.p. At least one source suggests that the Sioux hated the Germans at New Ulm because they sold the Indians so much liquor; see Jonas Pettijohn, *Autobiography, Family History and Various Reminiscences of the Life of Jonas Pettijohn among the Sioux or Dakota Indians. His Escape during the Massacre of August 1862. Causes That Led to the Massacre* (Clay Center, Kans.: Dispatch Printing House, 1890), 82–83.

[12] The issue of mutilation is discussed at some length in Anderson, *Kinsmen of Another Kind*, 267–68. For a detailed discussion of the killing of whites in the settlements, consult Satterlee, *A Detailed Account of the Massacre*, 23–43. See also Mary Schwandt Schmidt narrative (three different drafts exist), Mary Schwandt Schmidt Papers, MHS; Berghold, *The Indians' Revenge*, 106–16, 152–81; Carrigan, *Captured by the Indians*, [9–26]; White, "Captivity Among the Sioux," *Minnesota Collections* 9(1901):398–400; Tarble, "Story of My Capture and Escape," in *Garland Library*, 105:25–29, 38; Sweet, "Mrs. J. E. De Camp Sweet's Narrative," *Minnesota Collections* 6(1894):365; George W. Doud, Diary, August-September 1862, MHS.

[13] Marion Satterlee spent many years collecting names of victims and came up with about four hundred. He remained uncertain whether that included everyone killed and concluded that "less than 500 whites were killed, including deaths from wounds, fights, etc."; see Satterlee to Gertrude Bonnin, August 21, 1918 (quotation), and Satterlee list, Satterlee Papers. On the Lake Shetek massacre, see Neil Currie Papers, MHS; H[arry] J[acob]

Hibschman, "The Shetek Pioneers and the Indians," in *Garland Library* (1901; New York: Garland Publishing Co., 1976), 104:8–37. Consult also Satterlee, *A Detailed Account of the Massacre*, 50–59; Anderson, *Kinsmen of Another Kind*, 263.

[14] Evidence supporting this argument is overwhelming. See especially "Original Transcripts of the Records of Trials of Certain Sioux Indians Charged with Barbarities in the State of Minnesota," Senate Records 37A-F2, NARG 48 (hereafter "Trial Transcripts"); Pond, "The Dakotas . . . as They Were in 1834," *Minnesota Collections* 12(1905–08):329–30. Thomas A. Robertson concluded that prior to the Wood Lake battle, "orders [to attack] were not given by Little Crow, as is usually supposed, but by the Soldier lodge of whom the notorious Cut Nose [Mahpiya okinzin] . . . was the head"; see Thomas A. Robertson, Reminiscences. Antoine J. Campbell, who was with Little Crow throughout the war, verified this, testifying that all orders "used to come from what they [the Sioux] called the soldiers' lodge"; see Testimony of Antoine J. Campbell, Sisseton-Wahpeton Claims, docket no. 22524, p. 257. David Weston, an Indian participant in the war, testified that Little Crow "did not command the camp, or have any charge of the prisoners, or have anything to do with that people as a whole, except that he was there and had his own affairs"; see Testimony of David Weston, Sisseton-Wahpeton Claims, docket no. 22524, p. 316 (quotation), 314.

[16] Brown, "In Captivity," in *Garland Library*, 76:n.p.; White, "Captivity Among the Sioux," *Minnesota Collections* 9(1901):404, 421; Mary Schwandt Schmidt narrative; Bryant and Murch, *History of the Great Massacre*, 93; Daniels, "Reminiscences of Little Crow," *Minnesota Collections* 12(1905–08):526–27; Bishop, *Dakota War Whoop*, 35–36. The evidence suggests that during the period of initial success many farmer Indians joined the hostile forces and participated in battles, but on perceiving that the Mdewakanton soldiers could not prevail, they grew weary of the war. See "Trial Transcripts," Senate Records 37A-F2; Holcombe, ed., "Chief Big Eagle's Story," *Minnesota Collections* 6(1894):390–91; Riggs to Treat, August 24, 1862, ABCFM Papers; Brown, "In Captivity," in *Garland Library*, 76:n.p.

[17] White, "Captivity Among the Sioux," *Minnesota Collections* 9(1901):404.

[18] *Papers Relating to Talks and Councils Held with the Indians in Dakota and Montana Territories in the Years 1866–1869* (Washington, D.C.: Government Printing Office, 1910), 93–94. See also Mary Schwandt Schmidt narrative; "The Story of Mary Schwandt: Her Captivity during the Sioux 'Outbreak'—1862," *Minnesota Collections* 6(1894):470; White, "Captivity Among the Sioux," *Minnesota Collections* 9(1901):403–4; Brown, "In Captivity," in *Garland Library*, 76:n.p.

[19] The council on August 19 is described in "Lightning Blanket's Story," *Minnesota History* 38(September 1962):144. Little Crow's speech was recorded by Antoine J. Campbell and appears in Heard, *History of the Sioux War*, 144, and in Minnesota Valley Historical Society, *Sketches Historical and Descriptive*, 18. Mary Woodbury, Lawrence Taliaferro's daughter, recorded yet another speech that Little Crow supposedly made in which the chief said he would save the lives of the captives "for the sake of our good old Father" Taliaferro; see "Auto-Biography of Maj. Lawrence Taliaferro," *Minnesota Collections* 6(1894):254–55.

[20] "Trial Transcripts," Senate Records, 37A-F2; Holcombe, ed., "Chief Big Eagle's Story," *Minnesota Collections* 6(1894):390.

[21] Nancy McClure Huggan to William R. Marshall, May 1894, Nancy McClure Huggan Reminiscencs, MHS, printed as "The Story of Nancy McClure: Captivity among the Sioux," *Minnesota Collections* 6(1894):438–60.

[22] As the Brown party, made up mostly of mixed-bloods, was being moved to Little Crow's camp, the hatred for the mixed-bloods surfaced on several occasions. At one point, as the

Browns were attempting to find shelter, they were told: "Go on, go on, no Dutchman [a farmer or mixed-blood] wanted." See Brown, "In Captivity," in *Garland Library*, 76:n.p.; McClure, "Story of Nancy McClure," *Minnesota Collections* 6(1894):453. The one mixed-blood killed was Francis LaBathe, a trader; see Sibley to Adjutant General O. Malmross, September 8, 1862, Sibley Papers.

[23] Allanson, "Stirring Adventures," in *Garland Library*, 103:n.p.; Brown, "In Captivity," in *Garland Library*, 76:n.p.; *Inter-Lake Tribune* (Brown's Valley), September 12, 1912. Relatives of Little Crow later disputed the argument that he threw all his "energies" behind the war effort. See Elizabeth Lawrence, Reminiscences; Interview with White Spider, *St. Paul Pioneer Press*, October 24, 1897.

[24] White, "Captivity Among the Sioux," *Minnesota Collections* 9(1901):405–7; Sweet, "Mrs. J. E. De Camp Sweet's Narrative," *Minnesota Collections* 6(1894):368; Tarble, "Story of My Capture and Escape," in *Garland Library*, 105:33; Wakefield, *Six Weeks in the Sioux Tepees*, 32–33.

[25] Hubbard and Holcombe, *Minnesota in Three Centuries*, 3:323, 331–35; "Lightning Blanket's Story," *Minnesota History* 38(September 1962):144–45; Testimony of Antoine J. Campbell, 1901, Sisseton-Wahpeton Claims, docket no. 22524, p. 257; Thomas A. Robertson, Reminiscences. For information on Cut Nose and Gray Bird, consult Minnesota Valley Historical Society, *Sketches Historical and Descriptive*, 32, 40; Testimony of Antoine J. Campbell, Sisseton-Wahpeton Claims, docket no. 22524, p. 257; Thomas A. Robertson, Reminiscences. The official history of the Fifth Regiment suggests that a council took place two miles west of Fort Ridgely on Tuesday morning, August 19, and that Little Crow failed to convince the Mdewakantons to attack the fort at this time; see "Extracts," by Hubbard, *Minnesota in the Civil and Indian Wars*, 2:182.

[26] Quotation in Hatch to his sister, September 24, 1862, Hatch Papers. See also Folwell, *History of Minnesota*, 2:126–29; Hubbard and Holcombe, *Minnesota in Three Centuries*, 3:331.

[27] Folwell, *History of Minnesota*, 2:126–29; Hubbard and Holcombe, *Minnesota in Three Centuries*, 3:332–33; Report of Lieutenant-Governor Ignatius Donnelly, *HED*, no. 1, 37th Congress, 3d session, serial 1157, p. 205.

[28] Testimony of Timothy J. Sheehan, Sisseton-Wahpeton Claims, docket no. 22524, p. 275; Minnesota Valley Historical Society, *Sketches Historical and Descriptive*, 39; Hubbard and Holcombe, *Minnesota in Three Centuries*, 3:334–35; "Extracts," by Hubbard, *Minnesota in the Civil and Indian Wars*, 2:183–84.

[29] Big Eagle described the fight as a "grand affair"; see Holcombe, ed., "Chief Big Eagle's Story," *Minnesota Collections* 6(1894):392. Consult also *Richland County Farmer-Globe* (Wahpeton, N.Dak.), September 22, 1936; "Extracts," by Hubbard, *Minnesota in the Civil and Indian Wars*, 2:183–84. The testimony in the Sisseton-Wahpeton Claims, docket no. 22524, looks primarily at the role of the Sissetons and Wahpetons in the war. Heard suggests that Little Crow had sent Shakopee to get assistance from the Sissetons and Wahpetons; see Heard, *History of the Sioux War*, 83.

[30] Information on Little Crow's role in the battle is in "Extracts," by Hubbard, *Minnesota in the Civil and Indian Wars*, 2:184–85. See also Testimony of Sheehan and Charles Crawford, Sisseton-Wahpeton Claims, docket no. 22524, p. 275–77, 167–68; Holcombe, ed., "Chief Big Eagle's Story," *Minnesota Collections* 6(1894):391–92; "Proceedings of a Military Commission which convened at Fort Abercrombie, D.T., by Virtue of the Following Special Order (The Original Order is hereto marked 'A'), Trial of Wowinape, August 22, 1863," manuscript in MHS. One authority states that Little Crow was actually on the northeast

perimeter of the fort when the charge took place on the southwestern approach and believes that Little Crow was stunned by a cannonball and took no part in the fighting; see Hubbard and Holcombe, *Minnesota in Three Centuries*, 3:337; Brown, "In Captivity," in *Garland Library*, 76:n.p.

[31] Consult "Report of Charles E. Flandrau, August 23, 1862," *Minnesota in the Civil and Indian Wars*, 2:203–7; Asa W. Daniels, "Reminiscences of the Little Crow Uprising," *Minnesota Collections* 15(1915):329–33; Berghold, *Indians' Revenge*, 130–36; Hubbard and Holcombe, *Minnesota in Three Centuries*, 3:325–29.

[32] The activities of Little Crow are reported in Daniels, "Reminiscences of the Little Crow Uprising," *Minnesota Collections* 15(1915):333. See also Flandrau, "Report," August 23, 1862, *Minnesota in the Civil and Indian Wars*, 2:204–6.

[33] Brown, "In Captivity," in *Garland Library*, 76:n.p. Wakefield has a good account of the move, describing the caravan as the "confusion of Babel"; see Wakefield, *Six Weeks in the Sioux Tepees*, 32–33. See also Sweet, "Mrs. J. E. De Camp Sweet's Narrative," *Minnesota Collections* 6(1894):366–69. There is some question regarding the performance of Little Crow in the battles. While no mixed-blood or full-blood participant ever questioned his bravery and he was mentioned by several whites as being in the thick of the fighting, Hubbard and Holcombe in *Minnesota in Three Centuries*, 3:371, state that he was "not of much physical courage" and that he seldom took risks. There is little evidence to support the claim.

[34] Some testimony suggests that the meetings began on the evening of August 20. See testimony of Robert Hake waśte, 1901, Sisseton-Wahpeton Claims, docket no. 22524, p. 359.

[35] Brown, "In Captivity," in *Garland Library*, 76:n.p.; Gabriel Renville, "A Sioux Narrative of the Outbreak in 1862, and of Sibley's Expedition in 1863," *Minnesota Collections* 10(1905):596–99. Joseph Fortier argued that Gabriel Renville joined the hostiles in the attempted seizure of Fort Abercrombie; see Fortier, Reminiscence, December 8, 1892, Fortier Papers.

[36] "Declaration of Paul Màzakootemani," May 3, 1869, ABCFM Papers; Testimony of Amos E-ce-tu-ki-ya, Sisseton-Wahpeton Claims, docket no. 22524, p. 121–23. There is some confusion over how many councils occurred and where and when they occurred. Heard, in his *History of the Sioux War*, 150–53, describes the council that Paul and Strikes the Pawnee participated in. He suggests that it occurred sometime in early September. Other evidence contradicts this chronology. See Brown, "In Captivity," in *Garland Library*, 76:n.p., and Sisseton-Wahpeton Claims, docket no. 22524. See also S[tephen] R. Riggs, trans., "Narrative of Paul Mazakootemane," *Minnesota Collections* 3(1870–80):82–90.

[37] "Declaration of Paul Mazakootemani," May 3, 1869, ABCFM Papers; Heard, *History of the Sioux War*, 154; Renville, "Sioux Narrative," *Minnesota Collections* 10(1905):600.

[38] Testimony of Samuel Brown, Sisseton-Wahpeton Claims, docket no. 22524, p. 28–29; Brown, "In Captivity," in *Garland Library*, 76:n.p.; Renville, "Sioux Narrative," *Minnesota Collections* 10(1905):599–601; Allanson, "Stirring Adventures," in *Garland Library*, 103:n.p.

[39] Brown, "In Captivity," in *Garland Library*, 76:n.p.; Testimony of Joseph La Framboise, Sisseton-Wahpeton Claims, docket no. 22524, p. 148–49.

[40] Brown, "In Captivity," in *Garland Library*, 76:n.p.; Renville, "Sioux Narrative," *Minnesota Collections* 10(1905):600–1.

[41] Testimony of Joseph La Framboise, Sisseton-Wahpeton Claims, docket no. 22524, p. 148–49 (quotation). Brown describes the brief trouble that occurred; see Brown, "In Captivity," in *Garland Library*, 76:n.p. See also Thomas A. Robertson, Reminiscences; Renville, "Sioux Narrative," *Minnesota Collections* 10(1905):603–4.

[42] Renville, "Sioux Narrative," *Minnesota Collections* 10(1905):603.

[43] Testimony of Charles R. Crawford, Sisseton-Wahpeton Claims, docket no. 22524, p. 164–65.

[44] Extract of Sibley to his wife, August 28, 1862, Sibley to Malmross, September 1, 1862, Sibley Papers; Heard, *History of the Sioux War*, 133–37; Hubbard and Holcombe, *Minnesota in Three Centuries*, 3:343–44.

[45] White, "Captivity Among the Sioux," *Minnesota Collections* 9(1901):415; Heard, *History of the Sioux War*, 136; Renville, "Sioux Narrative," *Minnesota Collections* 10(1905):604; Holcombe, ed., "Chief Big Eagle's Story," *Minnesota Collections* 6(1894):393.

[46] Holcombe, ed., "Chief Big Eagle's Story," *Minnesota Collections* 6(1894):393. White troops were generally surprised by the bravery of the Indians and their willingness to sustain a frontal assault. For Sibley's quotation, see extract of Sibley to his wife, September 4, 1862, Sibley Papers. On the Birch Coulee debacle and on the controversy over the site selected for a camp, see Hubbard and Holcombe, *Minnesota in Three Centuries*, 3:343–51; "Battle of Birch Coulee—September 2, 1862," in *Minnesota in the Civil and Indian Wars*, 2:212–23; Robert K. Boyd, "How the Indians Fought: A New Era in Skirmish Fighting, by a Survivor of the Battle of Birch Cooley," *Minnesota History* 11(September 1930):299–304; Folwell, *History of Minnesota*, 2:151–56.

[47] Here and below, Folwell, *History of Minnesota*, 2:158–63; Hubbard and Holcombe, *Minnesota in Three Centuries*, 3:357–70; Marion P. Satterlee, *The Story of Capt. Richard Strout and Company, Who Fought the Sioux Indians at the Battle of Kelly's Bluff, at Acton, Minn., on Wednesday, September 3rd, 1862* (Minneapolis: Marion P. Satterlee, 1909), 1–9.

[48] Brown, "In Captivity," in *Garland Library*, 76:n.p.; Testimony of Antoine J. Campbell, Sisseton-Wahpeton Claims, docket no. 22524, p. 259.

[49] Sibley's letter was discovered by Charles Crawford, the mixed-blood son of Joseph Akipa Renville, who initially turned it over to the soldiers' lodge. The soldiers at first objected to sending an answer, but Little Crow was finally allowed to compose one. See Testimony of Thomas A. Robertson, Sisseton-Wahpeton Claims, docket no. 22524; Sibley to Malmross, September 8, 1862, Sibley to his wife, September 8, 1862, Sibley Papers; Holcombe, ed., "Chief Big Eagle's Story," *Minnesota Collections* 6(1894):397; John Wakeman, "Big Thunder's Story," January 23, (n.d.), MHS Scrapbook no. 2, p. 91.

[50] Sibley to Malmross, September 8, 1862, Sibley Papers.

[51] Sibley to Malmross, September 8, 1862, Sibley to his wife, September 8, 10, 1862, Sibley Papers; Thomas A. Robertson, Reminiscences.

[52] Brown, "In Captivity," in *Garland Library*, 76:n.p.; Renville, "Sioux Narrative," *Minnesota Collections* 10(1905):605; Thomas A. Robertson, Reminiscences; Holcombe, ed., "Chief Big Eagle's Story," *Minnesota Collections* 6(1894):397; Sibley to Malmross, September 13, 1862, NARG 393, LS, Sibley's Indian Expedition; Sibley to Charles Flandrau, September 11, 1862, Sibley Papers; Riggs to Treat, September 15, 1862, ABCFM Papers; Robinson, *A History of the Dakota*, 290–93.

[53] Testimony of Samuel Brown, Sisseton-Wahpeton Claims, docket no. 22524, p. 57. See also Brown, "In Captivity," in *Garland Library*, 76:n.p.

[54] Little Crow (by Antoine J. Campbell) to Sibley, received September 12, 1862, NARG 393, LR, Sibley's Indian Expedition; Riggs to his wife, September 13, 1862, transcript (original lost), Chippewa County Historical Society, Montevideo, Minn. Heard reported that Little Crow had attempted to ask for peace as early as September 1 when he was on the raid to the Big Woods, but no evidence supports this argument, and the events of that particular time make it illogical; see Heard, *History of the Sioux War*, 144.

[55] Sibley to Malmross, September 13, 1862, Sibley to "innocent" Indians, September 13, 1862, NARG 393, LS, Sibley's Indian Expedition; Riggs to his wife, September 13, 1862, Chippewa County Historical Society.

[56] Declaration of Paul Mazakutemani, May 3, 1869, ABCFM Papers; Brown, "In Captivity," in *Garland Library*, 76:n.p. Heard seems to have collected various accounts of Paul's many speeches made during the war and strung them together in one dialogue without attempting to determine chronology; see Heard, *History of the Sioux War*, 143–66.

[57] Brown, "In Captivity," in *Garland Library*, 76:n.p.; Minnesota Valley Historical Society, *Sketches Historical and Descriptive*, 54–55.

[58] Brown, "In Captivity," in *Garland Library*, 76:n.p.; Thomas A. Robertson, Reminiscences.

[59] Robinson, *A History of the Dakota*, 294 (quotations). Other evidence is in Testimony of Wicanrpimonpa, or Two Stars, Sisseton-Wahpeton Claims, docket no. 22524, p. 87; Renville, "Sioux Narrative," *Minnesota Collections* 10(1905):606–7; Folwell, *History of Minnesota*, 2:178. While large numbers of horses had been lost at Birch Coulee, two to three hundred of Sibley's cavalry had also left him after their terms of enlistment had expired; see Sibley to his wife, September 17, 1862, Sibley Papers.

[60] The standard account of the Battle of Wood Lake is Henry H. Sibley, "Battle of Wood Lake," in *Minnesota in the Civil and Indian Wars*, 2:240–53. See also Hubbard and Holcombe, *Minnesota in Three Centuries*, 3:401–7; Folwell, *History of Minnesota*, 2:178–81; Sibley to Ramsey, September 23, 1862, NARG 393, LS, Sibley's Indian Expedition. The report of multilation by white soldiers is found in Riggs to his wife, September 22, 1862, transcript (original lost), Chippewa County Historical Society; Heard, *History of the Sioux War*, 177.

[61] Brown, "In Captivity," in *Garland Library*, 76:n.p.; Thomas A. Robertson, Reminiscences; Wakefield, *Six Weeks in the Sioux Tepees*, 45.

[62] Contradictory evidence can be found regarding Little Crow's actions and statements on September 23 and 24. Brown, for example, reported Little Crow's initial support for the killing of the captives, even quoting him on the subject. Campbell, however, noted that Little Crow ultimately concluded that it would be "bad policy, for the whites will then follow us to the end of the earth and give us no peace. . . . It would be cruel and cowardly too." It seems likely that Little Crow, frustrated and angry over the defeat at Wood Lake, considered killing the captives on September 23 only to change his mind by the time he met Campbell; see Brown, "In Captivity," in *Garland Library*, 76:n.p.; Minnesota Valley Historical Society, *Sketches Historical and Descriptive*, 19. Other accounts of Little Crow's actions to save the captives, also originating with Campbell, are in *St. Paul Pioneer Press*, October 24, 1897, and Celia M. Campbell, Reminiscences, Celia Campbell Stay Papers, MHS.

[63] Brown, "In Captivity," in *Garland Library*, 76:n.p.

[64] Celia M. Campbell, Reminiscences, Stay Papers; *Independent Press* (Madison), June 15, 1923, p. 1.

[65] Celia M. Campbell, Reminiscences, Stay Papers; *Independent Press*, June 15, 1923, p. 1; *Mankato Weekly Record*, February 21, 1863.

[66] *St. Paul Pioneer Press*, October 24, 1897.

[67] *St. Paul Pioneer Press*, October 24, 1897.

Chapter 9. The Last Campaign

[1] *Nor'Wester* (Winnipeg), February 9, 1863. Thomas Robertson gives an interesting account of Little Crow's belief that the British would help. Robertson says that when the Mdewakantons were retreating up the Minnesota River towards Red Iron's village in September 1862, Little Crow could be seen "singing and dancing and as we got nearer we heard him saying, 'The British are coming to help me and they are bringing "Little Dakota".'" "Little Dakota" was a small cannon that was given to the Sioux in 1815 and apparently was carried out onto the Dakota plains and buried in the James River. See Thomas A. Robertson, Reminiscences.

[2] According to Antoine J. Campbell, Little Crow had pleaded with reluctant Indians near Camp Release to follow him. Many decided against his advice. See *Mankato Weekly Record*, February 21, 1863.

[3] Thomas A. Robertson, Reminiscences; Holcombe, ed., "Chief Big Eagle's Story," *Minnesota Collections* 6(1894):397; Barton, *John P. Williamson*, 58.

[4] Brown indicates that "several hundred of the hostiles had come over into our camp with their captives" in the two days after the Wood Lake battle; see Brown, "In Captivity," in *Garland Library*, 76:n.p. Consult also White, "Captivity Among the Sioux," *Minnesota Collections* 9(1901):420–22; [Thomas Scantlebury], *Wanderings in Minnesota During the Indian Troubles of 1862* (Chicago: F. C. S. Calhoun, 1867), 20–21; Sibley to General John Pope, September 27, 1862, NARG 393, LS, Sibley's Indian Expedition; Sibley to his wife, September 27, 1862, Sibley Papers.

[5] Brown, "In Captivity," in *Garland Library*, 76:n.p.; Holcombe, ed., "Chief Big Eagle's Story," *Minnesota Collections* 6(1894):397; Thomas A. Robertson to M. P. Satterlee, April 10, 1923, Satterlee Papers; Sibley to Whipple, March 11, 1863, Whipple Papers.

[6] Brown, "In Captivity," in *Garland Library*, 76:n.p.; Sibley to Pope, September 27, 1862, NARG 393, LS, Sibley's Indian Expedition; "Trial Transcripts," Senate Records, 37A-F2.

[7] Anderson, *Kinsmen of Another Kind*, 276–77; Sibley to Pope, October 7, 11, 1862, NARG 393, LS, Sibley's Indian Expedition; John Kingsley Wood, Diary, October 9–28, 1862, MIIS.

[8] "Trial Transcripts," Senate Records, 37A-F2; Sioux annuity rolls, 1860, NARG 75; Riggs to his wife, October 6, 13, 1862, Chippewa County Historical Society.

[9] Sibley to Flandrau, September 28, 1862, Sibley Papers; Sibley to Pope, September 28, 1862, NARG 393, LS, Sibley's Indian Expedition; Sibley to his wife, November 3, 1862, Sibley Papers; Sibley to Whipple, December 7, 1862, Whipple Papers. Sibley stuck by his faith in the commission into the next year even though the federal government questioned the procedure and decided to execute only a small portion of those condemned. See Riggs to Treat, February 20, 1863, ABCFM Papers; Sibley to Whipple, March 11, 1863, Whipple Papers.

[10] On the issue of rape, Washington officials concluded: "Though it is a fact well established in the minds of the people of Minnesota that all of the females captured were ravished by the savages, and that large numbers were engaged in the crime, yet the evidence only discloses two instances in which it was done. The evidence in many other respects is equally unsatisfactory." See J. P. Usher to Sibley, December 10, 1862, NARG 48, LS, Indian Division of the Department of the Interior. For the report of Minnesota's Congressional delegation, see M. S. Wilkinson, Cyrus Aldrich, and William Windom to President of the United States, n.d., *SED*, no. 7, 37th Congress, 3d session, serial 1149, p. 2–4. Sibley believed that all of the young women were raped; however, one of the white captives estimated that only two

were abused, the exact number who testified to that effect in front of the commission. See Sibley to his wife, September 27, 1862, Sibley Papers; Wakefield, *Six Weeks in the Sioux Tepees*, 55.

[11] "Trial Transcripts," Senate Records, 37A-F2; Abraham Lincoln to Senate of the United States, December 11, 1862, *SED*, no. 7, 37th Congress, 3d session, serial 1149, p. 1–2; Lincoln to Sibley, December 6, 1862, Sibley to Riggs, December 22, 1862, Sibley Papers; Monsignor A[ugustin] Ravoux, *Reminiscences, Memoirs and Lectures* (St. Paul: Brown, Treacy and Co., 1890), 72–81. For a contemporary account of the trials, see Heard, *History of the Sioux War*, 251–71.

[12] Eli Pickett to his wife, December 26, 1862, Eli K. Pickett Scrapbook, MHS. See also Heard, *History of the Sioux War*, 272–95; Colonel Stephen Miller to R. C. Olin, December 30, 1862, NARG 393, "Two or More Names File," Department of the Northwest, 1862–65.

[13] Anderson, *Kinsmen of Another Kind*, 277–78; Riggs, *Mary and I*, 190–97; "Indian Prisoners at Mankato," January 1863, NARG 94, AGO miscellaneous correspondence, Sioux Commission. For information on the prisoners during their stay at Davenport and removal to Crow Creek, see the letters of John P. Williamson in the Riggs Papers and Williamson Papers.

[14] Riggs to Treat, November 24, 1862, ABCFM Papers; Miller to Sibley, November 21, 1862, NARG 393, "Two or More Names File," Department of the Northwest, 1862–65; Scout lists, 1863, Brown Papers; Renville, "Sioux Narrative," *Minnesota Collections* 10(1905):611; Testimony of "Little Paul," or Wa-hna-xki-ya, Sisseton-Wahpeton Claims, docket no. 22524, p. 112; Olin to Lieutenant Colonel William Pfaender, February 19, 1863, NARG 393, "Two or More Names File," Department of the Northwest, 1862–65.

[15] Robinson, *A History of the Dakota*, 296. Robinson believed that Little Crow was involved in an attack on Fort Abercrombie on September 26, but he gives no source for this assertion (p. 296–97).

[16] Thomas A. Robertson, Reminiscenses (quotation). See also Testimony of "Little Paul," or Wa-hna-xki-ya, Sisseton-Wahpeton Claims, docket no. 22524, p. 112; William McTavish to Thomas Fraser, January 9, 1863, Winnipeg correspondence, Letterbooks, 1861–64, Hudson's Bay Company Archives (hereafter HBCA), Winnipeg, Manitoba; Disposition of Sisseton and Wahpeton bands, 1863, Brown Papers; Major G. Alexander to Olin, May 26, 1863, NARG 393, "Two or More Names File," Department of the Northwest, 1862–65.

[17] John Euni's "Narrative" is in *St. Paul Daily Press*, September 20, 1863. Other heavily edited and changed versions are "A Scrap of History: The Capture by the Sioux of John Schurch [Euni], in 1862," extract in *Minneapolis Tribune*, miscellaneous newspaper clippings, MHS; Bishop, *Dakota War Whoop*, 359–63. Dakota territorial officials wrote Abraham Lincoln on Christmas Eve, 1862, reporting that Little Crow's Mdewakantons were then encamped just above Fort Pierre. See Robert Huhn Jones, *The Civil War in the Northwest: Nebraska, Wisconsin, Iowa, Minnesota, and the Dakotas* (Norman: University of Oklahoma Press, 1960), 60.

[18] Charles Primeau and W. G. Guilberth to Major Pattee, November 5, 1862, NARG 393, LR, Northwest Department; Sam E. Adams, Letter, *St. Paul Pioneer*, January 31, 1863; *St. Paul Daily Press*, September 20, 1863; *St. Paul Pioneer*, February 12, 1863; Report of Francis La Framboise, February 13, 1863, NARG 75, LR, NS; *St. Paul Daily Press*, April 17, 1863.

[19] See Samuel J. Brown, "Little Crow's Trip to the Missouri," manuscript in the Satterlee Papers; *St. Paul Daily Press*, September 20, 1863. Other accounts confirming the trip are found in reports published in the *St. Paul Pioneer*, February 12, May 27, 1863. The newspaper misidentified the Mandans as Rees.

[20] The British never took the Dakota claim for assistance seriously. See Governor H. H. Berens to Duke of Newcastle, February 26, 1863, Dallas correspondence, inward, 1858–64, HBCA; *Nor'Wester*, February 9, 1863; Dallas to Viscount Monck, June 3, 1863, London correspondence, inward, 1862–65, HBCA.

[21] Father Mestre, "Relation of the Visit of the Sioux to St. Boniface," December 1862, Belleau Collection, Assumption Abbey Archives, Richardton, N.Dak.; McTavish to Thomas Fraser, January 9, 1863, Winnipeg correspondence, Letterbooks, 1861–64, HBCA. For a general discussion of the "international" problem created by the Sioux presence in Canada, see Alvin C. Bluek, Jr., "The Sioux Uprising: A Problem in International Relations," *Minnesota History* 30(Winter 1955):317–24.

[22] McTavish to Fraser, January 9, 1863, Winnipeg correspondence, Letterbooks, 1861–64, HBCA.

[23] Dallas to Fraser, December 20, 1862, April 29, 1863, London correspondence, inward, 1862–65, HBCA; Berens to Duke of Newcastle, February 26, 1863, Dallas correspondence, inward, 1858–64, HBCA.

[24] *Nor'Wester*, March 17, 1863. Dallas never wrote the letter requested by Standing Buffalo; see *St. Paul Daily Press*, June 3, 1863.

[25] *Nor'Wester*, February 9, 1863.

[26] *Nor'Wester*, February 9, March 17, 1863; Father André to Bishop Taché, March 4, 1863, Belleau Collection.

[27] Father André to Bishop Taché, March 4, 1863, Father Mestre letter, June 5, 1863, Belleau Collection; *St. Paul Daily Press*, June 3, 23, 1863.

[28] The initial report placing Little Crow at Devil's Lake is in Polette Campbell interview, *Nor'Wester*, February 9, 1863. For other evidence of the chief's movements and the role of British traders, see *St. Paul Daily Press*, April 17, 1863; *St. Paul Pioneer*, February 12, 1863; *St. Paul Daily Press*, May 27, September 20, 1863. Father André was quite displeased with the tendency of the two most important traders at St. Joseph, Gingras and one Bottineau, to offer "almost entirely their stores [to the Sioux] . . . so there is no more food to be bought [at St. Joseph]"; see Father André to Bishop Taché, March 4, 1863, Belleau Collection. One other report, a letter written by Sam E. Adams, in the *St. Paul Pioneer*, January 31, 1863, places Little Crow at Devil's Lake as early as mid-January. But it is secondhand information and is contradicted by Gingras, who traded with the Sioux at the lake on January 28 and specifically mentioned that Little Crow was expected soon but was still on the Missouri.

[29] *St. Paul Daily Press*, May 27, 1863; Dallas to Viscount Monck, June 3, 1863, London correspondence, inward, 1862–65, HBCA.

[30] McTavish to Norman Kittson, May 15, 1863, Winnipeg correspondence, 1863–64, HBCA.

[31] *St. Paul Daily Press*, May 26, June 3, 1863; Major G. Alexander to Olin, May 26, 1863, NARG 393, "Two or More Names File," Department of the West, 1862–65; Sibley to Brown, May 18, 1863, Brown Papers. Sibley believed that about half of the Sissetons and Wahpetons wanted peace by May.

[32] "Letter of Judge [Joseph] LeMay," *St. Paul Pioneer*, June 4, 1863; *St. Paul Daily Press*, May 28, June 3, 11, 1863.

[33] *St. Paul Daily Press*, June 23, 1863 (quotation); Father Mestre letter, June 5, 1863, Belleau Collection.

[34] Dallas to Sibley, June 3, 1863, London correspondence, inward, 1862–65, HBCA; *Nor'Wester*, June 2, 1863.

[35] *St. Paul Daily Press*, June 23, 1863.

[36] Dallas to Sibley, June 3, 1863, London correspondence, inward, 1862–65, HBCA; *Nor'Wester*, June 2, 1863.

[37] Dallas to Sibley, June 3, 1863, London correspondence, inward, 1862–65, HBCA; *St. Paul Daily Press*, June 23, 1863.

[38] William E. Lass, *Minnesota's Boundary with Canada: Its Evolution since 1783* (St. Paul: Minnesota Historical Society Press, 1980), 76–78; Dallas to Fraser, June 3, 1863, Dallas to Viscount Monck, June 3, 1863, London correspondence, inward, 1862–65, HBCA; McTavish to Kittson, May 22, 1863, Winnipeg correspondence, Letterbook, 1861–64, HBCA; Dallas to Fraser, February 24, 1864, in "Sioux Indians," Great Britain Colonial Office, printed document in MHS Library.

[39] Joseph LeMay, Letter, *St. Paul Daily Press*, June 25, 1863; *St. Peter Tribune*, July 29, 1863; S[tephen] R. Riggs, Letter, *St. Paul Daily Press*, August 4, 1863; Jones, *The Civil War in the Northwest*, 57–74.

[40] Riggs, Letter, *St. Paul Daily Press*, August 4, 1863; *St. Peter Tribune*, July 29, 1863.

[41] Riggs, Letter, *St. Paul Daily Press*, August 4, 1863; Statement of Wowinape, *St. Paul Pioneer*, August 13, 1863.

[42] A host of other explanations exist. Consult Father André to Sibley, August 5, 1863, Sibley Papers; Joseph Fortier, "Incident of Indian War," Fortier Papers; Eastman, *Indian Heroes and Great Chieftains*, 53–54; *St. Cloud Democrat*, April 5, 1866; Interview with White Spider, *St. Paul Pioneer Press*, October 24, 1897; "Journal of Sibley's Expedition Against the Sioux," August 10, 1863, NARG 393, LS, Sibley's Indian Expedition; Statement of Wowinape, *St. Paul Pioneer*, August 13, 1863. On the loss of horses, see Thomas A. Robertson, Reminiscenses.

[43] Brown, "In Captivity," in *Garland Library*, 76:n.p.

[44] For another example of the notion of "throwing one's life away," see Hugh A. Dempsey, *Charcoal's World* (Lincoln: University of Nebraska Press, 1979). Consult also Royal B. Hassrick, *The Sioux: Life and Customs of a Warrior Society* (Norman: University of Oklahoma Press, 1964), 308.

[45] Testimony of William L. Quinn and Joseph DeMarais, Sr., in "Proceedings of a Military Commission which convened at Fort Abercrombie D.T. by virtue of the following Special Order," hereafter identified as the "Trial of Wowinape," typed manuscript in MHS; Landes, *Mystic Lake Sioux*, 159.

[46] Testimony of Joseph DeMarais, Sr., in "Trial of Wowinape"; Statement of Wowinape, *St. Paul Pioneer*, August 13, 1863; Calvin Mooers, "Indian Warfare in the Red River Country, 1862–1866," *Detroit Society for Genealogical Research Magazine* 20(Summer 1957):139–40; *Hutchinson Leader*, October 6, 1905, p. 3.

[47] Statement of Wowinape, *St. Paul Pioneer*, August 13, 1863; *St. Paul Daily Press*, July 10, 1863; Satterlee, "Narratives of the Sioux War: The Killing of Chief Little Crow," *Minnesota Collections* 15(1915):368–69.

[48] Interview with White Spider, *St. Paul Pioneer Press*, October 24, 1897; Statement of Wowinape, *St. Paul Pioneer*, August 13, 1863; L[oren] W. Collins, *The Expedition Against the Sioux Indians in 1863* (St. Cloud: Journal-Press Print, 1895), 20–21.

[49] Lewis Harrington to William and Abbie Pendergast, July 5, 1863, A. Pendergast Papers, MHS; J. W. Murray, Letter, *St. Paul Daily Press*, August 21, 1863; *Hutchinson Leader*, October 6, 1905, p. 3; Receipt for the killing of Little Crow, March 26, 1864, State Auditor's Warrents, State Archives, MHS.

Epilogue

[1] *St. Paul Pioneer*, August 20, 1863; John W. Bond to Colonel Miller, August 16, 1863, printed in *St. Peter Tribune*, August 26, 1863; *St. Paul Daily Globe*, February 4, 1896.

[2] Interview with Alan R. Woolworth, June 12, 1984, St. Paul, Minnesota.

Appendix 1

[1] Landes, *Mystic Lake Sioux*, 100–4; Royal B. Hassrick, "The Teton Dakota Kinship System," *American Anthropologist* 46(1944):338–48; Raymond J. De Mallie, "Change in American Indian Kinship Systems: The Dakota," in *Currents in Anthropology: Essays in Honor of Sol Tax*, Studies in Anthropology, ed. Robert E. Hinshaw (The Hague and New York: Mouton, 1979), 221–41.

[2] Celia M. Campbell, Reminiscences, Stay Papers; De Mallie, "Change in American Indian Kinship Systems: The Dakota," in *Currents*, 232–33.

[3] De Mallie, "Change in American Kinship Systems: The Dakota," in *Currents*, 233–34; Deloria, *Speaking of Indians*, 24–26.

[4] Landes, *Mystic Lake Sioux*, 97.

[5] Landes, *Mystic Lake Sioux*, 31.

[6] Jane Williams to Satterlee, August 8, September 4, 1916, Satterlee Papers; Holcombe, *Minnesota in Three Centuries*, 2:180; Elizabeth Lawrence, Reminiscences. The fact that Taoyateduta was the son of Big Thunder's first wife is confirmed in Robinson, *A History of the Dakota*, 109–18, and Prescott, "Contributions to the History, Customs, and Opinions of the Dacota Tribe," in *Historical and Statistical Information*, 2:182–84.

[7] Sibley, *Iron Face*, 97–98.

[8] Williams to Satterlee, September 4, 1916, Satterlee Papers.

[9] Holcombe, *Minnesota in Three Centuries*, 2:170; Pond, "The Dakotas . . . as They Were in 1834," *Minnesota Collections* 12(1908):325; Riggs and Gideon Pond to Greene, September 10, 1846, ABCFM Papers; Taliaferro Journals, July 7, 1835.

[10] Holcombe, *Minnesota in Three Centuries*, 2:181–82; Prescott, "Contributions to the History, Customs, and Opinions of the Dacota Tribe," in *Historical and Statistical Information*, 2:183; Robertson to Satterlee, November 1, 1922, Satterlee Papers.

[11] *St. Paul Pioneer Press*, October 24, 1897.

[12] Notes on individuals tried by the Sioux Commission, "Little Dog," Satterlee Papers; Thomas A. Robertson, Reminiscences; Samuel J. Brown, "Little Crow's Famous Trip to the Missouri River," Satterlee Papers.

[13] Roll of Sioux prisoners, February 25, 1864, Brown Papers; Williams to Satterlee, September 4, 1916, Satterlee Papers; *St. Paul Pioneer Press*, October 24, 1897.

[14] See the list of Little Crow relatives in *St. Paul Daily Press*, April 10, 1864.

[15] Roll of Sioux prisoners, February 25, 1864, Brown Papers; *St. Paul Pioneer Press*, October 24, 1897; *Morton Enterprise*, April 25, 1902, p. 1; John Wakeman, "Big Thunder's Story," in Minnesota Historical Society Scrapbook, no. 2, p. 91.

[16] Sioux annuity rolls, 1849, 1854, 1856, 1857, 1860, NARG 75, Indian Annuity Rolls. Martin McLeod identified Tapateduta as a brother of Little Crow's trading at Lac qui Parle in 1848. Nothing more is known of this brother. See McLeod to Sibley, March 30, 1848, Sibley Papers.

[17] Affidavit of Mrs. Harry Lawrence, March 1952, MHS; Notes on individuals tried by the Sioux Commission, "Medicine Bottle," Satterlee Papers.

[18] Sioux annuity roll, 1860, NARG 75, Indian Annuity Rolls.

[19] Robinson, *A History of the Dakota*, 341–43; Daniels, "Reminiscences of Little Crow," *Minnesota Collections* 12(1908):514.

[20] Williams to Satterlee, September 4, 1916, Satterlee Papers; Riggs and Gideon Pond to Greene, September 10, 1846, ABCFM Papers; Riggs, *Tah-koo Wah-kan*, 25. John C. Wakeman, among others, identified Inyangmani as a Sisseton; see *St. Paul Pioneer Press*, October 24, 1897.

[21] Statement of Wowinape, *St. Paul Pioneer*, August 13, 1863; "Boarding School Students," 1847–59, Riggs Papers, Wowinape gave the number of children, noting first the two Wahpe-kute wives who had been "put away," and identifying his mother, Mazaiyagewin, as Little Crow's third wife.

[22] E[dward] D. Neill, "Dakota Land and Life," *Minnesota Collections* 1(1852; reprinted, 1902):226 (quotation). See also Statement of Wowinape, *St. Paul Pioneer*, August 13, 1863; Williams to Satterlee, September 4, 1916, Satterlee Papers.

[23] Statement of Wowinape, *St. Paul Pioneer*, August 13, 1863; Williams to Satterlee, September 4, 1916, Satterlee Papers; School reports, June 30, 1844, June 30, 1845, June 20, 1846, ABCFM Papers. The approximate date for Little Crow's third marriage was arrived at by consulting Neill, "Dakota Land and Life," *Minnesota Collections* 1(1902):226, and Riggs and Gideon Pond to Greene, September 10, 1846, ABCFM Papers.

[24] Statement of Wowinape, *St. Paul Pioneer*, August 13, 1863; Williams to Satterlee, September 4, 1916, Satterlee Papers; School reports, June 30, 1844, June 30, 1845, June 20, 1846, ABCFM Papers; Letter to the author from Alan R. Woolworth, February 22, 1985.

[25] Williams to Satterlee, September 4, 1916, Satterlee Papers; Statement of Wowinape, *St. Paul Pioneer*, August 13, 1863; List of men on "war path" with Cloud Man, September 1, 1862, Samuel J. Brown to Satterlee, July 7, 1915, Satterlee Papers.

[26] Williamson to Greene, June 20, 1846, Riggs to Treat, January 21, 1858, ABCFM Papers.

[27] Some confusion exists over the relationship of Mary Renville to Little Crow, but the most complete statement, and likely the correct one, is from Hughes, who wrote: "Mary Renville . . . is a cousin of Little Crow of the Indian Outbreak of 1862, her mother being a sister of Big Thunder, Little Crow's father." See Hughes, *Indian Chiefs*, 117. See also page 41, above.

[28] "Indian Reserve Papers," testimony taken in 1856, NARG 75, miscellaneous manuscripts; Annuity roll for Mdewakanton tribe, 1847?, Sibley Papers.

[29] Riggs, *Tah-koo Wah-kan*, 154–55; Joseph Tassé, *Les Canadiens*, 293; Gertrude Ackermann, "Joseph Renville of Lac qui Parle," *Minnesota History* 12 (September 1931): 231–32; William H. Keating, *Narrative of an Expedition to the Source of St. Peter's River* (1824; Minneapolis: Ross and Haines, 1959), 1:324–26; Taliaferro Journals, September 7, 1821.

[30] Bray and Bray, trans. and eds., *Joseph N. Nicollet*, 279–80.

[31] Stephen Return Riggs, "Dakota Portraits," *Minnesota History Bulletin* 2(November 1918):547–52, 561–68; Lorenzo Lawrence, Letter, *Iapi Oaye/The Word Carrier*, June 1878; "American Indian Hero Gone," *Iapi Oaye/The Word Carrier*, January 1885; Williamson to Bruce, August 5, 1840, NARG 75, LR, St. Peter's Agency; Williamson to Treat, April 1, 1853, ABCFM Papers.

[32] Thomas A. Robertson, Reminiscences.

[33] This relationship is difficult to establish and is possible only after looking at a series of documents. Fortunately, there were only about a dozen women converts to the Lac qui

Parle church in 1841 and virtually all of them can be identified. Thus Catherine is identified as Left Hand's wife through a process of elimination. In addition, in McLean to Ramsey, March 31, 1851, NARG 75, LR, MS, McLean notes that Lorenzo Lawrence was a member of the Little Crow band. Information on Catherine and Left Hand is found in Riggs, "Dakota Portraits," *Minnesota History Bulletin* 2(November 1918):532–37, 544; Riggs to Greene, March 26, 1839, Riggs and Gideon Pond to Greene, September 10, 1846, ABCFM Papers; Riggs, *Tah-koo Wah-kan*, 180–81; Riggs, *Mary and I*, 50–51. A problem with yet another polygamous marriage also surfaced at Lac qui Parle in 1850 when Wakanmani wanted to join the church. His situation was so like Left Hand's that he could easily be confused for Catherine's husband were it not for the fact that the chronology does not fit, and the missionaries do reveal the identity of one of Wakanmani's wives and their children. For information on Wakanmani, see Riggs, "Dakota Portraits," *Minnesota History Bulletin* 2(November 1918):547–52; Riggs letter, May 17, 1850, ABCFM Papers; Riggs, *Mary and I*, 139–41.

[34] Riggs to Treat, October 26, 1859, ABCFM Papers (quotation). See also Riggs to the American Board, January 2, 1862, ABCFM Papers; Williamson, "Joseph Napehshneedoota," *Minnesota Collections* 3(1880):188–89; Hughes, *Indian Chiefs*, 53.

[35] "Indian Reserve Papers," NARG 75, miscellaneous manuscripts; Wozniak, *Contact, Negotiation and Conflict*, 118–21; Celia M. Campbell, Reminiscences, Stay Papers.

[36] Sweet, "Mrs. J. E. De Camp Sweet's Narrative of Her Captivity," *Minnesota Collections* 6(1894):371; Parker, ed., *Recollections of Philander Prescott*, 35–36; Note cards on Sioux, "Ampetu-sota-dan," Satterlee Papers.

[37] "Indian Reserve Papers," NARG 75, miscellaneous manuscripts; Hughes, *Indian Chiefs*, 65–69, 87–101; Samuel J. Brown to Satterlee, April 9, 1915, Satterlee Papers.

Bibliography

MANUSCRIPTS

Assumption Abbey Archives, Richardton, North Dakota
   Belleau Collection (microfilm)
Bancroft Collection, University of California Library, Berkeley, California
   Andrew Drips Papers
Beinecke Rare Book and Manuscript Library, Yale University, New Haven, Connecticut
   Benjamin O'Fallon Letter, November 29, 1817
Bentley Historical Library, University of Michigan, Ann Arbor, Michigan
   Chauncey Bush Journal, 1837 (microfilm)
Chippewa County Historical Society, Montevideo, Minnesota
   Miscellaneous Correspondence
Columbia University Library, New York, New York
   Edwin James Diary and Journal (microfilm)
Detroit Public Library, Burton Collection, Detroit, Michigan
   American Fur Company Papers
   Ramsay Crooks Papers (microfilm)
Hudson's Bay Company Archives, Winnipeg, Manitoba
   A. G. Dallas Correspondence, Inward, 1858–1864
   A. G. Dallas Private Journals
   London Correspondence, Inward, 1862–1865
   Winnipeg Correspondence, Letterbooks, 1861–1864
Kansas State Historical Society, Topeka, Kansas
   William Clark Papers (microfilm)
Manitoba Provincial Archives, Winnipeg, Canada
   Celia Campbell Stay Reminiscences
Minnesota Historical Society, St. Paul, Minnesota
   Moses N. Adams Papers
   John Felix Aiton Papers
   American Board of Commissioners for Foreign Missions Papers (transcripts)
   American Fur Company Papers (photostats and microfilm)
   Alexis Bailly Papers
   Joseph R. and Samuel J. Brown Papers

Bibliography

Scott Campbell Papers
Miss Phoebe Frances Cory and Mrs. William H. Forbes Papers
  (Cory-Forbes Papers)
Neil Currie Papers
Jeremiah Chester Donahower Papers
George W. Doud Diary
William G. and George W. Ewing Papers (microfilm)
Charles E. Flandrau Papers
William Watts Folwell Papers
Joseph Fortier Reminiscences
Edwin A. C. Hatch Papers
Nancy McClure Huggan Reminiscences
Alexander G. Huggins Papers
Elizabeth W. Lawrence Reminiscences
Frederick P. Leavenworth Papers
Martin McLeod Papers
A. Pendergast Papers
Eli K. Pickett Papers
Gideon H. and Samuel W. Pond Papers and Diaries
Alexander Ramsey Papers (microfilm)
Stephen Return Riggs Papers
Louis Robert Papers
Thomas A. Robertson Reminiscences
William W. and Marion P. Satterlee Papers
Mary Schwandt Schmidt Papers
Selected Documents from the Office of Indian Affairs Regarding the Treaty of
  1851 (microfilm)
Timothy J. Sheehan Papers and Diary
Henry Hastings Sibley Papers (microfilm)
Celia Campbell Stay Papers
Lawrence Taliaferro Journals and Papers
Clark Thompson Papers
"Trial of Wowinape, August 22, 1863" (a manuscript)
Henry Benjamin Whipple Papers
J. Fletcher Williams Papers
Thomas S. Williamson Papers (microfilm)
John Kingsley Wood Diary
Alan R. Woolworth Files (private files)
National Archives, Washington, D.C., Documents on Microfilm
  Record Group 48, Letters Sent, Indian Division of the Department of the
    Interior
  Record Group 75, Documents Relating to the Negotiation of Ratified and Un-
    ratified Treaties with Various Tribes of Indians

238

Record Group 75, Special Files of the Office of Indian Affairs
Record Group 75, Letters Sent, Office of Indian Affairs
Record Group 75, Letters Received and Sent, Minnesota Superintendency
Record Group 75, Letters Received and Sent, Northern Superintendency
Record Group 75, Letters Received, St. Peter's Agency
Record Group 75, Letters Received, Upper Missouri Agency
Record Group 94, Letters Received and Sent, Adjutant General's Office
Record Group 107, Letters Received, Secretary of War, Unregistered
National Archives, Washington, D.C., Original Documents
Senate Records 37A-F2, Original Transcripts of the Records of Trials of Certain Sioux Indians Charged with Barbarities in the State of Minnesota
Record Group 75, "Indian Reserve Papers"
Record Group 75, Annuity Rolls for the Sioux
Record Group 75, Letters Received and Sent, Northern Superintendency
Record Group 393, Letters Received and Sent, Jefferson Barracks
Record Group 393, Letters Received and Sent, Department of the West and Western Department
Record Group 393, Letters Received and Sent, Letterbooks, and Miscellaneous, Fort Ridgely
Record Group 393, Letters Received and Sent and Letterbooks, Fort Abercrombie
Record Group 393, Letters Sent, Sibley's Indian Campaign
Record Group 393, Letters Received and Sent, Sibley Indian Expedition (Field Records)
Record Group 393, Letters Received and Sent, Northwest Department
Record Group 393, Department of the Northwest, "Two or More Names File"
Record Group 393, Letters Received, District of Minnesota
Newberry Library, Edward E. Ayer Manuscript Collection, Chicago, Illinois
Hercules L. Dousman Papers
Nathaniel Fish Moore Journal
John Howard Payne Reminiscences
State Historical Society of Wisconsin, Madison, Wisconsin
Hercules L. Dousman Papers
Thomas Forsyth Papers, Draper Collection (microfilm)

PUBLISHED PRIMARY SOURCES

Newspapers

Atlas (Boston), 1837
Daily Pioneer and Democrat (St. Paul), 1855–56
Daily Union (Washington), 1854, 1858, also *Washington Union*
Dakota Tawaxitkakin or *Dakota Friend*, 1851

Bibliography

Henderson Democrat, 1856–62
Hutchinson Leader, 1893, 1905, 1912
Iape Oaye/The Word Carrier, 1878, 1885, 1888
Independent Press (Madison), 1906, 1923
Inter-Lake Tribune (Brown's Valley), 1912
Mankato Independent, 1857–63, also *Mankato Weekly Independent*
Mankato Weekly Record, 1862–63
Minneapolis Journal, 1916, 1938
Minnesota Democrat (St. Paul), 1854
Minnesota Pioneer (St. Paul), 1849–55
Minnesota Statesman (St. Peter), 1861
Morris Sun, 1935
Morton Enterprise, 1902
National Intelligencer (Washington), 1837, 1854, 1858
Niles' Register (Washington) 1854, 1858; *Niles' Weekly Register* and *Niles' National Register* are also cited as *Niles' Register*
Nor'Wester (Winnipeg), 1861–63
Redwood Falls Gazette, 1907
Richland County Farmer-Globe (Wahpeton, North Dakota), Supplement of September 22, 1936
St. Cloud Democrat, 1866
St. Paul Daily Globe, 1896
St. Paul Pioneer, 1862–63
St. Paul Pioneer Press, 1897
St. Paul Press, 1862–63, also *St. Paul Daily Press*
St. Peter Tribune, 1862–63
Weekly Minnesotian (St. Paul), 1854
Weekly Pioneer and Democrat (St. Paul), 1861

Government and Congressional Documents

Adjutant General of Minnesota, *Reports*, 1863
Carter, Clarence E., and John P. Bloom, eds. *The Territorial Papers of the United States*. 28 vols. Washington, D.C.: Government Printing Office, 1934–.
Executive Documents for the State of Minnesota, 1862.
Kappler, Charles J., comp. and ed. *Indian Affairs, Laws, and Treaties*. 2 vols. Washington, D.C.: Government Printing Office, 1904.
Minnesota Board of Commissioners on Publication of History of Minnesota in Civil and Indian Wars. *Minnesota in the Civil and Indian Wars, 1861–1865*. 2 vols. St. Paul, 1890–93.
Papers Relating to Talks and Councils Held with the Indians in Dakota and Montana Territories in the Years 1866–1869. Washington, D.C.: Government Printing Office, 1910.

The Sisseton and Wahpeton Bands of Sioux Indians vs. the United States, 1901–07. Court of Claims docket no. 22524, bound testimony in Minnesota Historical Society Library.

United States Congress. House and Senate Executive Documents and Reports. Serial Set.

Books and Articles (Primary Sources)

Allanson, George C. "Stirring Adventures of the Joseph R. Brown Family." In *The Garland Library of Narratives of North American Indian Captivities*, edited by Wilcomb E. Washburn, vol. 103. [1930?]; New York: Garland Publishing Co., 1976.

Armstrong, Benjamin G. *Early Life among the Indians. Reminiscences from the Life of Benj. G. Armstrong. Treaties of 1835, 1837, 1842, and 1854. Habits and Customs of the Red Men of the Forest. Incidents, Biographical Sketches, Battles, Etc. Dictated to and Written by Thos. P. Wentworth*. Ashland, Wis.: Press of A. W. Brown, 1892.

Babcock, Willoughby M., ed. "Up the Minnesota Valley to Fort Ridgely in 1853." *Minnesota History* 11 (June 1930):161–84.

Beltrami, Giacomo C. *A Pilgrimage in America*. Americana Classics. Chicago: Quadrangle Books, 1962.

Berghold, Alexander. *The Indians' Revenge; or, Days of Horror. Some Appalling Events in the History of the Sioux*. San Francisco: P. J. Thomas, 1891.

Bishop, Harriet E. *Dakota War Whoop: Or, Indian Massacres and War in Minnesota of 1862–3*. St. Paul: D. D. Merrill, 1863; Minneapolis: Ross and Haines, 1970.

Boyd, Robert K. "How the Indians Fought: A New Era in Skirmish Fighting, by a Survivor of the Battle of Birch Cooley." *Minnesota History* 11 (September 1930):299–304.

————. *The Battle of Birch Coulée: A Wounded Man's Description of the Battle with the Indians*. Eau Claire, Wis.: Herges Printing, 1925.

[Brackett, George A.]. *A Winter Evening's Tale*. New York: The Author, 1880.

Bray, Edmund C., and Martha Coleman Bray, trans. and eds. *Joseph N. Nicollet on the Plains and Prairies: The Expeditions of 1838–39 with Journals, Letters, and Notes on the Dakota Indians*. St. Paul: Minnesota Historical Society Press, 1976.

Brown, Joseph Epes, ed. *The Sacred Pipe: Black Elk's Account of the Seven Rites of the Oglala Sioux*. Norman: University of Oklahoma Press, 1953.

Brown, Samuel J. "In Captivity: The Experience, Privations and Dangers of Sam'l J. Brown, and Others, while Prisoners of the Hostile Sioux, during the Massacre and War of 1862." In *The Garland Library of Narratives of North American Indian Captivities*, edited by Wilcomb E. Washburn, vol. 76. [1900?]; New York: Garland Publishing Co., 1977.

Bryant, Charles S., and Abel B. Murch. *A History of the Great Massacre by the*

Sioux Indians, in Minnesota, Including the Personal Narratives of Many Who Escaped. Cincinnati: Rickey and Carroll, 1864.

Buck, Daniel. *Indian Outbreaks.* 1904; Minneapolis: Ross and Haines, 1965.

Carley, Kenneth, ed. "As Red Men Viewed It: Three Indian Accounts of the Uprising." *Minnesota History* 38 (September 1962):126–49.

Carrigan, Wilhelmina B. ("Minnie"). *Captured by the Indians: Reminiscences of Pioneer Life in Minnesota.* Forest City, S.D.: Forest City Press, 1907.

Coleson, Ann. *Miss Coleson's Narrative of Her Captivity among the Sioux Indians! . . . in Minnesota.* Philadelphia: Barclay and Co., 1864.

Collins, Loren Warren. *The Expedition against the Sioux Indians in 1863.* St. Cloud, Minn.: Journal-Press Print, 1895.

Collins, Mary C. *The Story of Elizabeth Winyan, a Dakota Woman.* Chicago: American Missionary Association, n.d.

Connolly, Alonzo P. *A Thrilling Narrative of the Minnesota Massacre and the Sioux War of 1862–63.* Chicago: A. P. Connolly, 1896.

Dally, Nathan. *Tracks and Trails; or, Incidents in the Life of a Minnesota Territorial Pioneer.* Walker, Minn.: Cass County Pioneer, 1931.

Daniels, Arthur M., ed. *A Journal of Sibley's Indian Expedition during the Summer of 1863, and Record of the Troops Employed. By a Soldier in Company 'H', 6th Regiment.* Winona, Minn.: Republican Office, 1864.

Eastman, Charles A. *Indian Boyhood.* New York: Phillips and Co., 1902; New York: Dover Publications, 1971.

————. *Indian Heroes and Great Chieftains.* Boston: Little, Brown and Co., 1918.

Emerson, Charles L. *Rise and Progress of Minnesota Territory, Including a Statement of the Business Prosperity of St. Paul; and Information in Regard to the Different Counties, Cities, Towns, and Villages in the Territory, Etc.* St. Paul: C. L. Emerson, 1855.

Featherstonhaugh, George W. *A Canoe Voyage up the Minnay Sotor; with an Account of the Lead and Copper Deposits in Wisconsin; of the Gold Region in the Cherokee Country; and Sketches of Popular Manners.* 2 vols. London, 1847; St. Paul: Minnesota Historical Society, 1970.

Frémont, John C. *The Expeditions of John Charles Frémont.* Edited by Donald Jackson and Mary Lee Spence. Urbana: University of Illinois Press, 1970.

Gardner-Sharp, Abbie. *History of the Spirit Lake Massacre and Captivity of Miss Abbie Gardner.* Des Moines, Iowa: Iowa Printing Co., 1885.

Goff, Lyman. *An 1862 Trip to the West.* Pawtucket, R.I.: Pawtucket Boy's Club, 1926.

Gordon, H[anford] L. *The Feast of the Virgins and Other Poems.* Chicago: Laird and Lee Publishers, 1891.

Hachin-Wakanda [Lightning Blanket]. *Story of the Battle of Ft. Ridgely, Minn., August 20 and 22, 1862.* Morton, Minn.: O. S. Smith, 1908.

Hankins, Col. *Dakota Land; or, The Beauty of St. Paul. An Original, Illustrated,*

Historical and Romantic Work on Minnesota, and The Great North-West. 1868; New York: Hankins and Son, 1869.

Heard, Isaac V. D. *History of the Sioux War and Massacres of 1862 and 1863.* New York: Harper and Brothers, 1864.

Heilbron, Bertha L., ed. *With Pen and Pencil on the Frontier in 1851: The Diary and Sketches of Frank Blackwell Mayer.* St. Paul: Minnesota Historical Society, 1932, reprint, 1986.

Hibschman, H[arry] J[acob]. "The Shetek Pioneers and the Indians." In *The Garland Library of Narratives of North American Indian Captivities,* edited by Wilcomb E. Washburn, vol. 104. 1901; New York: Garland Publishing Co., 1976.

Huggan, Nancy. "Mrs. Huggan the Minnesota Captive." In *The Garland Library of Narratives of North American Indian Captivities,* edited by Wilcomb E. Washburn, vol. 86. 1894; New York: Garland Publishing Co., 1978.

Keating, William H. *Narrative of an Expedition to the Source of St. Peter's River, Lake Winnepeek, Lake of the Woods, &c. Performed in the Year 1823, by Order of the Hon. J. C. Calhoun, Secretary of War, under the Command of Stephen H. Long, U.S.T.E.* 2 vols. 1824; Minneapolis: Ross and Haines, 1959.

Kelly, Fanny Wiggins. *Narrative of My Captivity among the Sioux Indians.* 1871; Hartford, Conn.: Mutual Publishing Co., 1872.

Lamare-Picquot, F. V. "A French Naturalist in Minnesota, 1846." *Minnesota History* 6 (September 1925):270–77.

Lawrence, Mr. and Mrs. Harry. "The Indian Nations of Minnesota: The Sioux Uprising." In *Minnesota Heritage: A Panoramic Narrative of the Historical Development of the North Star State,* edited by Lawrence M. Brings. Minneapolis: T. S. Denison and Co., 1960.

Le Duc, W[illiam] G. *Minnesota Year Book for 1851.* St. Paul: W[illiam] G. Le Duc, 1851.

———. *Minnesota Year Book for 1852.* St. Paul: W[illiam] G. Le Duc, 1852.

Lee, L[orenzo] P., ed. *History of the Spirit Lake Massacre, 8th March, 1857, And of Miss Abigail Gardiner's Three Month's Captivity among the Indians, According to Her Own Account.* New Britain, Conn.: L. P. Lee, 1857; Iowa City: State Historical Society, 1971.

Long, Stephen H. *The Northern Expeditions of Stephen H. Long: The Journals of 1817 and 1823 and Related Documents.* Edited by Lucile M. Kane, June D. Holmquist, and Carolyn Gilman. St. Paul: Minnesota Historical Society, 1978.

Minnesota Historical Society. *Minnesota Historical Collections.* 17 vols. St. Paul: The Society, 1860–1920.

Missionary Paper. By the Bishop Seabury Mission. No. 23. Faribault, Minn.: Holley and Brown, 1862.

Neill, Edward D., ed. *The History of Minnesota: From the Earliest French Explorations to the Present Time.* 1858; Philadelphia: J. B. Lippincott and Co., 1873.

Bibliography

————, and Charles S. Bryant. *History of Fillmore County, Including Explorers and Pioneers of Minnesota, and Outline History of the State of Minnesota . . .; also Sioux Massacre of 1862, and State Education. . . .* Minneapolis: Minnesota Historical Co., 1882.

————, and J. Fletcher Williams. *History of Ramsey County and the City of St. Paul, Including the Explorers and Pioneers of Minnesota. . . , and Outlines of the History of Minnesota. . . .* Minneapolis: North Star Publishing Co., 1881.

Pettijohn, Jonas. *Autobiography, Family History and Various Reminiscences of the Life of Jonas Pettijohn among the Sioux or Dakota Indians. His Escape during the Massacre of August, 1862. Causes that Led to the Massacre.* 1889; Clay Center, Kans.: Dispatch Printing House, 1890.

Pike, Zebulon M. *The Journals of Zebulon Montgomery Pike, with Letters and Related Documents.* Edited by Donald Jackson. 2 vols. Norman: University of Oklahoma Press, 1966.

Pond, Samuel W., Jr. *Two Volunteer Missionaries among the Dakotas, or the Story of the Labors of Samuel W. and Gideon H. Pond.* Boston: Congregational Sunday-School and Publishing Society, 1893.

Potter, Theodore E. "Captain Potter's Recollections of Minnesota Experiences." *Minnesota History Bulletin* 1 (November 1916):419–521.

Prescott, Philander. *The Recollections of Philander Prescott.* Edited by Donald Dean Parker. Lincoln: University of Nebraska Press, 1966.

Ravoux, A[gustin]. *Reminiscences, Memoirs and Lectures.* St. Paul: Brown, Treacy and Co., 1890.

Renville, Mary Butler. *A Thrilling Narrative of Indian Captivity.* Minneapolis: Atlas Company Book and Job Printing Office, 1863.

Riggs, Stephen Return. *A Dakota-English Dictionary.* Edited by James Owen Dorsey. Washington, D.C.: Government Printing Office, 1890; Minneapolis: Ross and Haines, 1968.

————. "Dakota Grammar, Texts, and Ethnography." In *Contributions to North American Ethnology,* edited by James Owen Dorsey. Washington, D.C.: Government Printing Office, 1893.

————. "Dakota Portraits." *Minnesota History Bulletin* 2 (November 1918): 481–568.

————. *Grammar and Dictionary of the Dakota Language.* Washington, D.C.: Smithsonian Institution, 1852.

————. *Mary and I: Forty Years with the Sioux.* 1880; Boston: Congregational Sunday-School and Publishing Society, 1887.

————. *Tah-koo Wah-kan; or, The Gospel among the Dakotas.* Boston: Congregational Sabbath-School and Publishing Society, 1869.

Scantlebury, Thomas. *Wanderings in Minnesota during the Indian Troubles of 1862.* Chicago: F. C. S. Calhoun, Printer, 1867.

Schmidt, Mary Schwandt. "The Story of Mary Schwandt: Her Captivity during the Sioux Outbreak." In *The Garland Library of Narratives of North American*

Indian Captivities, edited by Wilcomb E. Washburn, vol. 99. 1894; New York: Garland Publishing Co., 1976.

Schoolcraft, Henry R., ed. *Historical and Statistical Information Respecting the History, Condition, and Prospects of the Indian Tribes of the United States.* 6 vols. Philadelphia: J. B. Lippincott, 1851–57, 1865.

————. *Narrative Journal of Travels through the Northwestern Regions of the United States, Extending from Detroit through the Great Chain of American Lakes, to the Sources of the Mississippi River, Performed as a Member of the Expedition under Governor Cass in the Year 1820.* Albany: E. and E. Hosford, 1821.

Seymour, E. S. *Sketches of Minnesota, the New England of the West. With Incidents of Travel in That Territory during the Summer of 1849.* New York: Harper and Brothers, 1850.

Sibley, Henry H. *Iron Face: The Adventures of Jack Frazer, Frontier Warrior, Scout, and Hunter.* Edited by Theodore C. Blegen and Sarah A. Davidson. Chicago: Caxton Club, 1950.

————. "The Unfinished Autobiography of Henry Hastings Sibley," edited by Theodore C. Blegen. *Minnesota History* 8 (December 1927):329–62.

Snelling, William J. *Tales of the Northwest.* 1830; Minneapolis: University of Minnesota Press, 1936.

[————?]. "The Fortunes of Mendokaychennah." *New-England Magazine* 3 (July–December 1832):290–96.

"Taoyateduta Is Not a Coward." *Minnesota History* 38 (September 1962):115.

Tarble, Helen M. "The Story of My Capture and Escape during the Minnesota Indian Massacre of 1862, with Historical Notes, Descriptions of Pioneer Life, and Sketches and Incidents of the Great Outbreak of the Sioux or Dakota Indians as I Saw Them." In *The Garland Library of Narratives of North American Indian Captivities*, edited by Wilcomb E. Washburn, vol. 105. 1904; New York: Garland Publishing Co., 1976.

Van Cleve, Charlotte Ouisconsin. *"Three Score Years and Ten": Life-long Memories of Fort Snelling, Minnesota, and Other Parts of the West.* [Minneapolis?]: Harrison and Smith, 1888.

Wakefield, Sarah F. *Six Weeks in the Sioux Tepees: A Narrative of Indian Captivity.* Shakopee, Minn.: Argus Book and Job Printing Office, 1864.

Wall, Oscar Garrett. *Recollections of the Sioux Massacre: An Authentic History of the Yellow Medicine Incident, of the Fate of Marsh and His Men, of the Siege and Battles of Fort Ridgely, and of Other Important Battles and Experiences, Together with a Historical Sketch of the Sibley Expedition of 1863.* Lake City, Minn.: Home Printery, 1908.

Whipple, Henry Benjamin. *Lights and Shadows of a Long Episcopate, Being Reminiscences and Recollections of the Right Reverend Henry Benjamin Whipple, D.D., L.L.D., Bishop of Minnesota.* New York: Macmillan, 1912.

White, Mrs. N. D. [Urania]. "Captivity Among the Sioux, August 18 to September

26, 1862." In *The Garland Library of Narratives of North American Indian Captivities*, edited by Wilcomb E. Washburn, vol. 104. 1901; New York: Garland Publishing Co., 1976.

[Williams, William]. "Report of Major Williams." *Palimpsest* 38 (June 1957): 265–72.

Williamson, John P. "Removal of the Sioux Indians from Minnesota." *Minnesota History Bulletin* 2 (May 1918):420–25.

Wisconsin Historical Society Collections. 31 vols. Madison: State Historical Society of Wisconsin, 1855–1931.

SECONDARY MATERIALS

Ackermann, Gertrude W. "Joseph Renville of Lac qui Parle." *Minnesota History* 12 (September 1931):231–46.

Anderson, Gary Clayton. "Early Dakota Migration and Intertribal Warfare: A Revision." *Western Historical Quarterly* 11 (January 1980):17–36.

————. *Kinsmen of Another Kind: Dakota-White Relations in the Upper Mississippi Valley, 1650–1862*. Lincoln: University of Nebraska Press, 1984.

————. "The Removal of the Mdewakanton Dakota in 1837: A Case for Jacksonian Paternalism." *South Dakota History* 10 (Fall 1980):310–33.

Andrist, Ralph K. *The Long Death: The Last Days of the Plains Indian*. New York: Macmillan, 1964.

Babcock, Willoughby M., Jr. "Louis Provençalle, Fur Trader." *Minnesota History* 20 (September 1939):259–68.

————. "Major Lawrence Taliaferro, Indian Agent." *Mississippi Valley Historical Review* 11 (December 1924):358–75.

————. "Sioux Villages in Minnesota prior to 1837." *Minnesota Archaeologist* 11 (October 1945):126–46.

Barton, Winifred W. *John P. Williamson: A Brother to the Sioux*. New York: Fleming H. Revell, 1919.

Berkhofer, Robert F., Jr. "The Political Context of a New Indian History." *Pacific Historical Review* 40 (August 1971):357–82.

Blegen, Theodore C. *Minnesota: A History of the State*. Minneapolis: University of Minnesota Press, 1963.

Brown, Dee A. *Bury My Heart at Wounded Knee: An Indian History of the American West*. New York: Holt, Rinehart and Winston, 1970; New York: Bantam Books, 1972.

Brunner, Edward H. "Mandan." In *Perspectives in American Indian Culture Change*, edited by Edward H. Spicer, 187–277. Chicago: University of Chicago Press, 1961.

————. "Two Processes of Change in Mandan-Hidatsa Kinship Terminology." *American Anthropologist* 57 (1955):840–50.

Carley, Kenneth A. *The Sioux Uprising of 1862*. St. Paul: Minnesota Historical Society, 1976.

Clayton, James L. "The Growth and Economic Significance of the American Fur Trade, 1790–1890." *Minnesota History* 40 (Winter 1966):210–20.

Danziger, Edmund Jefferson, Jr. *The Chippewas of Lake Superior.* Civilization of the American Indian 148. Norman: University of Oklahoma Press, 1978.

————. "Civil War Problems in the Central and Dakota Superintendencies: A Case Study." *Nebraska History* 51 (Winter 1970):411–24.

————. *Indians and Bureaucrats: Administering the Reservation Policy during the Civil War.* Urbana: University of Illinois Press, 1974.

Deloria, Ella C. *Speaking of Indians.* New York: Friendship Press, 1944.

De Mallie, Raymond J. "Joseph N. Nicollet's Account of the Sioux and Assiniboin in 1839." *South Dakota History* 5 (Fall 1975):343–59.

————. "Teton Dakota Kinship and Social Organization." Ph.D. diss., University of Chicago, 1971.

————, and Robert H. Lavenda. "Wakan: Plains Siouan Concepts of Power." In *The Anthropology of Power: Ethnographic Studies from Asia, Oceania, and the New World,* edited by Raymond D. Fogelson and Richard N. Adams, 153–65. New York: Academic Press, 1977.

Edmunds, R. David. *The Potawatomis: Keepers of the Fire.* Norman: University of Oklahoma Press, 1978.

Eggan, Fred. "Lewis H. Morgan in Kinship Perspective." In *Essays in the Science of Culture in Honor of Leslie A. White,* edited by Gertrude E. Dole and Robert L. Carneiro, 179–201. New York: Thomas Y. Crowell, 1960.

Ellis, Richard N. "Political Pressures and Army Policies on the Northern Plains, 1862–1865." *Minnesota History* 42 (Summer 1970):42–53.

Ewers, John C. "Influence of the Fur Trade upon the Indians of the Northern Plains." In *People and Pelts: Selected Papers of the Second North American Fur Trade Conference,* edited by Malvina Bolus, 1–26. Winnipeg: Peguis Publishers, 1972.

————. "Intertribal Warfare as the Precursor of Indian-White Warfare on the Northern Great Plains." *Western Historical Quarterly* 6 (October 1975): 397–410.

Feraca, Stephen E., and James H. Howard. "The Identity and Demography of the Dakota or Sioux Tribe." *Plains Anthropologist* 8 (May 1963):80–84.

Folwell, William Watts. *A History of Minnesota.* 4 vols. St. Paul: Minnesota Historical Society, 1921–30.

Forbes, Bruce David. "Evangelization and Acculturation among the Santee Dakota Indians, 1834–1864." Ph.D. diss., Princeton Theological Seminary, 1977.

Fox, Robin. *Kinship and Marriage: An Anthropological Perspective.* Harmondsworth, England: Penguin Books, 1976.

Fridley, Russell W., Leota M. Kellett, and June D. Holmquist. *Charles E. Flandrau and the Defense of New Ulm.* New Ulm, Minn.: Brown County Historical Society, 1962.

Gilman, Rhoda R. "Last Days of the Upper Mississippi Fur Trade." *Minnesota History* 42 (Winter 1970):122–40.

Bibliography

————. "The Fur Trade in the Upper Mississippi Valley, 1630–1850." *Wisconsin Magazine of History* 58 (Autumn 1974):2–18.

Gluek, Alvin C., Jr. *Minnesota and the Manifest Destiny of the Canadian Northwest: A Study in Canadian-American Relations.* Toronto: University of Toronto Press, 1965.

————. "The Sioux Uprising: A Problem in International Relations." *Minnesota History* 34 (Winter 1955):317–24.

Gray, John S. "The Santee Sioux and the Settlers at Lake Shetek: Capture and Rescue." *Montana: The Magazine of Western History* 25 (Winter 1975):42–54.

Hagan, William T. *The Sac and Fox Indians.* Norman: University of Oklahoma Press, 1958.

Hansen, Marcus L. *Old Fort Snelling, 1819–1858.* Iowa City: State Historical Society of Iowa, 1918; Minneapolis: Ross and Haines, 1958.

Hassrick, Royal B. *The Sioux: Life and Customs of a Warrior Society.* Norman: University of Oklahoma Press, 1964.

————. "Teton Dakota Kinship System." *American Anthropologist* 46 (1944): 338–48.

Henig, Gerald S. "A Neglected Cause of the Sioux Uprising." *Minnesota History* 45 (Fall 1976):107–10.

Herriott, Frank I. "Dr. Isaac H. Harriott, One of the Victims of the Spirit Lake Massacre, Killed on the Evening of Sunday, March 8, 1857." *Annals of Iowa* 18 (April 1932):243–94.

————. "The Origins of the Indian Massacre between the Okobojis, March 8, 1857." *Annals of Iowa* 18 (July 1932):323–82.

Hickerson, Harold. *The Chippewa and Their Neighbors: A Study in Ethnohistory.* Studies in Anthropological Method. New York: Holt, Rinehart and Winston, 1970.

————. *Mdewakanton Band of Sioux Indians.* American Indian Ethnohistory, Plains Indians, Sioux Indians 1. New York: Garland Publishing Co., 1974.

Holcombe, Return I. *Early History—Minnesota as a Territory.* Vol. 2 of *Minnesota in Three Centuries, 1655–1908,* edited by Lucius F. Hubbard, William P. Murray, James H. Baker, and Warren Upham. Mankato: Publishing Society of Minnesota, 1908.

Howard, James H. "The Cultural Position of the Dakota: A Reassessment." In *Essays in the Science of Culture in Honor of Leslie A. White,* edited by Gertrude E. Dole and Robert L. Carneiro, 249–68. New York: Thomas Y. Crowell, 1960.

————. "The Dakota or Sioux Indians: A Study in Human Ecology." *Dakota Museum Anthropological Papers,* no. 2 (Vermillion, S.D.), 1966.

————. "Yanktonai Ethnohistory and the John K. Bear Winter Count." *Plains Anthropologist* 21 (August 1976):1–64.

Hubbard, Lucius F., and Return I. Holcombe. *Minnesota as a State, 1858–1870.* Vol. 3 of *Minnesota in Three Centuries, 1655–1908,* edited by Lucius F. Hubbard, William P. Murray, James H. Baker, and Warren Upham. Mankato: Publishing Society of Minnesota, 1908.

Hughes, Thomas. *History of Blue Earth County, and Biographies of Its Leading Citizens.* Chicago: Middle West Publishing Co., [1909?].

———. *Indian Chiefs of Southern Minnesota.* Mankato: Free Press Co., 1927; Minneapolis: Ross and Haines, 1969.

———. *Old Traverse des Sioux.* St. Peter, Minn.: Herald Publishing Co., 1929.

Jennings, Francis. *The Invasion of America: Indians, Colonialism, and the Cant of Conquest.* New York: W. W. Norton, 1976.

Johnson, Roy P. "The Siege of Fort Abercrombie." *North Dakota History* 24 (January 1957):4–79.

Jones, Robert Huhn. *The Civil War in the Northwest: Nebraska, Wisconsin, Iowa, Minnesota, and the Dakotas.* Norman: University of Oklahoma Press, 1960.

Josephy, Alvin M., Jr. *The Patriot Chiefs: A Chronicle of American Indian Leadership.* New York: Viking Press, 1961; New York: Penguin Books, 1980.

Kane, Lucile M. "The Sioux Treaties and the Traders." *Minnesota History* 32 (June 1951):65–80.

Klein, Alan Michael. "Adaptive Strategies and Process on the Plains: The 19th Century Cultural Sink." Ph.D. diss., State University of New York, Buffalo, 1977.

Landes, Ruth. *The Mystic Lake Sioux: Sociology of the Mdewakantonwan Santee.* Madison: University of Wisconsin Press, 1968.

Lass, William E. "The Removal from Minnesota of the Sioux and Winnebago Indians." *Minnesota History* 38 (December 1963):353–64.

Lowie, Robert H. *Indians of the Plains.* American Museum of Natural History Anthropological Handbook no. 1. New York: McGraw-Hill, 1954.

Luebke, Frederick C., ed. *Ethnicity on the Great Plains.* Lincoln: Center for Great Plains Studies, University of Nebraska Press, 1980.

McManus, John. "An Economic Analysis of Indian Behavior in the North American Fur Trade." *Journal of Economic History* 32 (March 1972):36–53.

Mauss, Marcel. *The Gift: Forms and Functions of Exchange in Archaic Societies.* New York: W. W. Norton, 1967.

Meyer, Roy W. "The Canadian Sioux: Refugees from Minnesota." *Minnesota History* 41 (Spring 1968):13–28.

———. *History of the Santee Sioux: United States Indian Policy on Trial.* Lincoln: University of Nebraska Press, 1967.

Minnesota Valley Historical Society. *Sketches Historical and Descriptive of the Monuments and Tablets Erected by the Minnesota Valley Historical Society in Renville and Redwood Counties, Minnesota.* Morton: Minnesota Valley Historical Society, 1902.

Mooers, Calvin. "Indian Warfare in the Red River Country, 1862-1866." *The Detroit Society for Genealogical Research Magazine* 20 (Summer 1957):139–41.

Mooney, James R. *The Aboriginal Populations of America North of Mexico.* Edited by John R. Swanton. Smithsonian Institution Miscellaneous Collections, vol. 80, no. 7. Washington, D.C.: Government Printing Office, 1928.

Newcombe, Barbara T. "'A Portion of the American People': The Sioux Sign a Treaty in Washington in 1858." *Minnesota History* 45 (Fall 1976):82–96.

Bibliography

Nichols, David A. "The Other Civil War: Lincoln and the Indians." *Minnesota History* 44 (Spring 1974):2–15.

Oehler, Chester M. *The Great Sioux Uprising.* New York: Oxford University Press, 1959.

Paulson, Howard W. "Federal Indian Policy and the Dakota Indians: 1800–1840." *South Dakota History* 3 (Summer 1973):285–309.

Peterson, Jacqueline. "The People in Between: Indian-White Marriage and the Genesis of a Métis Society and Culture in the Great Lakes Region." Ph.D. diss., University of Illinois, Chicago Circle, 1980.

Powers, William K. *Oglala Religion.* Lincoln: University of Nebraska Press, 1975.

Prucha, Francis Paul. *American Indian Policy in the Formative Years: The Indian Trade and Intercourse Acts, 1790–1834.* Cambridge: Harvard University Press, 1962; Lincoln: Bison Book, 1970.

————. "American Indian Policy in the 1840s: Visions of Reform." In *The Frontier Challenge: Response to the Trans-Mississippi West,* edited by John G. Clark, 81–110. Lawrence: University of Kansas Press, 1971.

————. "Andrew Jackson's Indian Policy: A Reassessment." *Journal of American History* 56 (December 1969):527–39.

————. "Army Sutlers and the American Fur Company." *Minnesota History* 40 (Spring 1966):22–31.

————. *Broadax and Bayonet: The Role of the United States Army in the Development of the Northwest, 1815–1860.* Madison: State Historical Society of Wisconsin, 1953.

————. *The Sword of the Republic: The United States Army on the Frontier, 1783–1846.* The Wars of the United States. New York: Macmillan, 1968.

Ray, Arthur J. *Indians in the Fur Trade: Their Role as Trappers, Hunters, and Middlemen in the Lands Southwest of Hudson Bay, 1660–1870.* Toronto: University of Toronto Press, 1974.

————, and Donald B. Freeman. *"Give Us Good Measure": An Economic Analysis of Relations between the Indians and the Hudson's Bay Company before 1763.* Toronto: University of Toronto Press, 1978.

Robinson, Doane. *A History of the Dakota or Sioux Indians.* 1904; Minneapolis: Ross and Haines, 1956.

Roddis, Louis H. *The Indian Wars of Minnesota.* Cedar Rapids, Iowa: Torch Press, 1956.

Russo, Priscilla Ann. "The Time to Speak Is Over: The Onset of the Sioux Uprising." *Minnesota History* 45 (Fall 1976):97–106.

Sahlins, Marshall. *Stone Age Economy.* Chicago and New York: Aldine, Atherton, 1972.

Satterlee, Marion P. *A Detailed Account of the Massacre by the Dakota Indians of Minnesota in 1862.* Minneapolis: Marion P. Satterlee, 1923.

————. *The Story of Capt. Richard Strout and Company, Who Fought the Sioux Indians at the Battle of Kelly's Bluff, at Acton, Minn., on Wednesday, September 3rd, 1862.* Minneapolis: Marion P. Satterlee, 1909.

Schneider, David M. "What Is Kinship All About?" In *Kinship Studies in the Morgan Centennial Year*, edited by Priscilla Reining, 32–63. Washington, D.C.: Anthropological Society of Washington, 1972.

Skinner, Alanson. "Eastern Dakota Ethnology." *American Anthropologist* 21 (April 1919):167–74.

Stewart, William J. "Settler, Politician, and Speculator in the Sale of the Sioux Reserve." *Minnesota History* 39 (Fall 1964):85–92.

Stipe, Claude E. "Eastern Dakota Acculturation: The Role of Agents of Culture Change." Ph.D. diss., University of Minnesota, 1968.

Symes, Oliver C. *Ecology and Cultural Continuity as Contributing Factors in the Social Organization of the Plains Indians*. University of California Publications in American Archaeology and Ethnology, no. 48. Berkeley: University of California, 1962.

Syms, E. Leigh. "Cultural Ecology and Ecological Dynamics of the Ceramic Period in Southwestern Manitoba." *Plains Anthropologist* 22 (May 1977):1–142.

Tassé, Joseph. *Les Canadiens de l'Ouest*. 2 vols. Montreal: Berthiaume et Sabourin, 1882.

Taylor, Joseph H. "Inkpaduta and Sons." *North Dakota Historical Quarterly* 4 (April 1930):152–64.

Teakle, Thomas. *The Spirit Lake Massacre*. Iowa City: State Historical Society of Iowa, 1918.

Thompson, H. Paul. "Estimating Aboriginal American Population: A Technique Using Anthropological and Biological Data." *Current Anthropology* 7 (1966):417–24.

Trenerry, Walter N. "The Shooting of Little Crow: Heroism or Murder?" *Minnesota History* 38 (September 1962):150–53.

Trennert, Robert A., Jr. *Indian Traders on the Middle Border: The House of Ewing, 1827–54*. Lincoln: University of Nebraska Press, 1981.

Van Kirk, Sylvia. "The Role of Women in the Fur Trade Society of the Canadian West, 1700–1850." Ph.D. diss., University of London, Queen Mary College, 1975.

Vecsey, Christopher. "American Indian Environmental Religions." In *American Indian Environments: Ecological Issues in Native American History*, edited by Christopher Vecsey and Robert W. Venables. Syracuse, N.Y.: Syracuse University Press, 1980.

Viola, Herman J. *The Indian Legacy of Charles Bird King*. Washington, D.C.: Smithsonian Institution Press and Doubleday and Co., 1976.

Walker, James R. *Lakota Belief and Ritual*. Edited by Raymond J. De Mallie and Elaine A. Jahner. Lincoln: University of Nebraska Press, 1980.

West, Nathaniel. *Ancestry, Life, and Times of Hon. Henry Hastings Sibley*. St. Paul: Pioneer Press Publishing Co., 1889.

White, Richard. "The Winning of the West: The Expansion of the Western Sioux in the Eighteenth and Nineteenth Centuries." *Journal of American History* 65 (September 1978):319–43.

Bibliography

Willand, Jon. *Lac qui Parle and the Dakota Mission*. Madison, Minn.: Lac qui Parle County Historical Society, 1964.

Williams, J. Fletcher. *A History of the City of Saint Paul to 1875*. 1876; St. Paul: Minnesota Historical Society Press, Borealis Books, 1983.

Winchell, Newton H. *The Aborigines of Minnesota: A Report on the Collections of Jacob V. Brower and on the Field Surveys and Notes of Alfred J. Hill and Theodore H. Lewis*. St. Paul: Minnesota Historical Society, 1911.

Wood, W. Raymond. "Plains Trade in Prehistoric and Protohistoric Intertribal Relations." In *Anthropology on the Great Plains*, edited by W. Raymond Wood and Margot P. Liberty, 98–109. Lincoln: University of Nebraska Press, 1980.

Woolworth, Alan R. "A Disgraceful Proceeding: Intrigue in the Red River Country in 1864." *The Beaver*, Spring 1969, p. 54–59.

———, and Nancy L. Woolworth. "Eastern Dakota Settlement and Subsistence Patterns Prior to 1851." *Minnesota Archaeologist* 39 (May 1980):70–89.

Wozniak, John S. *Contact, Negotiation, and Conflict: An Ethnohistory of the Eastern Dakota, 1819–1839*. Washington, D.C.: University Press of America, 1978.

Index

Index

Chambers, John, treaty negotiator, 53, 54, 59
Chickasaw Indians, 71
Children, education, 10; tasks, 14; depicted, 47
Cloud Man (Maḣpiyawicaṡta), 24, 41, 86, 188, 190
Crawford, Charles R., 190, 227n49; depicted, 98
Crawford, Thomas, 190
Cree Indians, 162, 172
Crow Creek, Dak. Ter., 165
Crows, as namesake, 15
Cullen, William J., Indian superintendent, 84–87, 91, 92, 94, 95, 101, 108, 109, 112, 121
Curley Head, spokesman, 60
Cut Nose, warrior, 142, 143, 144, 145, 224n14; depicted, 148; captured, 164

DAKOTA INDIANS, in War of 1812, 9; name, 10; population, 11, 13; lands mapped, 12, 120; yearly cycle, 13–14; attitude toward strangers, 21; peace delegation, 25; intertribal relations, 26, 56, 162; political divisions, 89; traditional values, 109, 117, 134, 177; depredations, 111; hanged, 165; as scouts, 168; prisoners, 175
Dakota language, family terms, 16; alphabet, 38; taught, 42, 107
Dakota War of 1862, assessed, 2, 140; events leading to outbreak, 123, 127–34; outbreak, 135–38; casualties, 138–39, 146, 153, 154, 159; captives, 141, 142, 151–52, 156, 157, 158, 160, 161, 163, 169, 172; opposed, 151–53, 155–57; aftermath, 163–65. See also specific battles
Dakota-white relations, 3, 5, 130, 138; adoption, 21, 23; blood ties, 24; policy of accommodation, 35. See also Whites
Dallas, Alexander Grant, 171, 172, 175, 176
Daniels, Asa W., 37, 75, 78, 109
Davenport, Iowa, prison, 165
Death, mourning, 42
Debts, repayment, 53, 54, 64, 67–69, 92–93, 103, 112–13, 118, 121–22, 123
Denver, James W., Indian commissioner, 83, 86, 87
Disease, smallpox, 29, 50
Dowan, death, 33, 184
Dustin, Amos, family, 177

EARLE, JONATHAN W., farmer, 128
Eastman, Capt. Seth, artist, 60

Ebell, Adrian J., photographer, 124, 125, 126
Education, of children, 15–18, 19, 21; mission schools, 30, 32, 38, 42, 43, 46, 50; government schools, 31, 50, 107; boarding schools, 51, 53
Emma, Little Crow's daughter, 51
English language, instruction, 32
Estamuzza, Dakota Indian, 188
Euni, John, captive, 169
Extended Tail Feathers, Dakota Indian, depicted, 98

FARIBAULT, ALEXANDER, trader, 31, 37, 68
Faribault, David, trader, 59, 145
Faribault, Jean Baptiste, 21, 27
Flandrau, Charles, Indian agent, 82, 91–94
Folwell, William Watts, historian, 2
Food, plants gathered, 14; dietary patterns, 27, 28, 31, 34; annuities, 30, 77–78, 81, 118, 128; insufficient, 101, 116, 123, 172
Forbes, William H., trader, 92, 103, 113
Forest City, 111, 155
Forsyth, Thomas, trader, 199n5
Fort Abercrombie, attacked, 145, 168
Fort Ridgely, built, 75; battles, 143–46, 168
Fort Snelling, built, 9, 22, 23
Fox Indians, 21, 26, 40
Frazer, Jack, mixed-blood, 36–37, 68, 184
French, traders, 9
French Canadians, farmers, 32, 56
Frenier, Narcisse, 190
Fur trade, decline, 27; by Indians, 43; illegal, 52. See also Trade

GALBRAITH, THOMAS J., Indian agent, 113–14, 117, 121, 128, 144, 155; supports farmers, 116, 118; annuity distribution, 122–23, 127
Gambling, card games, 39
Garvie, Stuart B., trader, 92
Germans, settlers, 82, 101, 130, 138, 139; in war, 146
Gift giving, among kin, 17, 19, 24
Gingras, _____, trader, 231n28
Gleason, George, clerk, 136
Good Road, chief, 68
Gorman, Willis A., Indian superintendent, 69–72, 78, 79, 93, 209n48
Government, role of chiefs, 4–5, 15, 34; village council, 14–15, 25; spokesmen, 15, 119; councils eroded, 118, 133
Grand Partisan, chief, 25, 26

254

Index

Picture Credits